1964

W9-ADV-282

This book may be kept

ARISTOTLE

ARISTOTLE

BY JOHN HERMAN RANDALL, Jr.

FREDERICK J. E. WOODBRIDGE PROFESSOR
OF PHILOSOPHY, COLUMBIA UNIVERSITY

IN LITTERIS
LIBERTAS
1754·1893

COLUMBIA UNIVERSITY PRESS
NEW YORK 1960

FOR JOHN JACOB COSS

WHO LOVED AND PRACTICED

THE ETHICS

FOREWORD

This little book attempts to set forth what one man has found
to be the significance for the present day of the thought of the
second of the two major philosophers our so-called "Western"
civilization has managed to produce.

In the English-speaking world we have had in our generation
the chance to learn from some of the most distinguished scholars
in the long attempt to elucidate the text of Aristotle. In England
and the United States the leaders of this critical enterprise are
easily Sir David Ross and Werner Jaeger, whose contributions to
the study of Aristotle have been epoch-making. These eminent
classical scholars, however, have been primarily philologists;
philosophical analysis and interpretation of Aristotle's thought
has not been at the center of their concern. The same is largely
true of most of that band of Oxford Aristotelians whom J. A.
Smith and W. D. Ross originally gathered about themselves, to
make Aristotle a living force in a nonclassically trained century.
Of these perhaps H. H. Joachim was philosophically the most
penetrating.

This volume presents itself not as a philologist's but rather
as a philosopher's delineation of Aristotle. Of primarily philosophical expounders of Aristotle in our century, there stand out,
in the English-speaking world, perhaps A. E. Taylor, Harold
Cherniss, Kurt Riezler, and Richard McKeon. But the first two,
like most of the great interpreters of Greek philosophy in the
last couple of generations, have approached it as Platonists.
Though a student and admirer of Plato, the present writer is

forced to see much more than "Platonism," in the world and in Plato.

Other interpreters of Aristotle, like Mr. McKeon, Harry A. Wolfson, Dino Bigongiari, and the many competent students in this country and abroad who stand in a religious tradition and who have contributed so much to our knowledge of Aristotelian thinking, have come at Aristotle from the standpoint of the later medieval developments and problems. Though not unaware of the wealth and variety of medieval thought, so fascinating in itself, the present writer is not a medievalist. He seriously doubts whether Aristotle can survive translation into the Latin substantives of the scholastic tradition, or whether it is possible to state his fundamental functionalism in the Latin tongue. There are other judgments: Mr. McKeon once explained that in his commentaries Thomas Aquinas had really managed to state the Aristotelian philosophy in the Latin language of the thirteenth century.

The author has come to Aristotle, not from the problems of medieval philosophy, but from the problems of philosophers like Samuel Alexander and Whitehead in England, and like Charles S. Peirce, George Herbert Mead, and John Dewey in this country. He has found great stimulus for his own thinking [1] in Aristotle's careful analysis of language and communication against the broader context of his penetrating examination of processes, natural, living, and distinctively human—the processes which he sets off as those of human art. Hence this volume tries to point out some of the ways in which Aristotle's thought is relevant and suggestive for two of the most important present-day philosophical concerns, that with the analysis of language and that with the analysis of natural processes.

Plato and Aristotle, never so alive as today, are always a challenge to fresh interpretation. No student of the human achieve-

[1] He would hope that this is apparent in his *Nature and Historical Experience* (New York, 1958).

ment can foreswear the hope of eventually commenting on the
literary and philosophic genius of Plato. But further writing on
ancient philosophy offers a lesser temptation. Despite the many
suggestive accounts that scholars since Aristotle have given of
the course taken by pre-Socratic Greek thinking, it may well be
doubted whether the sources available to us permit the writing of
a critical history of the development of Greek philosophy. Work
in that field must inevitably take the form of rather speculative
reconstructions, based on the fragmentary remains of an unsatisfactory later "doxographical" tradition—a long series of textbooks
on the history of philosophy which went on repeating and distort-
ing each other. The forthcoming volume by Charles H. Kahn [2]
on Anaximander supplies a classic model for the way in which
the philosophy of the early Greeks may be critically and fruitfully
treated.

And fascinating as is Hellenistic philosophizing, that complicated field demands great special competence; most students
must remain content to learn from the experts. It would, to be
sure, be a delight to attempt a brief interpretation of Saint Augustine as the first modern philosopher. For Plato, Aristotle, and
Augustine are the three ancient philosophers that for most moderns continue to hold the greatest interest. Perhaps Cicero should
be added, as the very epitome of the Roman mind, so fascinating
and so influential, and so perverse.

It is an indication of the role of precision of language in Aristotle's thinking that no student of that thought is ever completely satisfied with any Englishing save his own. Yet it would
be presumptuous folly—indeed, *hybris*—for one who has not enjoyed the training of a classical philologist to fail to make full use
of the skill of the competent Greek scholars of our day. The outcome in this volume is a compromise. In the main there have been
employed the English translations of the Aristotelian texts—with

[2] Charles H. Kahn, *Anaximander and the Origins of Greek Cosmology* (New
York, 1960).

the *Physics,* the superior French of M. Carteron—that in each particular passage seemed closest to the meaning of the original. But there has been no hesitation to alter them, usually in the interest of bringing them nearer to what the Greek actually says. A literal translation is undeniably closer to Aristotle than a more polished English version. It can only be hoped that here there is not too often occasion to say, what has been at times remarked of some of the standard versions, that if the reader knows the Greek text, he can usually understand the English, and why it takes the otherwise puzzling course it does.

Greek words appear in these pages. It is hoped the terror they may provoke in the right-minded English reader will be not too overwhelming—and will pass. The writer is convinced that some Greek is necessary for any real understanding of Aristotle—those technical terms and phrases which through a variety of contexts and "ways of saying" retain a central flavor and connotation. He has never here included these Greek terms without an English equivalent. He wishes that life in twentieth-century America permitted the use of the Greek alphabet. But as George Sarton regretfully put it, the printing of Greek here today has become too onerous—for the printer, publisher, and reader alike. But the inclusion of the transliterated Greek words permits a checking in excellent texts like those of the Loeb Classical Library.

With a thinker whose thought has been for twenty-five hundred years such public property, it would be obvious folly to publish still another interpretation without trespassing on the good nature of other Aristotelian scholars. Richard P. McKeon and Herbert W. Schneider have been kind enough to go over the volume, and to make useful and illuminating suggestions whose incorporation seemed imperative. That they have not objected too violently to the general contentions expressed is probably due to the fact that we are all fellow-students of Frederick J. E. Woodbridge.

To certain younger scholars I am also greatly indebted. They have taken unusual care to correct in detail the carelessness of my labors. Arthur Hyman and Charles H. Kahn have examined the manuscript with painstaking thoroughness, and are responsible for whatever freedom from technical error the volume may now exhibit.

My colleagues Horace L. Friess and James Gutmann have been most helpful with chapter XII. To Paul Oskar Kristeller I owe as usual a great debt. He has forced me to face anew the philosophic problems raised by recent classical scholarship, as well as those posed by the long Platonic tradition. With so convinced a Platonist it is gratifying to be in such general agreement as to Aristotle's meaning, however we may differ in ultimate philosophical judgment. The indefatigable members of Columbia University Press have struggled to introduce a consistency of which neither I nor Aristotle proved capable. Would that Andronikos of Rhodes had enjoyed such a staff! My wife has performed rather more than usual of the thankless tasks for which wives volunteer.

Finally, pervasive obligation must be acknowledged to Frederick J. E. Woodbridge, careful scholar and profound philosophical interpreter of Aristotelian thinking, whose teaching has been extremely influential on those who were his students, though his actual writing on Aristotle was regrettably slender. The volume is dedicated to John Jacob Coss, who first introduced the writer to Aristotle, and to philosophy. In this, as in so much else, he owes to his teachers both initial stimulus and continuing inspiration.

J. H. R., JR.

Columbia University
September, 1959

CONTENTS

ARISTOTLE

Chapter I

THE ARISTOTELIAN APPROACH

TO UNDERSTANDING:

LIVING, KNOWING, AND TALKING

Aristotle came from the very edge of the Greek world. He was a Greek to the last fiber of his being, yet he remained the aloof, impartial observer, not deeply implicated in the struggles of that world. "All men," he starts the *Metaphysics,* "possess by nature the desire to know." I am not at all sure that is literally true: Aristotle never had the privilege of teaching in an American university. Had he had that chance to observe human nature, he might not have been so rash. But that sentence is certainly true of Aristotle's "nature." His great aim in life was to understand —to understand the world in which the Greeks found themselves. This was Aristotle's all-consuming passion. Indeed, his may well be the most passionate mind in history: it shines through every page, almost every line. His crabbed documents exhibit, not "cold thought," but the passionate search for passionless truth. For him, there is no "mean," no moderation, in intellectual excellence. The "theoretical life" is not for him the life of quiet "contemplation," serene and unemotional, but the life of *nous,* of *theōria,* of intelligence, burning, immoderate, without bounds or limits. There is in him a tremendous energy, an indefatigable industry, a sheer power of thought, that fascinates anyone who takes the trouble to understand what he is doing.

Dante called Aristotle *il maestro di color che sanno,* the master of them that know. He is the first of the great "Knowers" in the Western tradition. And they form a very small band: there are really only two others, Spinoza and Hegel. Possibly Thomas Aquinas belongs with them. But I am not sure of Thomas; about him there can be doubts, for after all he was a Christian saint, even if, like a good follower of Saint Dominic, he was a cherub filled with the knowledge of God, rather than like Saint Francis a seraph inspired wholly with the love of God.

Recent scholarship, notably that of Werner Jaeger, has made clear that our older picture of Aristotle as an industrious, conscientious, plodding fellow, who could not understand Plato, and could not feel Plato's imaginative power, his yearning and aspiration, his Eros, his poetry, was all wrong. In reality, as a young fellow Aristotle seems to have been caught by Plato, and to have been inspired by Plato's vision of truth. He got all that Plato had to offer, and thirsted for more: the whole of Plato was not enough for him. That is, Aristotle now appears as not less but more than Plato—he possesses more of understanding. As to wisdom, that may well be another matter. Perhaps Aristotle understood too much to be completely wise. If that be the case, it may serve as a consolation to the rest of us, who can so easily become appalled by the extent of Aristotle's understanding.

Aristotle's aim is to understand, to find out why things are as they are. It is not to control things, not to make them different from what they are. And that seems strange to us, for we are all confirmed Baconians. We are all convinced that the aim of knowledge is to build subways and sputniks, to cure disease, to reconstruct society. Now, of course knowledge can do such things, and many more not quite so admirable. But for Aristotle, that is not really why it is worth while and even divine to know. For instance, physics for him is not "practical" but "theoretical": it is not expected to *do* anything, except to give understanding. Such a conception of understanding, of intelligibility, naturally lost out in modern times, in an industrial society bent on trans-forming things, on extending the bounds of human empire over nature, to the effecting of all things possible. Aristotle sought intelligibility rather than power. Or better, we can say that for Aristotle the highest power a man can exercise over the world is to understand it—to do, because he sees why it must be done, what others do because they cannot help themselves.

Spinoza is the only other philosopher in our Western tradition who in this Aristotelian sense ever really tried to understand the world. Hence Spinoza is the only really important philosopher in modern times—though his thought is completely irrelevant to the problems that have exercised "modern philosophy." All the other "modern philosophers" have been trying to "prove" something, to prove some little theory. In one sense, Spinoza is more intelligent than Aristotle, because he understood the one thing that Aristotle failed to understand, the fact of mechanics. But then, Spinoza failed to understand life: he was precluded by his essentially mathematical, non-teleological, non-functional vision of the world from making living intelligible. And since life, which Aristotle understood thoroughly, is after all far more important than mechanics, for man at least, the palm for understanding must go to Aristotle. Hegel made the sublime attempt to understand absolutely everything. But unfortunately he lived among the post-Kantian idealists, and he mixed it up with the effort to prove an incredible theory.

Aristotle aimed to understand Greece: he never forgot that aim. He did not aim to understand something else—the Heavenly Beauty in the sky, the moral order in the universe, the divine creator of the world—any of those things which men would like to find in the world, but which so far as the evidence goes, are not there. Aristotle tried to understand the world of Greece, that *was* there. He started with that overwhelming fact, with that subject matter. And he managed in the end to give a complete and final expression of Greece and the Greek mind.

To understand the world of Greece meant for Aristotle three things: it meant an understanding of living, of knowing, and of talking. These are the three themes that, subtly interwoven, run through everything he ever set down.

To understand the world of Greece meant, first, an understanding of human life as something lived in human groups set in a physical environment. That is what men are encountered as being. They are not encountered as fallen angels, as wanderers from another realm. And they are not encountered as mere lumps of atoms, mere collections of electrons in motion. Those are theories about men, ways of understanding them. Both are extremely helpful, each in its own fashion. But neither is what we find, what Aristotle, and, one is tempted to add, what any true philosopher, is trying to understand. Groups of men in their natural setting—what the Greeks called "cities," *poleis*—formed the most insistent fact in the Greek world. Human life, with all the obvious and insistent traits it presents, is the central fact men are trying to understand, when they are seeking to understand the world in which they find themselves living. And no candid mind can view the great panorama of living beings in the world without seeking to ascertain the proper place of man among the multitude of other animate beings. Aristotle is convinced that no way of understanding the world, no scheme of "science," is worth its salt unless it provides the means for understanding living processes in general, and the processes of human living in particular. That is, for Aristotle the categories of "life" in general, and of "human life" in particular, are the most fundamental in any enterprise of understanding—because we who are trying to understand are neither angels nor electrons, but living men, and it is ourselves we are ultimately trying to know and understand. Like Socrates and like the Seven Wise Men of Greece, Aristotle makes the precept "Know Thyself" central in his vision of a world understood.

The "categories," the terms of understanding and explanation, which we employ must be such as to render the processes of human living, and the processes of life in general, intelligible in the same terms as any other natural processes. For Aristotle, life, and human life, do not present to us a problem to be solved, something to be somehow fitted into an "alien world," but rather a fact to be grasped and understood, indeed, the central fact. Throughout Aristotle there runs this controlling biological and functional point of view.

In the second place, to understand the world of Greece meant for Aristotle an understanding of intelligence and reason, of *nous,* as a natural and inevitable activity involved in human living, like breathing or digesting. This activity is the most fundamental fact in human life in general, and in Greek life in particular. Men are not only "physical" beings endowed with life—*empsycha,* "animate" beings—living in cities or *poleis*—"political animals." They are beings endowed also with intelligence, with *nous*—they are "rational animals," "political and rational animals."

Intelligence, knowing, is the most important and the most significant fact in the universe, the one big thing in the world for men, and for Greeks, trying to understand their world. For without it, there could be no importance or significance at all. The world can be understood, not in terms of what it means to God, or to a planet, but only in terms of what it means to men. If God—or if a planet—can "understand" the world, such beings must understand it in the same way in which man does. That is, the world is intelligible, and man's intelligence is a kind of flowering of the world's intelligibility.

During modern times, since Descartes—with the single exception of Spinoza, until our own century—it has been the accepted view that intelligence and knowing present a problem to be solved. The world, it has been held, is in fact a play of atoms and electrons, and could easily get along without "mind." Why, men have asked, is "mind," and thinking, added to what is quite perfect and complete without them? Why does it come in to complicate matters, to confuse us, to spoil the beautiful simplicity of it all, to raise insoluble problems? In such a world, "How is knowing possible?"

For Aristotle, that would be a wholly unintelligible question. Knowing is for him an obvious fact. What does it mean? How are we to construe and understand that fact? The real question, as he sees it, is, "In what kind of a world is knowing possible?" What does the fact of knowing imply about our world?

Modern philosophy, since the coming of the science of mechanics in the seventeenth century, has not been able to find any intelligible place for mind, for science itself, in the world that science describes. It has presented us with a host of impossible theories of "mind," of "consciousness" and knowledge. For Aristotle, that men can know their world is not a problem, but the most significant fact, both about men, and about the world. Men are animals that can know the world, and the world is a world that can be known. Knowing, intellectual grasp, *nous,* is itself cosmic and vital. "For *nous* is also a life," he says. And the world to be understood is primarily a world in which *nous,* "Reason," is a natural life. We can only appreciate the significance and the importance of this Aristotelian approach to the life of reason in nature after having journeyed on the long odyssey of "modern philosophy."

Thirdly, to understand the world of Greece means for Aristotle an understanding of language, of discourse, of *logos,* as the instrument of thinking and knowing. We think, we know, we understand, in terms of lauguage, by describing things in words, by making statements about things, by reasoning from one fact to another, by employing discourse. "Discourse" and "reason" are one and the same thing—in Greek they are designated by one and the same word, *logos.*

"Logic"—Aristotle's own term is "Analytics"—is the art of discourse, of using language, the Greek language. The world is the kind of world that can be talked about, in which things can be distinguished and defined, in which we can "reason" from one statement to another. The world lends itself to the grasp of language, it has a "logical" or "discursive" character, a systematic structure. Knowledge can find that structure, and express it in words and discourse: knowledge is, like language, systematic and "logical." "Knowing" is a matter of language, of stating; it is not a "having of sensations" or "sense data." And we can be said to "know" a thing, not when we perceive patches of color, as many British philosophers have assumed; and not when we have an "immediate experience" or "feeling" of it, or are "acquainted" with it, as William James and other "radical empiricists" have held; and not when by the exercise of an arbitrary "will to believe" we have made an "existential commitment" to it—Aristotle could understand British empiricism, since he had read the *Theaetetus,* and had profited by the reading; but I doubt whether even Aristotle could understand the notion of "existential truth."

No, we can be said to "know" a thing only when we can state in precise language what that thing is, and why it is as it is. Knowledge and language are a flowering of the world, an operation of its power to be understood and expressed. The Greek language, Aristotle is convinced—somewhat naively, we moderns think—is a perfect expression of the world's intelligibility. The structure of the Greek language and the structure of the world are ultimately the same, because the Greek language is a natural instrument for knowing and expressing the world's structure. This view too is doubtless naive. But is it really more naive than our modern conviction that the structure of mathematics and the structure of the world are the same?

Aristotle thus approaches every subject matter from the standpoint of living, of life as the foreground of nature; from the standpoint of knowing, of the way in which the mind grasps it, of the intellectual instruments it employs; and from the standpoint of talking, of the ways in which knowing proceeds, by means of language, making distinctions, arriving at an understanding, at a statement of what it can be said to be.

Chapter II

ARISTOTLE'S LIFE

AND CORPUS

1. The Legendary Life of Aristotle

We know, in actual fact, nothing whatever about the life of the author of the Platonic dialogues—we possess no certain knowledge of Plato the man. The ancient *Lives* of Plato that have come down to us from antiquity were written centuries after his death, when there existed a great Platonic school that had to have a worthy founder, and was accordingly furnished with one. They are made up of scraps of anecdote and illustrative stories that grew and improved in the telling over the centuries. In consequence, we now have a romance of Plato's career. It is itself a Platonic myth, just the kind of life that a man such as the author of the Platonic dialogues has come to be conceived should have lived. It is a myth, even though certain of the details should be in fact literally and historically accurate. What those details may be, we can never know.[1]

In contrast with the interest in the life of Plato that has given rise to this Platonic romance, men have never been greatly concerned with the historical career of Aristotle. It is true, stories have come down to us from the ancient scandalmongers.

[1] See Frederick J. E. Woodbridge, *The Son of Apollo* (Boston, 1929), ch. 1, "The Life of Plato." For a careful critical examination of the "evidence" on which conventional accounts of the life of Plato are based, furnishing a demonstration of the fact of our ignorance of Plato the man, see George Boas (with Harold Cherniss), "Fact and Legend in the Biography of Plato," *The Philosophical Review*, 57 (1948), 439–57.

As a young man, we are told, he squandered his patrimony in riotous living; he joined the army, and was thrown out of it; for a while he sold drugs and nostrums to make a living. Finally, at the age of thirty, he ended up in college—in Plato's Academy. Scholars have been worried by the reports that Aristotle quarreled with Plato: we are told, "He kicked off Plato as young colts do the mother mare who has born them." Now, we should like to see Aristotle as human, and not as a mere thinking machine. But unfortunately all these stories break down before the attacks of critical scholarship: they are to be found in our less reliable and more disreputable sources, while even our most truthworthy biographical information for this period leaves much to be desired.

The lack of serious interest in Aristotle's life during later antiquity, the absence of even any good stories, has been due to the universal assumption, bred of centuries of scholastic tradition, which began with the Hellenistic commentators on Aristotle, that his writings form an encyclopedia—that they are all of one piece. Even as recently as 1905 the leading French Aristotelian scholar, M. O. Hamelin,[2] could assume without question that the Aristotelian writings were all composed during the twelve years in which Aristotle was head of the Lyceum; and that he began at the "beginning," with the *Categories,* finished the *Organon,* and went right on through, following the order of our Bekker edition, ending with the *Poetics.* In contrast with Plato, who had achieved an intellectual "development" or *Entwicklung* at the hands of the evolutionary and genetically minded classical scholars of the nineteenth century, Aristotle was called a case of "arrested thought." It was assumed he never changed his mind or learned anything new, and so the higher critics kept away from him.

Today that is all changed. A few scholars, notably the English-

---

[2] O. Hamelin, *Le Système d'Aristote* (Paris, 1920; lectures delivered 1904-5, ed. Léon Robin).

man Thomas Case[3] and the German Werner Jaeger,[4] have shown how preposterous such a view was. Aristotle now enjoys as much right to an *Entwicklung* as anyone the higher critics have ever tackled. His right, indeed, is more securely based than is Plato's: for in his case we actually possess large fragments of his "early writings" as an external point of reference. Aristotle's "intellectual development" is based on actual documentary evidence, which is more than Plato can boast of—his *Entwicklung* is inferred entirely from internal evidence. And a close study of the chaotic and contradictory writings in the Aristotelian corpus themselves, in the light of these fragments of early works, makes clear that Aristotle did in fact pass through a process of intellectual growth and development that goes far to suggest possible genetic explanations of many of the outstanding contradictions in our Aristotelian texts, contradictions which for some two thousand years have puzzled the harmonizers in the successive scholastic traditions of interpretation. In what follows we shall first set forth Jaeger's general conclusions, and then state certain critical reservations.

Aristotle was primarily a scientific investigator and a scholar. But according to the reports he was also a friend of kings and princes; and he died the acknowledged intellectual master of the Greek world, with all Hellas at his feet. He was born in 384 B.C., in Stagira in Thrace. Stagira was an Ionian colony set in northern Greece, and Aristotle was an Ionian Greek. Nearly

---

[3] See his well worked out study in the article "Aristotle" in the 14th edition of the *Encyclopedia Britannica*.

[4] Werner Jaeger, *Studien zur Entwicklungsgeschichte der Metaphysik des Aristoteles* (Berlin, 1912); and *Aristoteles: Grundlegung einer Geschichte seiner Entwicklung* (Berlin, 1923; English trans. by Richard Robinson, 2d ed., Oxford, 1948; 2te veränderte Auflage, Berlin, 1955, based on Eng. ed.). Jaeger's method has been applied to other Aristotelian treatises by Friedrich Solmsen, *Entwicklung der Aristotelischen Logik und Rhetorik* (Berlin, 1929); F. J. C. J. Nuyens, *Ontwikkelingsmomenten in de Zielkunde van Aristoteles* (Nijmegen-Utrecht, 1939; French trans., *L'Evolution de la Psychologie d'Aristote,* Louvain, 1948); and Howard E. Runner, *The Development of Aristotle Illustrated from the Earliest Books of the Physics* (Kampen, Netherlands, 1951).

all the major Greek philosophers, with the exception of Socrates and Plato, had been Ionians: in any event, Aristotle was the heir of the already strongly developed Ionian interest in the facts of nature, an interest stretching back to the conventional "first" philosopher of the Greeks, Thales of Miletus.

Aristotle's ancestors, we are told, had been physicians to the rulers of Macedon; his father Nicomachus served King Amyntas in that capacity. He thus belonged to an old Asklepiad family, like the somewhat earlier Hippocrates of Cos; he is himself reported to have been trained as an Asklepiad, and to have been a member of that guild-like community. The Asklepiads all claimed descent from the great physician Asklepios, who figures in Homer and whose two sons ministered to the Greeks at Troy. Asklepios had himself just recently become a god on the Greek mainland, with his major shrine at Epidauros, and his spiritual powers were rapidly increasing. Hence, just as Speusippos credibly informs us that his uncle Plato was actually the son of Apollo himself, so in the Lyceum it was rumored that Aristotle's real begetter was Asklepios. Now Asklepios was himself the son of Apollo and of the daughter of the king of the civilizing Lapiths, whose battle with the barbarian Centaurs Apollo applauds on the eastern pediment of every properly built Greek temple. This makes Aristotle the grandson of Apollo, the divine reason and light, and the son of the god of healing and medicine, whose own strain united Apollo and the World Serpent. It also makes him the nephew of Plato.

The evidence for this genealogy may not seem incontrovertible to all classical scholars, who on most matters rarely arrive at unanimous agreement. But it is philosophically convincing. The divers elements it points to in Aristotle's ancestry—Apollo, Plato, Asklepios—are surely all present in Aristotle's heritage. He does indeed exhibit the temper of mind both of the Platonic dialectician, and of the observant physician with deep roots in the Earth. The physicians of the school of Hippocrates had already made the greatest achievements that empirical and experimental science was to attain before the Lyceum.

Aristotle grew up at the court of Amyntas, and was the friend of the king's son, Philip. The reports say that at the age of eighteen Aristotle came to Athens to secure the best education the Greek world had to offer, at the Academy supposed to have been set up by Plato. He studied there for twenty years, we are told, till the death of Plato. He was known as "the scholar" and "the reader"—he collected a large library of manuscripts, the first such collector of books we hear of after Euripides. He was known, appropriately, as the *"nous"* of the school. So runs the legend.

There is much doubt whether Aristotle actually studied in a school run by Plato, or not. The very existence of such a school, as well as what "studying with Plato" might mean, is a question that still vexes scholarship;[5] it is not without interest that Aristotle himself never mentions such an Academy, or his own study in it, and that most of his references to Plato himself are directed toward easily identifiable passages in the dialogues. But Aristotle was certainly seduced by the Platonic philosophy. Plato captured his allegiance, body and soul. He became a "Platonist": that is, he shared the mystic faith that is "Platonism," the devotion to "the Ideal," the aspiration after what is deathless and eternal—he shared and expressed these idealistic and religious interests. Aristotle was not an unimaginative fellow who was too stodgy to feel the appeal of "Platonism." Such a view, often and conventionally maintained, especially by those who regard themselves as followers of Plato, seems on the evidence to be all wrong. Rather, he appears as a young man to have been taken in by "Platonism" completely, to have given himself to its concern with imaginative vision.

As a "Platonist" Aristotle wrote a good many dialogues. We

[5] See the study by George Boas made with Harold Cherniss mentioned in footnote 1; and see Harold Cherniss, *The Riddle of the Early Academy* (Berkeley, California, 1945).

have the record of a number, and the fragments of at least eighteen.[6] All antiquity praised these dialogues of Aristotle for the "golden stream" of their eloquence, and judged Aristotle to be quite the equal of Plato as a writer—a fact to be remembered when we find our texts containing a metal heavier and less bright than gold. In these dialogues Aristotle seems to be in earnest, like the "later" Platonic dialogues. All Platonists are likely to be in earnest: they tend to fail to share the sense of the irony of life so strong in Plato himself. But Aristotle's dialogues are much more dramatic than the "later" dialogues of Plato: they seem to reflect real discussions, possibly in the Academy itself. They are thoroughly "Platonistic"—if not completely "Platonic"—in their spirit and ideas.

After Andronikos of Rhodes, Aristotle's first editor, these dialogues were misinterpreted as "exoteric" writings, containing false ideas for the general public, as contrasted with the "esoteric Aristotle," which Andronikos had at last gotten hold of, and would let you have on easy terms. This interpretation seems to have been a publicity device; the Greeks were quite capable of anticipating modern enterprise. Actually, Aristotle probably remained a Platonist until after the death of Plato. As such, he wrote a *Symposium,* a *Sophist,* a *Statesman,* a *Menexenus.* He wrote a *Eudemus,* modeled on the *Phaedo* and dealing with the deathlessness of the soul; a *Gryllos,* modeled on the *Gorgias* and dealing with rhetoric; a dialogue on justice, modeled on the *Republic.*

In the *Eudemus* the arguments of the *Phaedo* are simplified and reinforced; there is expressed a yearning for deathlessness, a faith, a taking seriously of the Pythagorean myths. Death is treated as a release; the soul is an immortal "substance" independent of the body. The *Eudemus* is in fact far more dualistic

[6] The standard edition of the Greek text of these fragments is edited by V. Rose in the Teubner series (1886); more recent editions by R. Walzer, and by Sir David Ross (1955). English translation by Sir David Ross as Volume XII of the *Oxford Translation of Aristotle* (1952).

than that most dualistic of all the Platonic dialogues, the *Phaedo*. It was used extensively by the later Neoplatonists, and hence considerable fragments have been preserved in their quotation— eight pages in Ross. The consolation Socrates is offering to his friends in Plato's picture of a man dying in such a way that he became deathless, Aristotle took quite literally. Yet his attitude is independent: he throws the proofs of the soul's deathless character into logical form. Aristotle was working at the problems he found in Plato's dialogues, but in his own spirit and manner. We must remember that according to the tradition, Aristotle is supposed to have been "studying" with Plato during Plato's "later" period, which exhibits a concern with method, with mathematics, and with natural science. In any event, the starting point of most of the Aristotelian treatises can be found in such "later" dialogues as the *Theaetetus*, in which is stated something very like his own analysis of sensing, and a close approach to his notion of science, *epistēmē*, as demonstration, *apodeixis:* "true opinion with *logos*," Plato puts it, which Aristotle translates as "knowledge of the that, *to hoti*, and of the reason why, *to dioti*." The *Sophist*, in raising the question of what it means *to be* anything, is asking the question with which Aristotle's First Philosophy sets out. The *Statesman* and the *Laws*, with their government of laws for this world as the closest approach to the rule of the divine *nous*, point to Aristotle's *politeia* or constitutional democracy; while the mixed life of the *Philebus* points to the complexities and relativities of Aristotle's mean and combination of moral and intellectual excellences.

Our largest collection of fragments—comprising some twenty-nine pages in Ross, largely taken from quotations in Iamblichus—come from the *Protreptikos*, or *Persuasion to Philosophy*, addressed to a certain Themiso, tyrant of Cyprus, to win him to the life of the philosopher-king. This work states the place of true knowledge, *epistēmē*, in life, and is a justification of *epistēmē* in the Platonic sense of an exact and practical wisdom.

It maintains the theory of Ideas, it emphasizes measurement and proportion, and seems very close to the *Philebus* ideal of the mixed life.

Ideas held in this early "Platonic period" of Aristotle's thought seem to be preserved in the *Organon,* especially in the *Posterior Analytics,* in which the doctrine of the *Theaetetus,* that *logos* must be added to "true opinion" or knowledge of facts to make *epistēmē* or "science," is worked out and made precise: the theory of science as demonstration in the *Posterior Analytics* presents a very Platonic "Idea" or ideal of science as completely formalized, on the model of geometry. The attitude of this Platonic period is reflected also in Book Lambda of the *Metaphysics,* with its Platonic feeling for the Idea of pure Good, "apart from" the world, which Aristotle calls "The Unmoved Mover," and describes in the "likely language" of the Platonic myth. Book Lambda expresses all Aristotle's early religious and theological interest. That interest is reflected also in the very notion of the science of what we call "metaphysics" as "the science of the things of *nous,*" as opposed to the things of the senses, the view that controls the thought in Books Alpha, Epsilon, and Kappa of the *Metaphysics.* This was Aristotle's earliest conception of the science which he then called "theology," the "science of divine things." And the Platonic period shines through the fourth and fifth chapters of Book III of the *De Anima,* about the *nous* that "makes all things," and is "separable," and deathless and eternal—and completely impersonal. These Aristotelian expressions of Platonism may all have taken first form while Aristotle was in the Academy, or shortly thereafter.

With Plato's death came Aristotle's *Wanderjahre.* Plato's nephew Speusippos became head of the Academy; his interests were strongly mathematical and Pythagorean, and Aristotle, whose temper belongs definitely to the Hippocratic, not the Pythagorean wing of Greek science, found them uncongenial.

He left Athens—apparently having made no break with Plato himself or his memory. We still have a touching elegy written for an altar to the "Friendship of Plato." Aristotle, the tradition tells us, continued to be held in the highest regard by the other members of the Academy. He remained away from Athens for twelve years: during this period he may well have begun to formulate his most characteristic "Aristotelian" doctrines. He first settled in Assos, near Troy, together with two fellow students from the Academy, Erastos and Koriskas. The tyrant of Assos was Hermias, quite a philosopher-king; at his court Aristotle taught and wrote and inquired, and married Hermias' niece. He stayed in Assos for three years, pursuing the problems of practical politics, and also biological investigation. Many forms of marine life described in the *History of Animals* have been found to be peculiar to that region near the Hellespont, and many place names mentioned are also located there.

Aristotle left Assos, and taught at Mitylene for five years. Here he won a reputation as a Pan-Hellenist, an advocate of a united Greece against the Persian might: this was the policy he had learned from Hermias, who was under great Persian pressure there at the edge of the Greek world. Then Aristotle was called to the court of Philip of Macedon, apparently on a political mission, not as a philosopher, but as a Greek patriot, whose advocacy of a united Hellas fitted in well with Philip's own ambitions. This devotion to a policy of union of Greek cities and empire, rather than to the old Greek *polis,* is not, of course, reflected in any of our Aristotelian texts, but permeates the tradition about Aristotle himself. He became tutor to Philip's son Alexander. Here at last a philosopher had found a real philosopher-king to educate—at least, a real king. The philosophical tradition likes to think that Aristotle had a great deal to do with making Alexander a genuine Greek, with a passion for spreading by force Hellenic ideals. The friendship endured, with some later coolness; on his excursions in the East, we are told Alexander always was careful to send biological specimens back to his old teacher.

The Persians had captured Hermias and put him to death. Aristotle wrote a hymn on this martyrdom, full of passionate Helenic patriotism. But in it there appears a new realization, that the Platonic "Ideas" are not the objects of science, *epistēmē*, but are religious ideals and symbols; that science is something quite different.

At this time Aristotle's teachings seem to have been in a transitional stage. "Platonism" was still a rational religion for him, but there is a growing desire to understand it more scientifically. From this period probably dates a dialogue *On Philosophy*, of which a portion amounting to twenty-one pages in Ross has been preserved. This starts with a history of philosophy, including that of the "orient": of Egypt, of Persia and the teachings of the Magi; and also including the Sophists. Plato is made to appear as the climax of Persian dualism. There also appears a critique of the "Ideas" of the Platonists taken as scientific concepts—the first such critique to appear in Aristotle. There is particular criticism of the Pythagorean number theory, which was held by Speusippos in the Academy; this is close to the critique in the *Metaphysics*, Book Alpha, and at the end of Book Nu. Aristotle speaks of himself as the true follower of Plato; Speusippos is departing from the master. Possibly those portions of the *Metaphysics* were written at this time.

In the dialogue *On Philosophy* Aristotle is also developing his own philosophy of nature. He still exhibits strong religious feeling, as we find it in the *Timaeus;* there are offered proofs of a God who is *nous,* the most perfect being. Religious aspiration is attached to the stars, the objects of astronomy: they are deathless and divine. To the end it is the stars and the planets that evoke religious emotion in Aristotle. The feeling is Platonic, but there is a science of "theology" there as the theory, the rationalization, of this feeling. Was this the time at which Aristotle first conceived the Unmoved Mover of Book Lambda? The temper and thought are very similar. Does the inception of the "active intellect" date from these days? In any event, the positions set forth in these passages seem the earliest part of the Aristotelian teaching to take form. The science of theology appears in the dialogue as even more fundamental than it is in Book Lambda of the *Metaphysics*. There are no traces of the central metaphysical distinctions of Books Zeta, Eta, and Theta.

Aristotle's speculative astronomy or cosmology was already formulated when the dialogue *On Philosophy* was written. This is the least "scientific" part of Aristotle, what has since the sixteenth century been in greatest disrepute. It clearly belongs to the early Platonic Aristotle, not to the mature investigator. The *De Caelo,* and perhaps the first two books of the *Physics*—the two containing the general theory of *physis*—may even have been written, Jaeger suggests, before Plato's death, while Aristotle was still in the Academy.

In 335 Aristotle returned to Athens, and set up a school and a kind of research foundation in the grove of the Lyceum, under the protection of the Macedonian statesman and proconsul Antipater. Here he taught for twelve years. In the mornings, we are told, he would lecture on logic and First Philosophy, as a methodological training for scientists. He talked in the Peripatos, a covered walk or loggia—whence the name of "peripatetic" for his school. In the afternoons he would give public lectures on rhetoric, politics, and ethics. All the while he engaged with his students and staff in extensive research.

Finally, in 323, after Aristotle had been teaching for twelve years, Alexander died. There was an anti-Macedonian reaction in Athens, and Aristotle fled to Chalcis, "lest," he is reported to have said, "the Athenians should sin twice against philosophy." He died the next year, a victim, we are told, of chronic indigestion. His character is reported to have been warm and affectionate: he was a kind husband and father, and a true friend, not a mere thinking machine. Rumor goes also that he had a bald head, thin legs, small eyes, and lisped; and that he dressed smartly.

The picture that emerges from the attempt of Jaeger and his followers to trace Aristotle's intellectual development is clear. Aristotle's philosophical system, the main outlines of his theoretical analyses, came near the beginning; they were probably worked out, Jaeger suggests, before he returned to Athens, during his middle period. He had made his early Platonic faith intelligible and scientific. He had created the analytical tools and methods for finding further knowledge: the theory of science that is now set forth in the *Organon,* his central metaphysical distinctions, perhaps his general theory of nature. These all came earlier rather than later: they proposed a program of investigation, and a technique for approaching and analyzing problems.

In Athens, tradition tells us, Aristotle seized the chance to engage in research and investigation, in the discovery, ordering, and explanation of facts, with the help of an organized research staff. Some of this research was antiquarian: he had compiled a list of the victors in the Olympic games, with their records. He prepared literary chronicles: he drew up lists of the competing dramatists and the prize winners. He investigated the facts of political science: he collected digests of the constitutions of 158 of the Greek city-states. The one on the *Constitution of Athens,* assumed to be by Aristotle himself, was discovered on papyrus in 1890, with appropriate excitement. He returned to the natural history that had interested him since the days in the Troad. The *History of Animals,* clearly at least begun at that earlier time, is the only such factual compilation that has been preserved. He collected psychological problems, and put together large histories of philosophy, and of the sciences.

Jaeger interprets this reported concern with empirical investigation as a turning in Athens from the elaboration of philosophic principles to the work of the special sciences, to the detailed application of his methods to the investigation of problems, to the use of his distinctions and concepts as techniques of analysis. He sees Aristotle as passing from philosophy to science; he compares the early treatment of the history of philosophy in Book Alpha of the *Metaphysics* with the later histories of the sciences. On such a view, Aristotle's true heirs were the great scientists of the Alexandrian period. The tradition, however, gives no support to any slackening of philosophical interest, nor does what we know of the concerns of many of his immediate successors like Theophrastos.

Jaeger's brilliant genetic hypothesis has revolutionized Aristotelian studies. For a generation it has indeed led to the expenditure of much time and effort in trying to determine just when Aristotle wrote a particular passage or book, effort that many scholars are beginning to suspect might well have been better spent in analyzing what he said in it. For the attempt to employ genetic techniques in detail soon made it clear that Jaeger's controlling assumption, that Aristotle's thinking progressed in a straight line from the "Platonism" of the dialogues to an exclusive emphasis on empirical research, is a great oversimplification. There is general agreement that the dialogues are "early," and that Aristotle "went on" from their Platonism. But the process of "going on," judged by any careful analysis of the treatises, was certainly very complex. It seems to have been not so much a movement "away from" Platonic notions as an addition to them, a putting of them in a broader factual context—with much necessary reconstruction, to be sure. There is not an Aristotelian document in which Platonic insights are not in some form deeply embedded; and their presence hardly bears witness to the date at which the book in which they are found took its present form. On the other hand, it seems clear that the biological research recorded in the *History of Animals* was at least begun while Aristotle was in the Troad and at Lesbos.

Aristotle thus seems to have displayed his passion for facts from the beginning of his independent thinking. And there is no evidence that he ever forgot the Platonic vision, or ever lost interest in refining and extending his philosophical principles. Both intellectual strands run through all Aristotle's thought. No doubt the resources of the Lyceum greatly enlarged the scope of his factual inquiries. And it is probable that his theoretical concepts underwent a critical reconstruction and sharpening. But if the details, especially the order, of that reconstruction can now be recovered at all, it is likely that they will be illuminated, not by attempting to assay the distance of passages from the position of the early dialogues, but by the methods Ross has increasingly employed: a careful examination of the references to works already written, and to the doctrines presupposed.

In any event, Aristotle emerges as a genuinely universal man, not only in the scope of his intellectual interests, but even more in the qualities of his mind. In it were combined the mystic feeling for the intellectual imagination that is *nous,* the keen dialectic and the precise distinctions of the *dialektikos,* and the careful observation and investigation of facts of the *physikos.* The Middle Ages could well call Aristotle "the Philosopher."

2. The Aristotelian Corpus in Legend, History, and Scholarship

The Aristotelian writings that have come down to us form a great contrast with those attributed to Plato. They exhibit nothing that could be called an artistic form, except for a few eloquent passages, like those about friendship in the *Ethics,* like the Platonic myth describing the Unmoved Mover in Book Lambda of the *Metaphysics,* and a few figures, such as, "One swallow does not make a summer." They are technical, laborious, and difficult, though in Greek they are nearly always quite clear, a fact no reader of the English translations would ever be led to suspect. They emphasize precise distinctions in the meaning of words, and the various subtle shades of significance which Greek usage gave them, very much in the spirit of present-day Oxford elucidation of English usages. They contain clear definitions of words and technical terms. Aristotle is always very keenly sensible of the fact of language as the instrument of thinking, and of the need for precision. He normally begins with ordinary Greek usage. But this usage needs to be sharpened and supplemented: "ordinary language" is Aristotle's starting point, not his conclusion.

The Aristotelian documents are fragmentary, and frequently break off; they are repetitious, and often display little clear order in their parts. Still more, they exhibit manifest contradictions, of approach, of mood, of theory, even of fundamental position and "doctrine." The obvious reason for this somewhat chaotic character is that our present text is not as Aristotle left it. The traditional legends that have come down to us about the history of the Aristotelian writings attempt to explain why. There is the romantic story of Strabo,[7] that the manuscripts were left to Aristotle's pupil Theophrastos, who in turn bequeathed them to a certain Neleus. He hid them in a cellar in Asia Minor, where worms and mold got at them. They were rediscovered there in Asia Minor by a collector of books, Apellikon, two hundred years after Aristotle's death. They were brought by Sulla to Rome, where a poor editor, Tyrannion, got them still further mixed up. They were finally edited and published in 70 B.C. by the eleventh Scholarch of the Lyceum, Andronikos of Rhodes, who put together the text of Aristotle as it has come down to us some two hundred and fifty years after Aristotle's death. Athenaeus adds, that some copies of the Aristotelian writings were purchased from Neleus by Ptolemy Philadelphus, for the great Library he

---

[7] Strabo XIII. I. 54, and Plutarch (*Sulla* 26). Strabo was a contemporary of Tyrannion, and presumably his student. For a recent critical discussion of this legend, see Felix Grayeff, "The Problem of the Genesis of Aristotle's Text," *Phronesis,* 1 (1956), 105–22.

was building up in Alexandria, but that they somehow got "lost" in the library. This seems quite credible: libraries have not changed much over the years.

All this while, the published dialogues of Aristotle were being widely read. It was to them that Cicero was referring when he spoke of Aristotle's *flumen orationis aureum,* "golden stream of eloquence," and Quintilian, when he praised Aristotle's *eloquendi suavitas,* "sweetness of eloquence." On the basis of these dialogues, Aristotle was taken as a thoroughgoing Platonist; the Platonists used and built upon them. The scientific lectures, we are told, were forgotten until the edition of Andronikos. It is reported that even the Lyceum had no copies of these treatises. This seems difficult to believe: it seems an excuse for the obvious petering out of the Lyceum. Perhaps Aristotle's own copies were given to Neleus.

When these documents were collected and published by Andronikos, the Aristotelian corpus was taken as a "system," a unified and consistent body of doctrine. The long line of commentators, from Alexander of Aphrodisias in the third century A.D. down, tried to "harmonize" them: this was the task of the whole "scholastic" enterprise, first in the Greek, then in the Syriac, the Arabic, the Jewish, and the Latin Christian traditions. Aristotle was made into a great system of thought, which finally came to dominate medieval Europe, and the influence of which has persisted in countless ways to this day.

But this system is scarcely Aristotle himself. The range and the open, growing character of Aristotle's thinking have been immensely illuminated by what scholarship has done in this generation, especially by the genetic studies of Werner Jaeger and Sir David Ross and their pupils. The emphasis they have given to an intellectual development in that thinking makes previous accounts quite literally "medieval." Most Aristotelian scholars would now accept a general "development" beyond the early dialogues, however sharply they may differ as to whether that development is traceable in the existing treatises, and as to just what course it followed. Critical reservations, however, have been growing about making too great claims for the application of a genetic analysis to the detailed chronology of the Aristotelian texts.[8] D. J. Allan[9] gives a brief account of this revolution in Aristotelian scholarship.

The works that form our text seem to be really rather full notes of lectures: Cicero calls them *commentaria,* "notebooks." Some are apparently Aristotle's own outlines and lecture notes: the first five chapters of Book Lambda of the *Metaphysics* seem to be of this character. Some seem to be brief summaries of what Aristotle has said for those who were not present. Some may well be students' notes, like those which make up much of Hegel's lectures, preserved in several different versions. Some, like the *History of Animals,* are probably in part reports of students' investigations.[10] In other words, there is to be found in the

[8] Thus Sir Ernest Barker sharply dissents: "Though there may be some natural propriety in the application of a genetic method to the problem (if it be a problem) of the composition and structure of the *Politics,* the results which are gained by its application seem highly dubious; and it is certain that the results obtained by one disciple of the method contradict, and contradict flatly, the results attained by another. The fact is that the use of the genetic method is vitiated by subjectivity. The inquirer who uses it becomes the prey of his own interpretation of Aristotle; and he gives or withholds chronological priority—in other words he makes *this* an early stratum, and *that* a later—on the grounds of his own inner feelings about the 'early' and the 'late' Aristotle." Sir Ernest Barker, *The Politics of Aristotle* (Oxford, 1946), p. xlii.

[9] D. J. Allan, *The Philosophy of Aristotle* (Oxford, 1952). See also the full and critical account in G. R. G. Mure, *Aristotle* (London, 1932), pp. 254–74.

[10] Felix Grayeff, in the article cited in footnote 7, concludes with the extreme hypothesis: "What has come to us as the *Corpus Aristotelicum* is, in fact, *hē bibliothēkē Aristotelous kai Theophrastou kai tōn met' autous,* i.e. the *Corpus Peripateticum,* or the School Library of the Peripatos. For contradictions, critical objections, discussions, differing viewpoints and varying standards are found in the Corpus to a degree that it seems impossible to attribute any part of it, i.e. any part of some length, to one individual author.

"It is likely that Tyrannion and Andronikos gathered and collected peripatetic lecture versions from wherever they could—and the main peripatetic centres, even at that time, were probably Rhodes and Athens (and perhaps Alexandria). The very large material which they had collected made their edition greatly superior to any earlier edition of the peripatetic writings. We may, therefore, assume that

corpus the activities of a whole school, dominated by a single great mind.

These notebooks were apparently planned and written originally as separate lectures on connected themes, in many cases not as the units we now possess. They were put together, with cross references inserted, partly perhaps by Aristotle himself, partly by the later editors. They finally attained almost their present form at the hands of Andronikos of Rhodes, to whom is attributed the construction of our texts of the *Politics* and of the *Metaphysics*. Andronikos invented the latter title for Aristotle's "First Philosophy," though he seems to have made only a ten-book collection, omitting Book Lambda. Hence our present versions preserve different layers of Aristotle's thought, sometimes worked over by Aristotle himself, sometimes fugitive writings collected under a common title, with a largely external unity. Thus the *Metaphysics*, "The Books that come after those on Physics," in the order of Andronikos' edition, corresponds

---

the influence of the early peripatetics on the Corpus Aristotelicum was even greater than has so far been realised; that, perhaps, it pertains to the whole of the Corpus Aristotelicum and that, broadly speaking, there may not be a single chapter in the Corpus which, as it stands now, is purely Aristotelian in origin. It is not improbable that the whole of the Corpus has passed through the hands of two or three successors and, in some cases, more than three, who amplified, criticized, explained and defended the text that was the basis of their own work." (pp. 118–19)

For the history of the early peripatetic school, see K. O. Brink in Pauly-Wissowa, *Realenzyklopädie,* suppl. VII (1940), "Peripatos," pp. 899–947. Grayeff summarizes: "We know that, for two or three generations after Aristotle, the peripatetic school flourished under Theophrastos, Straton and, perhaps, still under Lycon. It then slipped back and in spite of the intrinsic greatness of its teaching it was unable to compete with the Academy, the Stoics, the Epicureans. It appears that, after three generations, the peripatetic school ceased to be productive. . . . The platonising philosophers Theophrastos and Eudemos on the one side stood against Dicaearchos and Aristoxenos who were inclined to empiricism. . . . We also know that, at an early time, peripatetic philosophers were inclined to disperse and to establish themselves in different places. We know of Dicaearchos that he stayed in the Peloponnese for some time (Cic. Att. VI. 43), that Eudemos returned to Rhodes; and it is possible that Aristoxenos lived in Athens. The main centre of the school in the early period was, we can hardly doubt, Alexandria." (pp. 108–9)

quite literally to "Volume Eight" in the order of our own Oxford edition. Hence it appears quite as useless to attempt to harmonize all the writings contained in "Volume Eight" into a consistent body of doctrine, something the scholastic commentators have tried to do for centuries, as to endeavor to harmonize, say, the early Hegelian writings of John Dewey with *Experience and Nature* and his subsequent books.

If we accept the general picture made familiar by recent scholarship of an Aristotle pushing his thought "beyond" its initial Platonism, we see him setting out, a convinced Platonist, anxious to make "Platonism" intelligible by means of analytic thought, to get it all stated explicitly in words. He was trying to rationalize what for him was essentially a religious philosophy, as appears in the early "exoteric" dialogues. This was the same problem confronted by the medieval schoolmen: that is why Aristotle appealed to them so strongly. Reminiscent of this period of Aristotle's intellectual development are those elements in his thinking where he remains closest to the Platonic insights.

But unlike the schoolmen, Aristotle did not stop there. He proceeded to work out a much more naturalistic philosophy: the biological naturalism of the *De Anima,* Book II and Book III, chapters 9 through 13; the naturalism of individual things and processes of the *Physics,* and of Books Zeta, Eta, and Theta of the *Metaphysics;* perhaps the more naturalistic books of the *Politics.*

But Aristotle did not confine himself to the formulation of a matured naturalism. He directed it toward research, observation, and investigation, toward empirical science. In other words, Aristotle's logic, his geometrical theory of science, came rather early, with its very Platonic conception of the ideal of science as stated in the *Posterior Analytics.* This conception of demonstration is very close to the *Theaetetus;* there is almost no emphasis on the methods and procedures of inquiry and investigation. This extremely influential ideal of what a science should be, its

Platonic Idea, as it were, determined the aim of the modern scientific enterprise until the nineteenth century; and as the ideal of a completely "formalized" science it is still with us today, though it receives little support from our scientific enterprise as it has now developed.

But according to Jaeger Aristotle himself grew more and more empirical. In any event, the writings themselves make clear, he was never bound by his own theories: he used those theories as hypotheses, as tools, as "leading principles." He was impressed by the fact that although facts alone do not give understanding —he is no mere observationalist or positivist—facts are nevertheless far more certain than any theory. The final evidence is introduced when Aristotle can say, "but we see" that the consequences deduced dialectically from some theory or hypothesis are not the case. In Aristotle's own procedure, there is never any conflict between theory and facts: in his practice, theory is always modified to take account of facts. Aristotle's practice of inquiry thus belongs to nineteenth-century science, whereas the formal statement of his ideal belongs rather with the pioneers of the seventeenth century. It took the moderns some seven hundred years to get as far from "Platonism" to "Aristotelianism" as Aristotle himself was able to get during his own lifetime.

This account of Aristotle's intellectual development, which follows the main pattern of Jaeger's, seems initially extremely plausible. Perhaps it is indeed too plausible, as many judicious scholars are beginning to suspect. For it depends on the methods of the higher criticism of texts; and anyone at all familiar with that enterprise knows that there is no easier way to lose your balance and judgment. One normally ends, either by triumphantly proving one's own assumptions, or, if one is too honest for that, by having no unified manuscript left at all. With Aristotle we do, of course, possess considerable fragments of the early dialogues as external points of reference.

Moreover, experience has made clear that the results of this genetic method can hardly be taken literally, as establishing the actual order of composition of the existing documents and their component parts. Continuing lack of agreement in the conclusions of the able scholars who have made the attempt has brought a healthy disillusionment on that score. There are always "survivals of interest" in a man's later writings, early ideas he continues to hold to and tries to fit in with the fruits of further reflective experience. It would be rash to maintain that this is not preeminently true of the many Platonic conceptions found in the midst of Aristotle's most naturalistic passages.

Yet the general picture just set forth made a wide appeal as soon as Jaeger drew it. It has been seriously entertained by German, English, French, and American scholars, despite the difficulties that soon developed when men went beyond the general recognition that Aristotle presents a process of reconstructing "Platonism," to attempt to apply the genetic method to the dating of particular parts of the text. What accounts for this ready acceptance? The answer is clear: it has been so generally accepted, not merely because of the cogency of Jaeger's critical arguments, but ultimately because it strikes the student of Aristotle as both psychologically and philosophically true. We can never be certain that the passage about the so-called "active intellect" was *written* by Aristotle before the behaviorism that precedes and follows it. But it is a fact that "Aristotelianism" comes after "Platonism" and supplements it. The free imaginative speculation of the mind develops first, the chastened discipline of that imagination by facts, by verification, the hard work of controlled investigation, is achieved only later. This order is so profoundly true, both psychologically and historically, in the maturing of the thinking of an individual mind, and in the working out of an intellectual tradition, that it is easy to be convinced it must have been true in the case of Aristotle himself.

And yet—in spite of all the confusion of the documents, in

spite of the apparent record of an intellectual development, the
Aristotelian writings still manage to give the impression of
forming an organic whole. They are all bound together in a
unity of knowledge, of which the cross references are the symbol.
This fact of the organic unity of knowledge is for Aristotle himself the foundation of a central body of knowledge, "First
Philosophy." Each part, each separate science, is also an organic
whole: each has its own distinctive "first things," its distinctive
archai, "beginnings of understanding," *principia* or "principles,"
from which it radiates.

Does this mean that Aristotle is "systematic," is a great sys-
tematizer, is an "encyclopedist"? Yes, he was that during the
Hellenistic era and the Middle Ages, he became that in the hands
of Avicenna, Averroes, Maimonides, Albertus Magnus, and
Thomas Aquinas; he largely remained it in the grasp of the
nineteenth-century classical scholars. But we have only to compare Aristotle himself with any of the Hellenistic "systems" of
philosophy, which are true systems, to realize the vast difference.
Aristotle's own thinking is not closed, like theirs, but open. For
Aristotle knowledge is not a neat "system," but a living growth,
like a tree—it goes on and on, it is biological. *Nous* is a life,
the flowering of the world-life. Note Aristotle's keen sense of
the continuity and the cumulative growth of scientific inquiry.
Each science, and knowledge as a whole, is provisional and open.
Aristotle makes his many distinctions not to classify and cat-
alogue a subject matter—he is no Linnaeus—but as instruments
of living research.

Even logic, "Analytics," is for Aristotle not a science but
a *dynamis,* a "power"; a *technē,* an "art"; an *organon,* a "tool."
Aristotle's analysis is never an end in itself, but is always for
the sake of "knowing," of science. It may be suspected that
Aristotle would have had little sympathy with modern mathematical logic, which aims at beauty rather than use, and takes

the view of the Platonic tradition, that logic is a "science," the science of order.

The Aristotelian writings are "systematic" only in the common thread of the distinguishing and organizing power of analysis. Aristotle's formal classifications, like that of the sciences into theoretical, practical, and productive, made in one context, are often in another context discarded for a more appropriate classification. And no science is for him complete: the individual "inquiries" of Aristotle are in no sense systematic. They start with problems, *aporiai;* they grow and radiate from those problems. But he never answers more than a small part of the problems he initially states; and he ends by defining further problems. The Aristotelian corpus can be said to present a totality, not of results, but of problems. It is the problems that are for him primary, the systematic interest secondary. For the later Hellenistic systems, it is the systematic interest that is the primary concern.

What this means is that Aristotle is not a "scholastic," and that to grasp the range and significance of his thought it is important not to try to turn him into one. For he is not adequately understood merely as that "syllogistic gentleman with a category for every emergency," [11] whom the tradition has for the most part made out of him. This element is indeed there: concern with precise talking does form a central strand of his thinking. But what strikes a student today as even more fundamental is that other strand that forces us to call him the outstanding *functionalist* in the Western tradition. In modern terms, he can be viewed as a behaviorist, an operationalist, and a contextualist, with a thoroughgoing philosophy of process. The sense in which these present-day labels can be applied significantly to important aspects of Aristotle's thought will be a major theme of the following pages.

[11] The phrase comes from F. J. E. Woodbridge.

Chapter III

SCIENCE AS RIGHT TALKING:

THE ANALYSIS OF DISCOURSE

*1. Aristotle's Platonic Idea of Science
as Demonstration*

It was Aristotle who really invented the idea of "a science": he
sets forth that idea in the *Posterior Analytics,* one of the two
central writings that are collected in the *Organon,* the other
being the *Prior Analytics.* Plato has much to say about "science,"
epistēmē, true knowledge. But for him "science" is a single body
of knowledge, unified in the light of what he calls "the Idea of
the Good." Plato has no conception of separate "sciences": such
distinct bodies of knowledge he calls "arts," *technai.* And the
whole Platonic tradition has always had a strong drive toward
the unification of all knowledge into a single consistent system:
the latest instance is furnished by what today is called the "Unity
of Science" movement. Such a unification into a single deductive
system has always been the aim of what Platonists have called
"metaphysics." The classic modern illustration is the *Principia
Mathematica* of Whitehead and Russell.[1]

[1] Cf. the statement of a leading recent Platonist, A. E. Taylor: "We may say
that what the *Republic* calls 'dialectic' is, in principle, simply the rigorous and un-
remitting task of steady scrutiny of the indefinables and indemonstrables of
the sciences, and that, in particular, his ideal, so far as the sciences with which he
is directly concerned goes, is just that reduction of mathematics to rigorous de-
duction from expressly formulated logical premisses by exactly specified logical
methods of which the work of Peano, Frege, Whitehead, and Russell has given us
a magnificent example. . . . Such a unification of the sciences as the *Republic*
contemplates would require a combination of the reduction of mathematics to

In contrast, Aristotle formulates the notion of a whole series of separate and distinct "sciences," all of which possess certain methods and certain distinctions in common, but each of which has also its own distinctive *archai* or "principles," and its own determinate subject matter. The working-out and statement of what such a type of "science" involves seems to have come at the middle of Aristotle's career. The formulation of his ideal or aim in the *Posterior Analytics,* except for this pluralistic conception of many "sciences," is very Platonic: that work might well be called Aristotle's attempt to delineate the Platonic Idea of "a science itself," much as the central aim in the *Republic* is the attempt to delineate the Idea of "Justice itself." When Aristotle had embarked upon his own program of investigation, he found the actual practice of science, of inquiry and analysis, much more empirical. There is in the *Posterior Analytics* no concern with questions of method and procedure: Aristotle's gaze is fixed entirely on what a completed and perfected science is like. And the model is of course Greek geometry—what was to be codified in the next generation as "Euclid." This is Aristotle's model of "a science" of those things that are "always or for the most part," *aei ē hōs epi to poly.* This does not conflict with Aristotle's own position in the medical rather than the mathematical tradition of Greek science. For to Aristotle, medicine is not a "science," but the greatest illustration of an "art," a *technē.*

The *Posterior Analytics* undertakes to analyze what science is, and how to use language, *logos,* as an instrument, an *organon,* to formulate and express it. In the *Posterior Analytics* Aristotle thus answers the question raised in the *Theaetetus:* What is *epistēmē,* science? Aristotle's answer runs: We "just know," we have genuine "science," *epistēmē,* when we can state in precise

logic with the Cartesian reduction of the natural sciences to geometry." A. E. Taylor, *Plato: The Man and His Work* (London, 1926), p. 293. Descartes is of course one of the greatest of thinkers in the Platonic tradition.

language not only *that* things are so, *hoti,* but also *why* they are as they are, *dioti,* and why they have to be that way. We possess science when we can prove and demonstrate statements about them, by relating those statements to other statements of which they are the necessary consequences.

"Science" is thus for Aristotle a knowledge of the whys, the *dioti*'s, the "reasons for" true statements. It is a knowledge of the dependence of true statements on more fundamental truths, on "first things," *ta prōta,* or "causes," *aitia.* Science, that is, is like geometry, the model Aristotle clearly has in mind, as the one such fully developed and formalized science the Greeks had managed to achieve, in which theorems are demonstrated from initial axioms and definitions. This is of course a very Platonic conception of science, of *epistēmē.* It is Platonic, not only in taking with Plato geometry as the model, but also in pursuing the third definition of science proposed in the *Theaetetus,* that science is "true opinion with *logos."* The two elements of Plato's proposed definition appear in Aristotle as the knowledge of the *fact that, to hoti,* and of the *reason why, to dioti.* The *Theaetetus* had bogged down in the attempt to analyze the *logos* that must be added to factual knowledge to convert it into "science." Aristotle undertakes to analyze this *logos* of the *Theaetetus,* its character, and what is involved in it.

Science is thus for Aristotle not the mere observation of facts, of the *fact that, to hoti:* it is not mere observation or sensing. In observing the *fact that* something is the case, we sense or observe "this here thing, here and now," *tode ti:* in his illustration, we observe this particular eclipse. But we cannot, through mere observation alone, sense what is true of this kind of event always and everywhere, of "eclipses" as a class. We do not, by merely observing this particular eclipse, recognize what is true of every instance of an eclipse, what is true in "the nature of the case," so that it *must* be true in this particular instance. By merely observing this instance, we do not recognize the "universal" characteristics of any eclipse: we do not recognize the "cause" of eclipses.

Hence from observation alone we cannot really find out what an eclipse is: we cannot on the basis of mere observation state the definition of an eclipse. We cannot state what "causes" the observed fact. We observe particular instances of definite kinds of event. But "science" does more than this: science states something about a certain "kind" of event or thing. Science brushes aside what is irrelevant, extraneous, and incidental—what is "accidental"—about the particular instances observed, and states what is "essential" to being that "kind" of thing or event. Science thus states its "reason why," its *dioti;* it states what that kind of thing really is.

Science is thus demonstration, *apodeixis.* As in geometry, it demonstrates the *reasons why, ta dioti,* things are as they are observed to be, and why they must be so, and it demonstrates these reasons why from "first things," *ta prōta.* It demonstrates them from things that come before the conclusions, and are hence logically prior to those conclusions. It demonstrates them, consequently, as stated in Latin, *"a priori."* It demonstrates its conclusions from the "beginnings" of demonstration and of explanation, from *archai* of demonstration. *Archē* in Greek means "beginning." As Aristotle says, a quarrel is the "beginning" or *archē* of a fight; and the keel is the "beginning" or *archē* of a ship.[2] *Archē* meant also, "rule" or "control"; and this connotation also enters into the flavor of Aristotle's "beginnings" of demonstration. These *archai* of demonstration and science appeared in Latin as *"principia,"* or principles—the Latin term for "beginnings." In English, they mean the "beginnings" of understanding and intelligibility.

Hence for Aristotle every science comprises three factors: 1) that "about which" it establishes some theorem or conclusion, its *peri ho:* the particular and determinate subject matter about

[2] *Metaphysics* Delta, ch. 5: 1013a 5.

which that particular science proves conclusions. In each case, that subject matter is a certain "kind" of thing, about which it demonstrates the properties and causes. A science contains also 2) "what" it establishes as conclusions, *ha:* the causes and properties of that particular kind of thing. And it exhibits 3) that "from which" it demonstrates its conclusions, its *ex hōn:* namely, its first things, or *archai,* its principles.

We have to start always with a certain subject matter, a certain kind of thing. This subject matter is what we are trying to understand. We have to know what we are talking about: we have to be able to point to that subject matter, to denote it, as in the case of "living things" (*empsycha*) in the *De Anima,* or "natural things" (*physika*) in the *Physics.* This subject matter is just what Plato, employing his dramatic method, makes us "see" dramatically; though for Aristotle, just what that kind of thing is, and how to state what it is, the formulation of its definition, will come at the end of our inquiry, when we have completed that inquiry successfully.

That "from which" we demonstrate the properties of a subject matter, the *archai* or "first things," are of two kinds. They include those common to all the sciences, like the axiom, "If equals be taken from equals, the results will be equal"; and those peculiar or proper to a particular science, like the geometrical axiom, "A straight line is the shortest distance between two points." The common *archai* include those "from which" any demonstration proceeds, the *archai* of demonstration itself, usually implicit: the *archai* of logic, logical principles. The proper *archai* include those things "about which" we demonstrate conclusions: number, magnitude, lines, etc.—i.e., a determinate subject matter. The *archai* thus embrace definitions as well as axioms.

All sciences have certain things in common. They all exhibit certain universal distinctions and concepts, to be employed in making any subject matter intelligible. These common distinctions are treated and examined in what Aristotle calls "First

Philosophy," and we have come to call "metaphysics." They all exhibit also certain universal methods of proof, certain tools of reasoning, certain *archai* of reasoning and convincing, of "dialectic" or argument. This common method of proof is the syllogism, which Aristotle treats in the *Prior Analytics,* which deals with reasoning in general, and contains his treatment and exposition of his great discovery of the instrument of proof, the syllogism. This examination is "prior" to the treatment of demonstration in the *Posterior Analytics,* because, as Aristotle puts it, "The syllogism is the more general. The demonstration is a kind of syllogism, but not every syllogism is a demonstration." [3]

The proper *archai,* peculiar to a single subject matter, mark off the distinctive subject matters of the different sciences. These are distinguished in terms of their own *archai* or principles. Thus the *archē* of nature or *physis* sets off natural things as the subject matter of Natural Philosophy or Physics, the *archē* of life or *psychē* sets off animate things or *empsycha* as the subject matter of biology, the *archē* of welfare or *to eu zēn* sets off the subject matter of Ethics, the *archē* of the *polis* sets off the subject matter of Politics, etc. Each kind of thing, natural motions, living processes, living well, the city, has *archai* appropriate to it in terms of which it can be understood, "reasons why" it displays the properties and characteristics it does.

Aristotle distinguishes three different kinds of reasoning or syllogism, the dialectical, the eristic, and the demonstrative or scientific. These three kinds of reasoning do not differ in their form; the difference between them lies in the character of the premises from which they proceed. And when Aristotle discovered the principle of the syllogism, and worked out the first three figures of the now standard four, he included all three kinds of syllogism in his formal analysis of reasoning in general, in the *Prior Analytics.* But he seems to have begun with

[3] *Prior Analytics* I, ch. 4: 25b 28–31.

dialectical reasoning, in the earliest of his three treatments of reasoning, in the *Topics,* or "places" for finding arguments. The *Topics* has been shown to be clearly earlier than the other two treatments, in the *Prior* and the *Posterior Analytics.* It is obviously the work of a young man, and was clearly written before he had discovered the principle of the syllogism; though in our collection of books in the text of the *Organon,* it is placed after the two works on analytics.[4]

Dialectical reasoning is the reasoning of conversation and argument, *to dialegesthai,* in which the participants try to agree on premises. It is the reasoning of discussion, of the Sophists, of Socrates, of the Socratic dialogues, of that whole Greek world of talk and discussion and political argument. In the *Topics* Aristotle conceives "dialectic" as the science of what happens, not when we are thinking by ourselves, but when we are talking with others, and trying to convince one another. Its problem is to find good arguments to support our position. That is, its problem, like that of Socrates, is to find the premises your opponent will agree to, from which you can force him to admit the conclusion you want. The problem of dialectic is thus the lawyer's problem. Aristotle defines the syllogism: "A syllogism is an argument in which, certain things having been assumed, something other than these fellows of necessity by virtue of the things assumed." [5] In dialectical arguments, the things assumed must be "opinions that are generally accepted, *endoxa,* accepted by all, or by the majority, or by the most notable and illustrious of them," [6] to which you can hence get your opponent, or the court, to agree.

Dialectical arguments of this sort, clearly growing out of Socrates' way of questioning and arguing orally, probably played an important part in instruction in the Academy. In the *Phaedrus,* Plato expresses distrust of the written word, and prefers the

[4] See the lucid and brilliant account of the development of Aristotle's logical thought in Ernst Kapp, *Greek Foundations of Traditional Logic* (New York, 1942), ch. 1.

[5] *Prior Analytics* I, ch. 1: 24b 18–19.   [6] *Topics* I, ch. 1: 100b 23, 24.

Socratic "dialectic" of questioning and arguing.[7] What Aristotle
added to this educational practice was a systematic introduction
to "dialectic" or argument, in the *Topics*. That treatise announces
its subject as "useful for intellectual training, and for arguing
with men on the basis of their own opinions." [8]

The problem of such dialectical reasoning is clear. The conclusion to be admitted by your opponent is there to begin with,
to en archē. What is sought is the questions to ask, the propositions, the *protaseis*, to get him to admit. The questioner has to
"think backward" to the premises that will prove his point.
Hence Aristotle's first conception of what we call "logic," in the
Topics, was the dialectical syllogism that arises in conversation
and argument. This conception dominates his notion of the
logikos or *dialektikos*, and of thinking *logikōs* or *dialektikōs*
—the arguer who "discusses" questions, as contrasted with the
physikos, who thinks *physikōs*, the investigator of natural
processes.

The second form of reasoning Aristotle distinguishes, the
"eristic" or contentious syllogism, is treated in the last book of
our *Organon, De Sophisticis Elenchis, On Sophistic Refutations*,
or *On Fallacies*. This book seems to have been written after the
Topics, but before the discovery of the principle of the syllogism,
and to have been appended by Aristotle to the *Topics*. It is
directed against the confusions about words that had been
professionally abused by certain of the Sophists—against what
Plato is satirizing in the *Euthydemus*, where the eristic syllogism
is advanced by the two brothers: "Your dog has puppies, therefore he is a father. He is your dog, therefore he is your father." [9]
Such eristic reasoning starts from "opinions that seem to be
generally accepted, but are not really accepted; or seems to
reason from accepted opinions, but does not really reason from
them." [10]

So far, Aristotle had not found any general principle of valid

[7] *Phaedrus* 274 B-277 A.
[9] *Euthydemus* 298 E.
[8] *Topics* I, ch. 2: 101a 27-33.
[10] *Topics* I, ch. 1: 100b 24-26.

reasoning. He gives a fourfold classification of arguments in the *Topics*, with a really amazing variety of forms. They all aim at the search for possible premises, starting from a conclusion desired and given. They do not seek for the conclusions that will follow from given premises. This central problem of the dialectical syllogism is generalized in Aristotle's treatment of reasoning or the syllogism in general, in the *Prior Analytics*, and is carried over into the treatment of scientific reasoning, or demonstration, *apodeixis*, in the *Posterior Analytics*.

The demonstrative syllogism, *apodeixis*, which produces genuine knowledge, science or *epistēmē*, hence does not aim to lead from known premises to a conclusion up to then unknown. On the contrary, in the demonstrative syllogism also the conclusion is an observed fact previously known, a "that," a *hoti*. The scientific explanation, the "reason why," the *dioti* or "cause," will when found form the premise from which that observed fact can be demonstrated as a conclusion. Thus the scientific syllogism derives facts already known through observation, "thats," from "reasons why," or *archai*. It is not a logic of the discovery of new facts, but a logic of proof, of "formalizing" or systematizing facts already known. Thus the observed fact, given by experience, that the planets do not twinkle, is derived from two premises, "What is near does not twinkle," and "The planets are near." The observed fact follows from these premises as a conclusion. No new facts are ever derived from given premises in any syllogism: if they were, that would be a *petitio principii*, a begging of the question. Something new has however been added: not new facts, but the connection, the demonstration, the proof and explanation.

Now, if demonstration is to produce genuine knowledge, *epistēmē*, certain conditions are necessary. The "first things," the *archai*, the premises of the demonstrative syllogism, or *apodeixis*, must be true. It is this truth of the premises or *archai* that is what distinguishes demonstration and science from mere dialectic, in which the *archai* are only "probable" and "accepted" —that is, which are what we call mere "postulates." In demonstration the *archai* must also be "prior," in the sense that the facts in the conclusion can be logically derived from them. They must be "better known" and "more certain" than the facts being demonstrated. They must be themselves "undemonstrated" and "immediate," not mediate, not themselves links in a chain of proof, but genuine starting points. And they must be "causes" of the facts in the conclusion, in any of Aristotle's four senses of "cause," if they are to give genuine explanation or "reasons why." That is, the *archai* must possess all these characters in the statement of a completed science, in completed proof or *apodeixis*, in a formalized science like Euclidean geometry, which is Aristotle's model.

This is the statement of the ideal of a perfected science, of the Platonic Idea of a "science itself," *autē hē epistēmē*. This is what a science aims to become when it has been completely formalized or "demonstrated." It is not, of course, a statement of scientific method, of the procedures to be followed in inquiry and discovery, though it has often been so misread. And as Aristotle himself went on, he naturally grew more and more interested in something quite different from this ideal of demonstration, in the methods of inquiry. For Aristotle, the syllogism is in no sense a method of investigation, but a method of proof. In our actual method and procedure of inquiry, Aristotle insists, the *archai* of proof are not the starting point at all. "For us" the establishment of just what are the *archai* of demonstration and proof is the last step in inquiry. When found, they then become the logical starting point of understanding and proof. They are logically but not methodologically prior.

In Aristotle's actual investigations, and in his treatises or lectures, his *archai* always function very much as what we should today call "hypotheses." They are relative to their subject matter, and to their primary function of making it intelligible. The subject matter, the observed facts, what "we see," as Aristotle always puts it, are always ultimate and controlling for him. "For us," in our procedure of inquiry, what comes first temporally is the observation of the facts, the subject matter, and its structure. The task of "science" and demonstration is to fit these observed facts into a system of knowledge: it is to formalize our observations. The *archai* or principles emerge in this process of systematizing, as the unproved premises of proof. And they in turn lead on to the observation of further facts, in the process of the endless growth of inquiry and knowledge.

This Aristotelian conception of science, as set forth in the *Posterior Analytics,* is still the Platonic Idea, the ideal, of our modern scientific enterprise. It states precisely what Newton did, in discovering the mathematical *archai,* the *principia mathematica,* from which the facts observed by Copernicus, Kepler, and Galileo could be demonstrated. And the physicists of our day, like Einstein, have been merely finding still more fundamental *archai,* showing that Newton's *principia* are not immediate and ultimate, but mediate and derived from those still more fundamental *archai.* Thus our science too has proceeded from facts, from "thats," to "reasons why," to *archai,* and then back again to more facts.

Whence are these *archai* derived? How do we arrive at them? Aristotle's answer to this question, obviously fundamental for his whole conception of science, is that we learn them from observation of facts, of particular instances, by *epagoge,* which is usually translated into Latin as "induction." We have the power of perceiving particular "thats" by our senses. These perceivings remain as a "memory," and generate a *logos,* a meaning. "Many like memories make one experience, one *empeiria.*" That is, by "experience" of facts, by repeated observations, we become aware of the *arche,* the universal, that is implicit in them. "When the observation of instances is often repeated, the universal that is there becomes plain." [11] That is, in every perception of a partic- ular "that" we perceive the universal in it. But that universal only becomes "plain" and "evident" by repetition. By repeated ex- perience of it, it stands out from what is irrelevant and incidental —from what is "accidental"—in each instance. It is, says Aristotle, in a famous figure, just as in a battle, where the men are fleeing from the enemy in disorder. But then one man takes a stand, others join him, and finally the original order of the battle line is reestablished. The point of this figure is that the Greek for "original order" is *archē.*

This process of learning *archai* Aristotle calls *epagogē,* "in- duction." The Schoolmen, to distinguish it from another process Aristotle also calls *epagogē,* and which we call "complete enu- meration"—for instance, finding what all the planets possess in common by considering each of them in turn—called it "abstrac- tion," and held that we arrive at *archai* by a process of abstrac- tion. This was unfortunate, for the process Aristotle has in mind has nothing to do with the process of logical abstraction, or stripping away the particulars from the universal. It means seeing more than the mere thats, not seeing less; it is not a process of denuding, but the discovery of additional meaning. It means seeing not only the particular instances, but seeing also the intelligible structure of the particulars that is implicit in the various thats. It is very much like what Hegel called the "con- crete" universal: Hegel was very consciously trying to get back to Aristotle in emphasizing the concrete as opposed to the ab- stract universal.

This process of *epagogē,* which applies particularly to the dis- covery of mathematical *archai,* is helped in more complex fields by the further process of dialectic—by the dialectical examination of suggested *archai.* This Aristotle calls the "scientific" use of dialectic. For it is by dialectic that we examine proposed *archai,*

[11] *Posterior Analytics* II, ch. 19: 100a 5, 6; 100b 4, 5.

or explanatory hypotheses, as we should say. Dialectic develops
their implications, and brings to light any self-contradiction in
them; it then confronts the consequences dialectically derived
from the hypotheses with the facts. "It raises searching difficulties." We can examine *archai* only by comparing them with
their factual consequences. The *archai* to be examined are the
"accepted opinions," the *endoxa,* "of the most notable and
illustrious men," the *archai* of Aristotle's "predecessors," the
Eleatics or *logikoi,* and Empedocles and Democritus, the
physikoi. "For dialectic," he concludes, "is a process of criticism
(*exetastikē*) wherein lies the path to the *archai* of all inquiries." [12]
In the *Topics,* Book I, chapter 2, Aristotle states precisely the
procedure he himself follows in the first book of each of his
inquiries; he there selects the hypotheses or proposed *archai*
advanced by his predecessors, and subjects them to a searching
"dialectical" examination, modifying them and reconstructing
them until they are satisfactory to serve him as the *archai* of
that subject matter.

This is how we arrive at and formulate the *archai.* How do we
know that these *archai* are true? They must be true if we are
to find a genuine demonstration or *apodeixis,* genuine science.
This is clearly a quite different question from the one, how
do we arrive at them? It is a logical, not a psychological or
methodological question. Aristotle's answer is, in examining
particular facts by means of the *archai* arrived at by the process
we have just been describing, we "recognize" the significance,
the explanatory power of those *archai.* It is *nous,* working with
and in the midst of facts, working in the subject matter itself,
that "sees" the truth of the *archai. Nous* does not "see" the truth
of *archai* by holding them up, in isolation from the facts they
explain, and just staring at them; it "sees" their truth in the
subject matter.

This is an exact, analytical statement of the point of the

[12] *Topics* I, ch. 2: 101b 3, 4.

metaphor that Plato uses, that knowledge is like remembering something, like recognizing what we have known all along. We find universals in experience. We add two apples to two apples, and find we get four apples; we add two marbles to two other marbles, and we get four marbles. In this way we come to learn that two and two are four: we "see" it in a kind of intellectual vision, we "recognize" its truth. But two and two are not four *because* of the apples, or *because* of the marbles: the apples are clearly irrelevant to the truth of the arithmetical proposition.

Plato had put this, it is "like remembering," like "being reminded" of the truth, by experience, by observed facts. Aristotle puts it, we "recognize" the universal, the *archē,* by *nous,* by an intellectual seeing. These are two different ways of trying to express the element of recognition, of insight, in knowledge. We "see" the point, we say: it now "makes sense." This function of *nous* is like "seeing the point" of a story or joke. We either see it or we don't.

Aristotle's formulation was taken over by the great scientific pioneers of the seventeenth century, from Galileo and Newton on. Their method was to take a few instances, like that of the ball rolling down an inclined plane, and to analyze those instances, in order to "see" the mathematical relations involved. Galileo's *Two New Sciences* is full of examples of the sort. How, then, is the relation or law seen there in the instance to be proved to be true? By "experience"? No, experience can only "illustrate" the law, it cannot "prove" its truth. One or two crucial instances will suffice to "reveal" the law, and make us "recognize" its truth. No matter what their theory of method, scientists have always done something just like this, even when they have been bulldozed by theorists of an "empirical" method like Bacon, Hume, or Mill, into giving lip service to other views.

"We see, we recognize, that it is so." We grasp its truth by *nous,* by intellectual intuition, by insight: *nous,* working with and in experienced facts, is more certain than deductive proof.

than demonstration. "Science," *epistēmē,* is systematized, "formalized" reasoning; it is demonstration, *apodeixis,* from *archai.* But those *archai* themselves are established and validated as *archai,* not by reasoning or demonstration, but by *nous:* by "seeing" that it is so, that this is the way in which the facts can be understood. So Aristotle concludes, "It is not science, but *nous,* that is the *archē* of science itself." Hence science or demonstration and *nous* are the two necessary components of what Aristotle calls "theoretical wisdom," *sophia.*

This is what science, *epistēmē,* is: proof, demonstration from true principles. How does such science proceed and operate? It operates through language, *logos;* through using language, *logismos;* through using language in a certain connected fashion, through *syllogismos.* This is the instrument of reasoning in general, and of demonstration in particular, that Aristotle discovered, and set forth in the *Prior Analytics,* the syllogism. But before explaining it, Aristotle found it necessary to make certain general distinctions about the different kinds of thing that can be said in *logos,* about the different kinds of predicate, or "category." When we talk about anything, we can say various types of thing about it. We can tell either what it is, *ti esti;* or else we can say something else about it. Aristotle distinguishes in the *Categories* nine other types of statement we can make about anything, nine other types of "category" or predicate, besides the first and most fundamental kind of thing we can say, what it is, its *ti esti:* how big it is, of what sort it is, of or to what it belongs, where it is, when it is, etc. The list of ten categories given in the first book of the *Organon,* and repeated elsewhere in Aristotle, though sometimes with a list of fewer predicates, seems to have been drawn up originally to give a convenient way of avoiding the fallacies of eristic reasoning, to which the Sophists were much given.

Now, most of these things we can truly say about anything are irrelevant, they are incidental or "accidental," to that kind of thing's being what it is. A man is a man, no matter where or when he is, what is the color of his hair or his skin, what he happens to be doing, etc. These true statements that are ir- relevant to what he is, which Aristotle calls *symbebēkota,* "accidents," are no concern of the science of man. But there are some things we can say about a man that are involved in a man's being a man: they are bound up with what he is, with his *ti esti,* his "what." That he will die, for instance, that he is mortal, belongs to his "what," to what makes him what he is, his *ti ēn einai.* This property is "essential" to being a man: without it no man would be a man—were he immortal he might be a god, for example, but he would not be human. Such a property is an "essential property" of man; and such essential properties, or *idia,* of man are just what any science of man is concerned to demonstrate.[13]

If, then, we are not content to rest with the "fact that" men are mortal, that they will eventually die, which we have all learned from experience; if we demand "science," a "reason why" men are mortal, we can put it, Men are mortal, because men are animals, *empsycha,* and all animals or animate things are mortal. Men, that is, belong to that kind of being that has that kind of property, and hence they all exhibit that property also: it is es- sential to being a man that men are mortal. This is proof, demon- stration; this is, in fact, what Aristotle calls a syllogism. He says:

Whenever three terms are so related to one another that the last is in the middle as in a whole, and the middle either is or is not in the

---

[13] The adjectival meaning of "essential" is thus primary for Aristotle; from this root meaning is derived the noun meaning, "essence." See "nature," pages 173 ff. But the term "essence" is a Latin invention. The reader is puzzled, when he ap- proaches the text of Aristotle's Greek, to find that there is no Greek term for "essence" in his writing. There are half a dozen terms which can be so translated into Latin, ranging from the simplest, *to ti esti,* the "what," the answer to the question *ti esti?* to the most precise, *to ti ēn einai,* what makes anything what it is. What most complicates the matter, and has over the centuries given rise to great confusion, is the fact that the key term usually translated "essence," *ousia,* is also used by Aristotle to mean what was put into Latin as "substance." The relation between these two very different senses of *ousia* becomes a central prob- lem, in Books Zeta and Eta of the *Metaphysics,* of Aristotle's First Philosophy. See pages 116–23.

first as in a whole, there must be a perfect syllogism of the extremes.
I call that term middle which is itself in another and contains another in itself; in position also it comes in the middle.[14]

In the illustration, the "middle" is "animals." Proof consists in
finding such a "middle." The middle, *to meson,* is the "reason
why," *to dioti,* the connecting link, between the conclusion and
the premises. The aim of science is to find such links, such mid-
dles: to trace such an intelligible structure between things.

The precise wording of the basic Barbara syllogism in the
Prior Analytics is:

> If A is predicated of (or "belongs to") all B,
> and B is predicated of (or "belongs to") all C,
> then A is necessarily predicated of (or "belongs to") all C.

That is, Aristotle's conception of the syllogism in the *Prior
Analytics,* as Jan Łukasiewicz has shown in his brilliant book,
*Aristotle's Syllogistic from the Standpoint of Modern Formal
Logic,*[15] is that of a purely formal instrument, or, as we should
say, of a purely formal calculus. It is consistently formal, where
the later tradition became confused and introduced various material elements. There are in the *Prior Analytics* no psychological
terms, no laws or forms of "thinking." There are no singular
terms, for the same term must be used both as a subject and a
predicate, and a singular term cannot be used as a predicate.
There are no concrete terms in the statement of the syllogism,
only letters, variables. Aristotle's introduction of variables into
formal logic was as epoch-making as their later introduction
into arithmetic. In the one case, "formal" logic was created, in
the other, algebra.

Aristotle presents the syllogism as an implication, not as an
inference. It takes the form: If A and B, then "necessarily" C;
not the form: A and B are, "therefore" C is. The "necessarily,"

[14] *Prior Analytics* I, ch. 4: 25b 32–36.
[15] Jan Łukasiewicz, *Aristotle's Syllogistic from the Standpoint of Modern Formal
Logic* (Oxford, 1951; 2d ed. enlarged, Oxford, 1957).

anankē, emphasizes the fact that the implication is true for all values of the variables: in our modern terminology, it is a universal quantifier. Aristotle defines a proposition, a *protasis,* as "a statement affirming or denying something of something." Its elements he calls "terms," *horoi,* the "limits" or "boundaries," the "termini" of the statement. He avoids all psychological or metaphysical overtones, all words like "notion," "concept," in their Greek equivalents. Aristotle's analysis of propositions into "terms" in the *De Interpretatione* is the most "nominalistic" book of the *Organon.*

The outcome of Łukasiewicz's close textual analysis may be stated in historical terms. Aristotle's own "logic," in the *Prior Analytics,* is best presented in the "terminism" of William of Ockham, as Ernest Moody has contended in his study of Ockham's logic,[16] and not in the Platonizing reconstructions of the Aristotelian position to be found in Thomas Aquinas or Duns Scotus.

Aristotle's syllogistic is thus a consistent, purely formal "dialectic." But Aristotle is no advocate of a logic without ontological implications—quite the contrary! This is the instrument of proof, of demonstration, of science. In what kind of world can you use it successfully? What kind of structure of things can be so expressed?

The syllogism will operate in a world exhibiting "kinds" of thing, *eidē,* and more inclusive "kinds," *genē,* a world in which are to be found real species and genera, a world in which individual things are what they are because they are of a certain kind, because they belong to a certain species. And this species is what it is because it in turn belongs to a more inclusive kind, to a certain genus. In such a world, science is not concerned with the individual or particular thing as such, with all its "accidental" or incidental qualities and relations. It is concerned rather with this structure of kinds, with what a given species is, and what

---

[16] Ernest A. Moody, *The Logic of William of Ockham* (New York, 1935).

are the differentia marking it off from all other species in the same genus, and with all the properties that species or kind possesses because of what it is, because of its genus and differentia.

The outcome of such scientific inquiry will be a formal definition, a statement of what a thing is, its *ti esti*, its "what it is," its "essence" or "nature," *physis*. It is not necessary in such a definition to state all the properties of a kind, not even all the essential properties, in order to state "what the kind of thing really is," its *ti ēn einai*. It is sufficient to state enough to indicate its position in this stucture of kinds: to state the kind to which that species of thing belongs, its genus, and what marks it off as a distinctive species.

Because all the properties of man follow either from the fact that "man is animal," *empsychon*—this is his genus—or that he possesses the power of *nous*—this is the distinctive trait, setting man off from all other animals—because all the traits of man "follow from," and can be "demonstrated from," these two traits, man's "essence" will be so stated in his definition: "Man is an animate being endowed with the power of *nous*." More traditionally, this runs: "Man is a rational animal."

The object of science is to show how these properties are connected with the essence of the subject matter through its structure of kinds. For example, it will be to show how "mortality" is connected with man because of man's "animality" as a middle. The demonstration of a property thus eventuates in finding its *logos,* which means at once its "reason why" and its "definition" —*logos* meant both in Greek. For what a property is, and the reason why it is a property of that kind of thing, are identical. The "nature" of a property and the "cause" of a property are the same, and are expressed in the definition of that kind of thing.

This is the particular idea of science Aristotle developed out of his discovery of the syllogism. Science is the demonstration of properties from essences stated in definitions. And such a science implies a definite and determinate kind of world. The relations of the syllogistic instrument of science to the conception of science itself, and to the kind of world in which that instrument functions, are summed up in the following statement:

Aristotle was above all a naturalist. He asserted that the universal is united with particular existences, binding them together into a permanent whole (the species), and keeping within definite and fixed limits the changes which occur in each particular existence. The species is the true whole of which the particular individuals are the parts, and the essence is the characteristic form. Species fall within a graded order of genera as particular individuals fall within the species. Thinking is the correlate of these relations in nature. It unites and differentiates in judgment as species are united and separated in reality. Valid knowledge or demonstration necessarily takes the form of the syllogism because the syllogism merely expresses the system in which, by means of an intervening essence, individuals are included in species. Definition is the grasp of the essence which marks one species off from another. Classification and division are counterparts of the intrinsic order of nature.[17]

2. *Aristotle's Actual Practice of Inquiry*

As distinguished from his early setting forth of the Platonic theory or ideal of science, in the *Posterior Analytics,* Aristotle's actual practice of inquiry must be learned from observing the procedures he employs in his scientific treatises, and from the incidental *obiter dicta* on method that are scattered throughout his writings.[18] This contrast is fruitful and significant, especially

[17] John Dewey, article on "Logic" in *Encyclopedia of the Social Sciences,* IX, 599. It is doubtful whether Aristotle thought of the universal as "keeping within definite and fixed limits the changes which occur in each particular existence."
[18] For an excellent brief introduction to Aristotle's methodology, see Émile Boutroux, *Historical Studies in Philosophy* (London, 1912), "Aristotle," especially section V, "Method and the Point of View." The best full treatment of Aristotle's methodology is Rudolf Eucken, *Die Methode der aristotelischen Forschung in ihrem Zusammenhang mit den philosophischen Grundprincipien des Aristoteles* (Berlin, 1872). Eucken started his career as an excellent Aristotelian scholar.

if like many of the earlier Schoolmen one is tempted to treat the *Posterior Analytics* as stating the method Aristotle is proposing to follow in his procedure.

The first step in any of Aristotle's inquiries is to determine the object of investigation. In the *De Anima,* for instance, this is the *archē* of living and of knowing; in the *Ethics,* it is the *archē* of human conduct, the end at which man aims, acting well, *eu praxein.* The object of investigation is always an end or function of the subject matter: what that kind of thing does, how it operates. And the problems of that science are how everything in the subject matter, all the facts there displayed, are related to and involved in that function. The inquiry thus seeks to analyze the factors involved in a certain function. Hence it is important at the outset to establish norms: in the *Physics,* natural motion; in the *De Anima,* knowing; in the *Ethics,* the "prudent" or intelligent man. The norm is always a perfected activity, functioning without interference from outside, without *bia,* "violence" or "compulsion."

The second step in inquiry is to examine previous "opinions" or hypotheses as to the best way to understand the subject matter in question, the *archai* proposed by Aristotle's predecessors among the Greeks. These *endoxa* of outstanding thinkers are to be taken seriously, since men by nature desire to know, and since they can by nature completed with art arrive at the truth. Aristotle develops the explanatory possibilities of previous hypotheses and theories into actuality, and builds upon them in his own formulations. He accepts proposed *archai* or hypotheses, as he accepts everything else, as material to be worked over, to bring out the best in them. He thus accepts Greek scientific hypotheses, as he accepts Greek life, ideals, and institutions, as materials given to be developed. What is often felt as the "conservatism" of the Aristotelian spirit and temper is the conservatism inherent in trust in experience, in facts long encountered.

There is indeed in Aristotle a strong sense of the continuous development of the arts and the sciences, of what today we call the "continuity of inquiry"—investigation is a living process that goes on and on. Thus in Book Alpha Minor of the *Metaphysics* he says:

While no one person can grasp truth adequately, we cannot all fail in the attempt. Each thinker makes some statement about nature, and as an individual contributes little or nothing to the inquiry. But the combination of all the conjectures results in something big (*ti megethos*). . . . It is only fair to be grateful not only to those whose views we can share, but also to those who have gone pretty far wrong in their guesses. They too have contributed something: by their preliminary work they have helped to form our scientific way of thinking (*hexis*).[19]

Again, in the *Sophistic Refutations,* Aristotle says:

In the case of all discoveries the results of previous labors that have been handed down from others have been advanced bit by bit by those who have carried them on, whereas the original discoveries generally make an advance that is small at first though much more useful than the development which later springs out of them. . . . When this is once discovered, it is easier to add and develop the remainder in connection with it. This is in fact what has happened with regard to rhetorical speeches and to practically all the other arts: for those who discovered the beginnings of them advanced them in all only a little way, whereas the celebrities of today are the heirs (so to speak) of a long succession of men who have advanced them bit by bit, and so have developed them to their present form.[20]

The third step in inquiry is to undertake a "dialectical" examination of proposed *archai* or *endoxa,* of suggested hypotheses, to bring out all the difficulties and problems, the *aporiai,* to which they lead. This is the scientific function of "dialectic," in Aristotle's usage of that term: to bring out the consequences that

---

[19] *Metaphysics* Alpha Minor, ch. 1: 993b 1–4.
[20] *Sophistic Refutations* ch. 34: 183b 17–32.

follow from hypotheses or proposed *archai*. Thus it has been well remarked that the first book of any Aristotelian treatise, or the first chapters dealing with any particular theme, as in the *Physics,* take the form of a kind of compressed Socratic dialogue, which raises all the questions, and then proceeds to solve some of them by making precise distinctions. In Aristotle's actual procedure, that is, satisfactory and adequate *archai* are always arrived at by *nous,* not merely working with facts, but working also in the midst of a critical examination of all the available hypotheses to account for the facts. This dialectical examination will reveal which hypotheses are contradictory, which are untenable because "we see" that the consequence predicted does not occur, and what facts and problems the satisfactory *archē* must meet and take into account.

The fourth step in inquiry is to find the relevant facts. Aware of the available hypotheses, Aristotle proceeds to seek to find what is, and to trace the intelligible structure of facts in order to reveal why it must be as it is. In this procedure, Aristotle tries to be as "objective" as possible. Since he conceives knowing as a direct grasp of the intelligible structure that is actually present there in a subject matter, as a literal "assimilation," a "becoming like," of the mind to the intelligible structure of things, he tries to follow the natural connections of things. In the *Politics* for example, he tries to follow the order of genesis of a *polis*. For him, knowing is not, as for the empiricists, a description of the succession of occurrences. It is not, as for Kant, an interpretation of facts in terms of a scheme of intelligibility. It is rather a direct intellectual vision of rational connections between facts.

Hence for Aristotle the order to be followed, the method of inquiry, must grow out of the subject matter itself. There is no "universal method," such as Platonists, like the father of modern philosophy, Descartes, can view with what Henry More called "inexsuperable confidence." The scientist must not exercise his imagination to cook up a theory, and then try to prove it; he must surrender his mind to the structure of the subject matter he is investigating. It was against this Aristotelian principle of method that the seventeenth-century scientists revolted: they insisted that there is one universal method for all subject matters of importance, the method of mathematics. They thus started our modern science on its glorious career, and our modern philosophy on its preoccupation with the consequent "problem of knowledge."

Aristotle insists we must go to the facts, not to some bright hypothesis about them. Every great scientist, until our own scientific revolution at least, when obviously inventing some wild idea, some "anticipation of nature," to use the phrase of Francis Bacon, has insisted that his idea was forced upon him by the encountered facts. The classic case is Isaac Newton, who "feigned no hypotheses," but deduced everything from phenomena. The present-day logic of science, that takes science as a postulate system, as a set of assumptions arbitrarily chosen, has been given the lie by every real scientist, who has always insisted that his hypothesis is to be "seen" in the facts, seen by the scientific *nous*.

The final step in inquiry is to explain the subject matter, to exhibit the intelligible structure of facts. Here Aristotle lays down at some point or other every methodological principle of exact investigation. Observation must come first, in a preliminary denotation of the subject matter; it must be rigorous, thorough, unprejudiced. Explanation must explain the observed facts, and not something else: it must explain motion, for example, and not why we are mistaken in thinking we observe motion. The experienced facts, what "we see" (*horōmen*), are ultimate and controlling, even in ethics. Explanations must never deny nor contradict the facts of observation. They must be clear and distinct. They must be the logically simplest explanations. They must fit in with other *archai;* they must be *verae causae.* Hypotheses must be entertained tentatively, until they actually succeed in making the facts intelligible.

Why then did Aristotle not only fail to make discoveries that seem to us through long familiarity obvious; why did he make positive mistakes? He had a fruitful method, what most scientists would still today call the "right" method. The method of the seventeenth-century pioneers was very consciously formulated by studying the *Organon.* The answer is clear: Aristotle was too much of an empiricist. He was clearly the greatest observational scientist until the nineteenth century; and our modern scientific enterprise was born in the rejection of such "empiricism" for some form of "rationalism"—in the rejection of trust in sheer observation for faith in mathematical demonstration.

All of Aristotle's errors of fact are due to his confidence in observation, in what "we see," combined with the lack of any instruments of observation, and consequently the lack even of any sense of the need of instruments, or of their very possibility. Thus he accepted spontaneous generation, because he "observed" it, even though it contradicted his correct general theory.

Modern science represents the triumph of rationalism, of theory, over the mere observation of facts. As former President James B. Conant of Harvard has put it, the advance of science means the reduction of the element of "empiricism" in the body of science, its replacement by rational theory, its "formalization," we say. Nothing so clearly reveals the inadequacy of the common notion, inherited from a misunderstood Francis Bacon and John Stuart Mill, that science is merely an observation and description of facts, as the work of Aristotle. This is the view that first we observe facts, and then try to generalize a theory: the "facts" are so, they are "hard data."

Actually, the relevant "facts" in a science are continually being altered. They depend on our instruments of observation, on our previous assumptions, on our accepted standards and criteria of what can be admitted as a "fact," on our theories of what to look for, on our complex schemes of scientific verification and their institutionalized tests. Think of the host of assumptions involved in the statement, "The atomic weight of oxygen is 16." Yet that is about as well attested a "fact" as we possess. Indeed, as against Aristotle, sense observation is quite literally the last thing on which our science rests: we would agree with him that what "we see" (*horōmen*) comes at the very end of our dialectic. And here "observation" has become not a seeing, not sense, but measurements, an active process, involving complicated mathematical systems of coordinates, delicate instruments, and innumerable corrections.

In a few places, Aristotle observed some very suspicious "facts." He made astoundingly accurate observations of the structure and habits of a host of living things. Yet he also announces that man has only eight ribs, that women have fewer teeth than men, and that they possess an empty cavity in the back of their heads. Critics of Aristotle like Bertrand Russell make the most of these aberrations. Perhaps Aristotle merely observed Greek women and their distinctive excellence, which under the conditions of Greek culture was scarcely intellectual. But in general it seems that these egregious errors reveal a willingness to trust common opinion on some of the simpler and more familiar "facts," while he examined more unfamiliar matters himself.

Aristotle denied all theories opposed to sense observation, such as that light has a velocity, that the earth is in motion, etc. He did not conceive the possibility of closer observation, and so he assumed a finality in his explanations for everything. He had no sense of the possibility of correction by more accurate means of observation, of that corrigible character of all scientific conclusions, that has become so strongly entrenched in our own scientific enterprise. He had no means of measuring qualities: he had no thermometer with which to measure heat, nothing with which to measure the wave length of different colors; and he had no means of detecting exact conservation or persistence throughout change. Consequently, he naturally trusted the complete qualitative changes he observed.

He could hence attain no notion of the uniformity of law throughout the cosmos. The motion of the heavenly bodies was clearly uniform, and he so treated it. But the motion of sublunar bodies was clearly not. Hence Galileo could effect a revolution by pointing out, that as a result of Copernicus, "The earth is now in the heavens!" and hence equally subject to law.

Since without instruments of observation it was impossible for Aristotle to attain any exact solutions to problems, any mathematical formulations, any precise verification, he did not seek for such results. All this is clearly the consequence of the persisting influence on Aristotle's thought of the lack of instruments of observation.

Above all, Aristotle rejected the Pythagorean faith of the Platonists and the Platonic tradition, that the order of nature is and must be mathematical in character. He rejected Pythagoreanism because it is obviously not founded on observation, on sense, and is impossible for an empiricist in any strict sense. And our modern science came into existence, from the twelfth century on to the seventeenth, with the abandonment of complete reliance on sense observation for some form of the Pythagorean faith in the mathematical structure of nature. Many present-day philosophies of science would, like Aristotle, call themselves "empirical." But an "empiricist" interpretation of science has become possible again only with the working out of what we call today a "logical" or "mathematical" empiricism. That essential element Aristotle lacked. The great vision of Leibniz in the seventeenth century still remains to be fulfilled: to work out a mathematical expression of the fundamental Aristotelian concepts for the understanding of the world that has generated us men as beings with the natural desire to understand.

Chapter IV

ARISTOTLE'S FUNCTIONAL CONCEPTS:

LIVING AND DESIRING

For Aristotle, understanding and thinking are not only the product of *logos,* of language, terms, propositions, and demonstrations, of what things can be said to be. Understanding is also a biological process, a natural activity practiced by men in a world that is intelligible, a characteristically human way of living in an environment that sustains it.

The fact that knowing or understanding can itself be analyzed in these two quite different ways illustrates that double approach and aspect that appears throughout all Aristotle's investigations. His inquiries are carried on with two different sets of concepts. Things can be understood in the way they can be talked about, and they can also be understood as taking part in a dynamic process of change. They lend themselves to intelligible expression in terms of language, and they also have a career, a kind of life. Aristotle therefore developed and used one set of distinctions appropriate to talking, to discourse or *logos,* and also another set of distinctions appropriate to becoming, to living. The first or logical concepts and distinctions are well illustrated in the *Organon* in general and in the *Posterior Analytics* in particular, which seeks to consider what science or true knowledge is, regarded from the point of view of the way language is used as an instrument to express it. The second set, the functional or biological concepts and distinctions, are illustrated in the *De Anima,* which Aristotle himself announces as an introduction "to the whole domain of truth, and more particularly, to the study of nature, *psychē* being as it were the *archē* of all living things." [1] They are applied in the *De Anima* to living processes in general, and also to knowing, considered not as the creation of language, but as itself a living process, as a natural activity in a knowable world.

The *Posterior Analytics* and the *De Anima* taken together thus furnish an excellent introduction to the double method and the double set of concepts of Aristotle. The various relations between these two sets of distinctions, and between them and the common world they have been developed to render intelligible, furnish the theme of the central core of that compilation of writings we know as Aristotle's *Metaphysics,* Books Zeta, Eta, and Theta, in which what Aristotle himself calls "First Philosophy" appears as an inquiry into just these ultimate distinctions.

However, it is not quite accurate to speak of Aristotle as using a "double method." The relation between the two approaches in his inquiries is actually much more intimate than that would suggest. For his investigations normally follow the same pattern in any field. Starting always with what things can be said to be, and with the careful analysis of that saying—starting, that is, with an analysis of the language in which things are talked about and stated—he always finds that this linguistic analysis, clarifying and essential as it is, sooner or later reaches a point where it raises questions that cannot be answered through the analysis of language alone. He then asks, "Well, how did this come into being?" He is led to examine the further context of discourse, in which we must "see" that subject matter, those things in their genesis and operation, co-operating with other things in the world of natural processes, before we can arrive at an adequate statement of what they are. That is, the formal analysis with which Aristotle always begins his inquiries into any field, the formal analysis of the language in which we express what is there, drives him to a "physical" or functional analysis of what

[1] *De Anima* I, ch. 1: 402a 4–8.

is there itself. Starting with what the *logikos* or talker, the *dialektikos* or dialectician, has said and continues to say about a subject matter, he is led to what the *physikos,* the "natural philosopher" or investigator of natural processes, can find in the world. This contrast between the *logikos* and the *physikos* runs throughout Aristotle. In his view, the *logikos* can formulate the questions, but ultimately it is the *physikos* who must answer them.

The relation between the *Analytics* and the *De Anima* can be stated in another way, to bring out a further point. The *Analytics* are concerned with talking, or dialectic, and with good talking or demonstration. The *De Anima* is concerned primarily with living and knowing. Good living, so far as man is concerned, Aristotle treats in the *Ethics* and the *Politics,* so that we shall find his discussion of human living in the *De Anima* naturally leading us into those practical sciences. Good knowing is for him identical with the good talking treated in the *Posterior Analytics*.

1. What Is Life?

The *De Anima* or, in Greek, *Peri Psychēs,* is about what the Greeks called *psychē*. At the outset Aristotle defines *psychē* as the *archē* of *zōa,* living things: as that which sets off and distinguishes "living" beings from those that are not living. The Greeks made their distinction between what they called *ta empsycha,* "animate" things, the things that possess *psychē,* and *ta apsycha,* "inanimate" things, the things without *psychē*. Animate things behave and act in a different way from inanimate things: characteristically, the Greeks made their distinction in terms of two ways of behaving and functioning, whereas we moderns distinguish the "organic" from the "inorganic," in terms of two different kinds of structure. The difference between *ta empsycha,* the animate, and *ta apsycha,* the inanimate, is clearly that the first possess *psychē* or *anima,* the second do not. The first possess "life," the second do not. What is this "life" or *psychē?* What is its nature and essence, and what are its properties? This is the question with which Aristotle starts out.

The *De Anima* is thus an introduction to the sciences which deal with living things, with especial reference to human living. Its title, *Peri Psychēs,* should really be translated, *On Living and Knowing.* For Aristotle, starting in the first book, as always, with what earlier Greek thinkers had said about life or *psychē,* finds that the term had been used to attempt to explain living and knowing. It had been taken as that *archē* which would not only distinguish the animate from the inanimate, but would also make living and knowing intelligible. For Aristotle is not inquiring merely into a term or a thing, least of all into what we may mean when we use the term "soul." He is inquiring into a subject matter which that term *psychē* as an *archē* sets off as the field for a distinctive inquiry or science, namely, the processes of living and of knowing. Most of the first book of the *De Anima* is devoted to the examination of the opinions of his predecessors in this inquiry. Since the outcome of this particular examination, unlike most of his inquiries into earlier hypotheses, is that earlier thinkers have not succeeded in making living and knowing intelligible, it is chiefly of historical interest, and he begins his own analysis with a fresh start in Book II.

"Life" or *psychē* thus means for Aristotle the complex but determinate power which all living things, all *empsycha,* exhibit. It is the power possessed by living organisms of moving themselves, and of discriminating between other things, of "sensing" them, and, in man, of "knowing" them, so important a part of human living. As the *archē* of animals, of *zōa,* it is the determinate power in terms of which the various specific activities and behaviors of different kinds of living organisms are to be understood. This distinctive power possessed by living things, their "life" or *psychē,* is a cardinal instance of that kind of *archē* in terms of which the activities of all natural things, all *physika,* are to be understood: *psychē* is an instance of the "nature" or *physis* of natural things, which is their power of acting in definite and discoverable ways. For *ta empsycha,* animate things, belong to the larger and more inclusive class of *physika,* natural things, and the "nature" or *physis* of living bodies to act in specific ways is their *psychē,* their "life," their tendency to act and function in a determinate manner. Thus every "life" is the "nature" of the living body whose life it is; but not every "nature" is a "life," only the "natures" of living bodies.

Hence for Aristotle *psychē* meant two things: 1) the power or *archē* of living, "life"; and 2) the power or *archē* of what he calls "discriminating," *to kritikon:* the power of selective response, which includes both sensing and knowing. Since traditionally *psychē* has been turned into Latin as *anima,* and into English as "soul," it is important to realize at the outset that Aristotle is *not* talking about the "soul" as centuries of Christian supernaturalism, to say nothing of Cartesian dualism, have led us to conceive it. That conception of a "soul" quite independent of any body, as he encountered it in the Pythagoreans, he could not take seriously. He calls the notion "absurd":

Such theories attach the *psychē* or "soul" to, and enclose it in, body, without further determining why this happens and what is the condition of the body. . . . The supporters of such theories merely undertake to explain what kind of thing the *psychē* is. Of the body which is to receive it they have nothing more to say: just as if it were possible for any soul taken at random, according to the Pythagorean tales, to pass into any body. But each body seems to have its own distinctive form (*eidos kai morphē*). It is just like saying that carpentry can pass into flutes: for the art must employ its own instruments, and the *psychē* its own body.[2]

---

[2] *De Anima* I, ch. 3: 407b 15–26. *Eidos kai morphē* is the technical phrase translated into Latin as *forma,* and into English as "form." It means, in this case, what makes the body what it is, a particular living body of a particular kind. Aristotle's view is that *psychē* or life is the "form" of the living body.

Thus for Aristotle the *psychē* is not the *archē* of religion. He is not investigating the Christian *anima* or "soul," but rather, "living," "sensing," and "knowing" taken as biological processes. He is asking, "Just what is life?"

Now, if life or *psychē* is the power of living and knowing, then it is clearly not a thing, like the living organism or body, but rather an activity or function of the living organism. It is not an *ousia* or "substance" capable of existing independently by itself, but rather the "form" of the living organism. That is, life is not an additional "thing" besides the living body, but the body's power to do what the living body does, its function (*ergon*), its operation (*energeia*), its culminating end (*entelecheia*).[3] The "life" of that living body is what makes it that kind of a body, and hence is that body's "form."

Aristotle uses two examples to make his meaning clear. If the living organism, instead of being, as it actually is, a complex organization of many organs, were instead a single natural organ, like the eye, then "vision," the power of seeing (*opsis*), would be its "life" or *psychē*. Or if it were an instrument made by art, say, an axe, then the power of cutting would be its "life" or *psychē*. Exactly the same is the relation of the living organism to its "life" or *psychē*. It is the relation of the instrument or organ to its function, its power of functioning—the relation of the flute to fluteplaying.

Hence Aristotle's first and formal definition of "life" or *psychē* runs: "Life is the first entelechy of a natural body possessing the power to live (*dynamei zōēn echontos*)."[4] Life

---

[3] These three terms are one of Aristotle's families of terms which mean the same thing in a scale of increasing emphasis. *Ergon*, the common term for "work" in Greek, is the term Aristotle uses for what we call "function." *Energeia* means literally the "putting to work" of a "power," or in Latin, its "operation." "Power" and its "operation," *dynamis* and *energeia*, are for Aristotle polar concepts, like the corresponding abstract Latin terms, the actualization of a potentiality. Entelechy (*entelecheia*) is a term invented by Aristotle to denote the most complete functioning or culmination of a thing—in Latin, "actuality."

[4] *De Anima* II, ch. 1: 412a 27, 28. For "entelechy," see footnote 3 above.

is the *first* entelechy, as the *power* to live and know; the second entelechy is the operation of that power, "actual" living and knowing—as we still say. The difference between the first and the second entelechy is the difference between possessing a function, and exercising that function: it is the difference between possessing knowledge when asleep, and knowing when awake. "Life," *psychē,* is a function in both senses, but it is primarily the power to perform the function.

2. *Aristotle's Functionalism*

Now an organic body can exist, for a while at least, without life or *psychē:* it can be dead. But life, *psychē,* obviously cannot exist without a living body. Life, as the *archē* of the living body, is that in terms of which the body's actions and behavior are to be understood. But life, *psychē,* is itself not understood in terms of the body and the body's structure. In general, an activity or function, for Aristotle, though it always involves an instrument with a determinate structure, so that that kind of instrument is necessary to the performance of that function, and without that instrument the functioning cannot occur—there can be no fluteplaying without a flute—is not to be understood merely, or adequately, in terms of its necessary instrument alone. He puts it: "Activities and functions are logically prior to powers [and their instruments]." [5] That is, we understand powers in terms of their operations. We understand the power of sight or vision in terms of the activity of seeing, and likewise the instrument by means of which vision operates, the eye. We understand the power of thinking, *nous,* in terms of the activity of thinking, and likewise the instrument by means of which thinking operates, the images or *phantasmata.* Aristotle is a thoroughgoing functionalist and operationalist.

Moreover, activities and functions are themselves understood

[5] *De Anima* II, ch. 4: 415a 18–20.

in terms of that toward which they are directed, of that to which they are a response, their "correlative objects" (*ta antikeimena*). Seeing is understood in terms of what is seen, the visible; nutrition (or metabolism) is understood in terms of what is assimilated as food; desiring is understood in terms of what is desired; thinking is understood in terms of what is thought. There is some object or objective in the environment, in the situation or context, to which the activity is a response, and toward which it is directed. The activity cannot be understood without reference to such an environment or context and to the objective to be found in it. Aristotle is a thoroughgoing contextualist or objective relativist. It is in terms of this objective or end in the context that we understand the activity; and it is in terms of the activity that we understand the power. Aristotle's Greek is able to indicate these relations through appropriate suffixes. Thus it is through its objective or end, "the desired" (*to orekton*), that we understand "desiring" (*to oregesthai*); and it is through desiring that we understand the power of desiring (*to orektikon*). Likewise, it is through what is sensed (*to aisthēton*) that we understand sensing (*to aisthanesthai*); and it is through sensing that we understand the power of sensing (*to aisthētikon*). It is through what is known (*to noēton*) that we understand knowing (*to noein*); and it is through knowing that we understand the power of knowing (*to noētikon*, or *nous*).

In general, for Aristotle the living organism is understood in terms of its "life" or *psychē*, its unified functioning in response to stimuli in its environment—how it acts and behaves in its context. In other words, for Aristotle life or *psychē* is the behavior of the organism as a whole in its environment. Aristotle is thus a thoroughgoing behaviorist. He is, of course, a functional and contextual behaviorist, not a mechanistic behaviorist. For him, life is the power of living and knowing, the power of selective response of the organism to the world. It is a natural function, like the breathing or the digestion that are aspects of life—"parts" of it, Aristotle puts it.

Modern behaviorists are mechanists: they explain the function by the structure of the mechanism or instrument involved. They emphasize what Aristotle calls the "by which," the efficient cause, which, though always necessary, is never for Aristotle sufficient for understanding. Aristotle analyzes function or process (*kinēsis*) in terms of all four of the factors or "causes" he distinguishes. In some respects, present-day Gestalt psychologists are closer to Aristotle than any other modern school. They likewise hold that there is a structure in the world that is grasped by "insight," by *nous*. But, unlike the Gestaltists, Aristotle has no objection to mechanism in itself: physical mechanisms of a determinate character are for him always involved in any function, and necessary to its understanding. And Aristotle is in no sense opposed to analysis: his analysis is in fact keen and sharp.

3. The Scale of Life

Now, if we go beyond the formal definition of life as the function of the living body, its power to act and operate in a characteristic way, its "first entelechy," to ask why it acts as it does, we are led to a number of characteristic specific and determinate operations and functions which different kinds of living organisms perform, and which taken together define what life is. Life as the function of the body in general, is broken down into, and is to be understood in terms of, these various specific powers of operating: nutrition or metabolism, growth, reproduction, desiring or motion as a whole, sensing, knowing, etc. These specific powers are to be described in terms of the specific operations they make possible and lead to, under the appropriate stimulus of some factor in the environment. Aristotle calls these specific powers "parts" of the *psychē,* parts of the fundamental power of the organism as a whole, "parts of the soul." The *psychē* is thus a group of various powers, to be understood through their analysis in detail.

But not all living organisms perform all these operations, or have all these powers. Aristotle distinguishes three main levels of living. There is first the level of the life common to all living organisms, all *empsycha,* plants, animals, and men alike: the life that is nutrition, growth, and reproduction. There is secondly the level of the life that is restricted to animals, which includes in addition, the power of sensing, of selective response to stimuli. There is thirdly the life restricted to men alone among animals, which includes in addition *nous,* the power of responding to universals and meanings, the power of acting with deliberation, with conscious forethought, of acting rationally. These three levels of life came to be called in Latin vegetative life, sensitive life, and intellectual life. Each "higher" functioning includes the lower functionings, in that it does not take place without them. Aristotle characteristically puts this: "Alike in figures and in organisms (*empsycha*) the earlier form exists potentially in the later, as, for instance, the triangle exists potentially in the quadrilateral, and the nutritive power in the power of sensing." [6]

The nutritive life (*threptikē psychē*) is the first and most widely distributed power of life; its functions are reproduction and the assimilation of nutriment. Aristotle was fascinated by the process of reproduction: as the cardinal instance of the most fundamental kind of change, *genesis,* the coming into being of a new substance, it offered the supreme challenge to his whole analysis of process. And characteristically, Aristotle tries to fit his naturalistic analysis into a truly Platonic framework:

[6] *De Anima* II, ch. 3: 414b 29–32. Note this Aristotelian way of putting what our evolutionary thinking would lead us to state the other way round. We should say, the more complex form exists potentially in the simpler or "earlier."

For it is the most natural function in all living things, if perfect and not defective or spontaneously generated, to make another being like itself, animal producing animal, plant producing plant, in order that they may, so far as they can, participate in the eternal and the divine. For that is what all things desire, and that is the final end of all their activity. . . . Since then things are incapable of sharing individually in the eternal and the divine, because nothing in the world of perishables can remain one and the same in number, they partake in the eternal and the divine in the only way they can, some more, and some less: each persists not in itself yet in another like itself, which is one with it not in number but in kind.[7]

4. Aristotle's Dynamism

The two highest functions involved in living, sensing and knowing, which he groups together as *to kritikon,* the power of selective or discriminating response, and treats as "passive powers," powers of being acted upon, by sensed objects (*aisthēta*) and by noused objects (*noēta*) respectively, Aristotle treats before dealing with life as an active power, as the mover of the organism (*to kinoun*), which he does not get to until the last five chapters of the *De Anima.* But these two passive powers of sensing and knowing must be seen in the context of the active power of desire (*orexis*), for they modify and direct it: that is why they are grouped together as *to kritikon,* the power of discrimination and selecting.

Before considering life as the mover, Aristotle asks as to the senses in which life can be called the cause (*aitia*) and the *archē* of the living body. Since cause and *archē* are said in many ways, we must distinguish the three ways in which life can be said to be a cause. Life is the cause of living bodies as the whence of their motion, as their end or final cause, and as their form or formal cause: that is, as the mover, the end, and the essence. Life is the formal cause of living bodies, since their being means life.

[7] *De Anima* II, ch. 4: 415a 26–415b 7.

Life is the end of living bodies, since they exist for the sake of living. And life is the mover, whence come all the activities that make up living.

In his general analysis, Aristotle distinguishes four factors in the process of motion in animals:

Motion implies three things, first, the mover (*to kinoun*); secondly, that by which it moves; and again thirdly, that which is moved (*to kinoumenon*). The mover is itself twofold: first, that which is unmoved, and secondly, that which moves and is moved. The unmoved mover is the practical good; that which moves and is moved is the power of desiring (*to orektikon*). For the animal which is moved is moved in so far as it desires, and desire (*orexis*) is a kind of motion or operation (*energeia*). Finally, the thing moved (*to kinoumenon*) is the animal. The organ with which desire moves it, once reached, is a part of the body.[8]

What moves the living organism to action, therefore, the mover (*to kinoun*), is thus twofold. There is something in the situation, *to orekton,* the object of desire; and there is something in the organism itself, "desire" (*orexis*). The ultimate mover, the ultimate spring of action, is the desired, *to orekton:* some stimulus in the situation, some end of conduct, some practical good, which is not itself moved or affected by being desired, and is hence an "unmoved" mover. The immediate mover, the immediate spring of action, is desire itself, awakened by the stimulus of the desired. Desire acts through some organ of the body; the organism as a whole responds and seeks the object of its desire. The instrument or efficient cause involved, the "by which," is the bodily organs by which the organism is moved.

Aristotle here speaks of life, *psyche,* and its "parts," like desire, as "moving" the organism, not mechanically—the various organs of the body, like the legs, do that—but in the sense in which any particular function can be said to "move" the body. Desiring something moves the organism to get it, just as seeing

[8] *De Anima* III, ch. 10: 433b 13–19.

a snake makes us avoid it, or running enables us to escape. All these functions, like desire, or like their sum, life itself, Aristotle calls "moved movers," in contrast to the unmoved mover in any process, the object of desire. A function he considers as a motion or process that can initiate other motions.

The "unmoved mover" in any process is thus in one sense a factor in that process: it is the stimulus (though not a mechanical stimulus), the point toward which the process is directed. The process is defined and understood in terms of that particular unmoved mover. In another sense, however, the unmoved mover is outside the process, "external" to it; it is itself unmoved, not affected by the process (*apathes*).[9]

Thus for Aristotle's analysis, every individual process has its own unique unmoved mover. The name is a generic term for a factor to be found in every process. There are untold billions of unmoved movers in Aristotle's world. When he generalizes, he gives to them a mythical unification, as in Book Lambda of the *Metaphysics*. And this mythically unified Unmoved Mover possesses the same traits as the factor in every process: in one sense it is immanent in every process, in another it is transcendent, and external to all processes. But even in Book Lambda Aristotle at once goes on to speak in chapter 8 of fifty-five unmoved movers. Aristotle's is a pluralistic philosophy, not a monotheistic theology.

The action of all living organisms is thus a response to some stimulus. In those animals that do move as a whole, including men, their movement proceeds from an impulse or drive, what Aristotle calls a *hormē;* such a *hormē* or drive he sees implanted in everything that exists by nature. Every natural thing, every

---

[9] Compare Whitehead's very similar Aristotelian analysis of process. For him, the relation between an "eternal object" and an "actual occasion" is "internal-external." That is, an actual occasion, or process, is itself constituted by the eternal objects ingredient in it: in this sense, the two are internally related. But the eternal objects are not themselves affected by their ingression into the process: in this sense, they are externally related to it.

physikon, has its own distinctive drive or *hormē,* to act in its own proper and determinate way. This Aristotelian *hormē* is the counterpart in his conception of the world, his vision of the cosmos, of the "inertia" of masses in the Newtonian philosophy of nature.

In animals—in life lived on the sensitive level—this universal *hormē* appears as *orexis,* desire (the Latin translation was *appetitus*), the desire for or the aversion to something in the environment, *to orekton,* the desired. In seventeenth-century philosophizing, this Aristotelian "desire" takes the form of Thomas Hobbes's "endeavor toward or fromward"—in many fundamental respects Hobbes remained a good Ockhamite Aristotelian. It appears as Spinoza's *conatus,* though with Spinoza's rejection of natural teleology, it becomes a *conatus sese conservandi,* an endeavor to persist in its form of being, rather than, as in Aristotle, a drive to achieve its own characteristic form of being.

5. *Human Action as Intelligent Response to the Object of Desire*

All human action therefore likewise proceeds from desire (*orexis*), and is likewise a response to the stimulus of some object of desire. But man, possessing the power of *nous* as well as the power of sense, is able to respond to the desired "intelligently." Being, because of his possession of this power of *nous,* "aware of the future," and not being, like other animals, limited to an immediate and present stimulus, man can respond to what will be: he can desire a future good. And *nous,* knowing the structure of things and events, can use that structure in its practical deliberation to achieve the object of desire (*to orekton*).

Man can thus act from desire, as he always must, even when he is acting from that "desire to know" which all men possess by nature; but he can act from desire modified by reflection and deliberation on the best way to attain the object of his desire. Man can act from an intelligent response to the object of his desire. Man can act from forethought, from the intelligent choice of means: he can act from *proairesis,* intelligence in the service of desire. This power of *proairesis,* so fundamental in Aristotle's analysis of human conduct, of, literally, "forechoice," the intelligent choice of means, when it has grown into a settled habit, a *hexis,* and become a "second nature," becomes that excellence or intellectual "virtue" we call *phronēsis, providentia,* "prudence" —foresight and intelligence.

In the life of action, the practical life, in human *praxis* or conduct, such *phronēsis,* such prudence or practical intelligence, is the highest intellectual excellence or "virtue." Theoretical knowledge of the structure of things supplies the means for attaining the object of desire. "Practical *nous*" or intelligence applies this scientific knowledge of means in particular cases, in particular problems and situations. Theoretical *nous,* which considers what is always or for the most part, thus serves practical *nous,* which considers what is variable and contingent, and can be otherwise—what in our language is relative—that is, the particular and relative goods of particular human situations, the relative goods which are the object of desire in intelligent conduct. Thus the analysis at the conclusion of Book III of the *De Anima* states a thoroughgoing instrumentalism in terms of the ends and procedures of practical *nous.*

Having carried his analysis of "the mover" from the *hormē* that moves all natural beings through the *orexis* or desire that moves all animals to the desire modified by practical intelligence that moves man, Aristotle considers the nature of the relation between desire and intelligence in human action. What is the cause of the motion of the organism as a whole?

It is not the power of reasoning or what is called *nous* that is the mover. For the theoretical *nous* thinks nothing that is practical and says nothing about what is to be avoided or pursued, whereas motion always implies that we are avoiding or pursuing something. But even when it thinks something of the sort, it does not forthwith order avoidance or pursuit. Thus it often thinks of something alarming or pleasant without prompting to fear; the only effect is a beating of the heart or, when the thought is pleasant, some other bodily movement. Besides, even if *nous* issues the order and reasoning (*dianoia*) bids us avoid or pursue something, we are still not thereby moved. Rather, men act from appetite (*epithymia*), like the incontinent man (*ho akratēs*). . . . Nor again is it desire alone which controls motion. The self-controlled, though they feel desire and appetite, do not do that which they have the desire to do, but obey *nous*.[10]

Are there then two different movers, *desire* and *nous?* No, Aristotle concludes; there is one single mover, the power of desiring.

For it is the object of desire (*to orekton*) that moves, and through this reasoning moves, since the object of desire is the starting-point of reasoning. . . . Now *nous* does not seem to be a mover without desire. For deliberation (*boulēsis*) is desire; and when anyone is moved in accordance with reasoning (*kata ton logismon*), he is also being moved in accordance with deliberation. But desire may move one in opposition to reasoning, for appetite is a kind of desire. . . . Hence it is always the object of desire that moves, but this may be either the good or the apparent good. Not all good, however, but practical good; practical good is what is relative and can vary. . . . Now desires arise which are contrary to each other, and this occurs whenever reason and the appetites are opposed, which takes place in those beings that have a sense of time (*chronou aisthēsis*). For *nous* bids one resist because of the future (*dia to mellon*), while appetite has regard for only the immediate present. For the pleasure of the moment appears to be both pleasant and good without question, since one does not see the future. Therefore, while in kind the mover will be one, the power of desiring as desire, and ultimately the object of desire (this moves without itself being moved, through being thought of or imagined), in number there is a plurality of movers.[11]

[10] *De Anima* III, ch. 9: 432b 26–433a 8.
[11] *De Anima* III, ch. 10: 433a 18–433b 13.

To explain how reasoning can thus form a link between the object of desire and an actual act, Aristotle tries to connect his formal analysis of reasoning with this functional analysis of "moving" through what he calls the "practical syllogism." In this, the major premise is universal, while the minor is particular.

For, while the former asserts that such and such a person ought to perform such and such an act, the latter asserts that this particular act is such an act, and that I am such a person. Now it is the latter opinion that at once moves me to action, not the universal. Or is it both, but is the first more at rest, while the other is not? [12]

6. Practical Intelligence as an Intellectual Excellence

It is in the sixth book of the *Ethics,* where he is considering the excellences or "virtues" of practical intellect as *hexeis,* "habits" or acquired powers, that Aristotle analyzes most carefully the relations between desire and *nous* in human conduct. There are three factors in the *psyche* which control human action and the attainment of truth: sense, *nous,* and desire. Sense is never the *arche* of human conduct, but only of purely animal responses to stimuli.

Pursuit and avoidance in desiring correspond to affirmation and denial in reasoning (*dianoia*). Hence since moral excellence is a habit of mind with regard to forechoice (*hexis proairetike*), and forechoice is desire accompanied by deliberation (*orexis bouleutike*), it follows from this that both the principle (*logos*) must be true and the desire right, if the forechoice is to be good, and that desire must pursue the same things that principle affirms. We are here speaking

---

[12] *De Anima* III, ch. 11: 434a 16–21. Compare the fuller treatment of the practical syllogism in *De Motu Animalium* ch. 7: 701a 7–701b 1. It is also introduced in explaining the action of the incontinent man in *Nicomachean Ethics* VII, ch. 3: 1147a 24–1147b 6. In explaining the cause of incontinence "physically" (*physikos*), Aristotle concludes, "Thus it comes about that when men fail in self-restraint, they are in a sense acting under the influence of a principle (*logos*) or opinion, but an opinion not in itself but only accidentally opposed to the right principle (for it is the appetite and not the opinion that is really opposed)."

of practical reasoning and of the attainment of truth with regard to conduct. . . . Now the *arché* of human action (the efficient, not the final cause) is forechoice, and the *arché* of forechoice is desire and reasoning directed to some end. Hence forechoice never occurs without *nous* or reasoning, or without moral habits (for acting well and the opposite never occur without reasoning and character).

Thought by itself however never moves anything, but only thought directed to some end, and concerned with action. . . . Hence forechoice may be called either *nous* served by desire (*orektikos nous*), or desire served by reasoning (*orexis dianoëtikë*), and just such an *arché* is man.[13]

Proairesis, "forechoice," is clearly the key term here. In an earlier discussion, Aristotle has said:

Perhaps we may define *proairesis* as voluntary action preceded by deliberation; since forechoice occurs with reason and reasoning. Indeed, previous deliberation seems to be implied by the very term *proairëton,* which denotes something *chosen before* other things. . . .

As then the object of forechoice is something within our power which after deliberation we desire, forechoice will be a deliberate desire of things in our power; for we first deliberate, then select, and finally fix our desire according to the result of our deliberation.[14]

It is thus clear that Aristotle's "forechoice," *proairësis,* is in his careful analysis the closest of all his terms to the American conception of "intelligence" as the intellectual power of dealing with the problems of practical life. When this power of intelligent choice has become a fixed habit, a *hexis,* it emerges as one of the five intellectual excellences, *phronësis,* practical intelligence:

Practical intelligence (*phronësis*) is indeed the same power of mind (*hexis*) as political intelligence, though their definition is different. Of practical intelligence as regards the city, one kind, as supreme and directive, is called the intelligence of the lawgiver; the other, as

---

[13] *Nicomach. Ethics* VI, ch. 2: 1139a 19–1139b 7.
[14] *Nicomach. Ethics* III, chs. 1, 3: 1112a 14–18; 1113a 9–13.

dealing with particular occurrences, has the name political intelligence, that really belongs to both kinds. The latter is concerned with action and deliberation, and this is why it is only those men who deal with particular facts who are spoken of as taking part in politics. . . . Practical intelligence also is commonly understood to mean especially that kind of intelligence that is concerned with oneself as an individual; and this kind is given the name, *phronēsis* (in the sense of Prudence) which really belongs to all the kinds, while the others are distinguished as intelligence in household management (*oikonomia*), the intelligence of the lawgiver, and political intelligence, the latter being subdivided into deliberative intelligence and judicial intelligence. . . . For people seek their own good, and suppose that it is right to do so. Hence this belief has caused the word "prudent" (*phronimos*) to mean such men. Yet probably as a matter of fact a man cannot pursue his own welfare without being intelligent in household management and even in political affairs. Moreover, even the proper conduct of one's own affairs is a difficult problem, and requires intelligent consideration.[15]

Practical intelligence is thus the highest intellectual excellence of every form of human conduct and action. Aristotle draws a distinction between "making things," which is art (*technē*), and "performing actions," which is conduct (*praxis*), based on the fact that the one aims to make an external product, while the other aims at the action itself. But in every other respect art and practical intelligence are alike: they are both kinds of what we Americans have come to call "know-how." They both deal with what is variable, contingent, and relative, and they both aim at a particular outcome (in the artistic syllogism, just as in the practical, while the major premise is universal, the minor must be particular). In all these respects, both practical intelligence and art differ from the third intellectual excellence, theoretical wisdom (which for Aristotle is a combination, as we saw in chapter II, of science or demonstration from *archai*, and *nous*,

[15] *Nicomach Ethics* VI, ch. 8: 1141b 24–1142a 12.

which judges the *archai* themselves). Theoretical wisdom deals with what is always or for the most part, what cannot be otherwise, and what is universal.

The distinctions between these three forms of intelligence, scientific, practical, and artistic, Aristotle sets forth:

Now it is held to be the mark of a man of practical intelligence to be able to deliberate well about what is good and advantageous for himself, not in some one department, for instance what is good for his health or strength, but what is advantageous as a means to living well (*to eu zēn*) in general. . . . So that the man of practical intelligence in general is the man who is good at deliberating.

But no one deliberates about things that cannot be different, nor about things not within his power to do. Hence, since science involves demonstration, while things whose *archai* are variable are not capable of demonstration, because everything about them is variable and relative, and since one cannot deliberate about things that are of necessity, it follows that practical intelligence is not the same as science, nor as artistic intelligence. It is not science, because matters of conduct are relative; and it is not art, because doing and making are different in kind, since making aims at an end different from the act of making, while in doing the end cannot be other than the doing itself: acting well (*eupraxia*) is itself the end. It remains therefore that practical intelligence is a rational habit of mind that attains truth about action in relation to things that are good and bad for man.[16]

We have now followed Aristotle's dynamism from his recognition of that basic drive or *hormē* to realize its own nature most completely, which he finds exhibited by every natural body, through the desire or *orexis* in which that drive is exhibited on the level of animal living, to its fullest development on the level of rational living in man, in the three forms of intelligence, theoretical in science and wisdom, practical, and artistic. Aristotle examines the relations between these three forms of intelligence, but he makes no attempt to rank them in an order of value; his protest is against any one of them attempting to dominate

[16] *Nicomach. Ethics* VI, ch. 5: 1140a 25–1140b 8.

the others. It is true that what is most distinctive about man is the desire to know which all men possess by nature—when one gets an imaginative grasp of the sweep of Aristotle's dynamism, and realizes the basic importance of desire in the whole panorama of living beings, the first sentence of the *Metaphysics* hits one in the face. And it is true that the *Ethics* ends by making clear Aristotle's own preference for the life of *theōria,* that sheer knowing in which man transcends the limits of human nature and becomes like the gods. From the standpoint of theoretical wisdom, practical intelligence orders the conditions of the life of knowing.

But from the standpoint of practical intelligence, which has to deal with the variable and relative goods ultimately of each situation, theoretical wisdom or science supplies the knowledge of what every form of being and every situation must take into account, that structure of things that is the same for all and cannot be otherwise. In its deliberation about ends and means, practical intelligence must turn to science for what it has discovered about means. And practical intelligence can find in the conditions of its operation a humility that is in its own way as much an expression of a Platonic religious feeling as the participation of theoretical *nous* in the *nous* of the gods:

Wisdom must be a combination of Nous and Science: it must be a consummated knowledge of those things that are most exalted. For it is absurd to think that political or practical intelligence is the loftiest kind of knowledge, since man is not the best thing in the world. And as "wholesome" and "good" mean one thing for men and another for fishes, whereas "white" and "straight" mean the same thing always, so everybody would denote the same thing by "wise," but not by "intelligent"; for each kind of beings will describe as intelligent and will entrust itself to, one who can discern its own particular welfare; hence even some of the lower animals are said to be "intelligent," namely those which display a capacity for forethought as regards their own lives.

It is also clear that theoretical wisdom cannot be the same thing as political intelligence; for if we are to call knowledge of our own interests wisdom, there will be a number of different kinds of wisdom, one for each species: there cannot be a single such wisdom dealing with the good of all living things, any more than there is one art of medicine for all existing things. It may be argued that man is superior to the other animals, but this makes no difference: since there exist other things far more divine in their nature than man, for instance, to mention the most visible, the things of which the celestial system is composed.[17]

[17] *Nicomach. Ethics* VI, ch. 7: 1141a 19–1141b 2.

Chapter V

THE POWER OF SELECTIVE RESPONSE:

SENSING AND KNOWING

The power to respond with discrimination to the object of desire is the power to know. Knowing takes place on two levels, that of sensing, and, in the case of animals that possess the power of *nous*, that of the operation of *nous*, which Aristotle calls *noēsis*, and which we may for convenience call "nousing." [1] Aristotle groups the two powers together under the common heading of *to kritikon*, the power of selective response. Still more important, in his analysis of these two powers and their operation, he attempts throughout to deal with "nousing" on the analogy of the more accessible process of sensing.

1. Sensing

Sensing is an activity characteristic of all animals—and some borderline plants—which possess "sense," *aisthēsis*, the power of sensing or perceiving; Aristotle never makes our modern, post-Jamesian distinction between the two. This power exists "potentially" in the organism, until it is set in operation or "actualized" by some sensible object in the environment, some *aisthēton*. Then the "sense" (*hē aisthēsis*) conceived as the functioning of the sense organ, *to aisthētērion*—that is, the sense as the sensing of the sense organ—becomes "like" the sense object. The sense quality which the object potentially possesses becomes actual in

---

[1] I borrow the device of turning *nous* into an English verb from the man who first taught me Plato and Aristotle, Wendell T. Bush.

the sensing of the sense organ. For example, the wall is potentially white; it has the power of being seen as white. The power of vision (*opsis*) can, by means of the eyes, see "whiteness." For Aristotle, we do not see "in" our eyes, we see "with" our eyes.

In the process of sensing, there is a co-operation of these two powers, in which the power of the wall to be seen white and the power of vision to see whiteness receive a common fulfillment. The potential whiteness of the wall, and the potential whiteness of the power of vision, are actualized in a single process, "seeing the whiteness of the wall." The "actual" color has its locus in the seeing of the eye, not in the wall; that is, in the co-operation of the two powers. But the color of the object, and the color in the seeing of the eye, are one and the same color. Just so, the axe has the power of cutting, and the tree has the power of being cut. But the actual cutting takes place, in Aristotle's way of formulating it, in the tree. In general, the activity of the mover has its locus in the thing moved, not in the mover itself.[2] "For the operation of the agent and the mover occurs in what is acted upon; this is why that which causes motion (*to kinoun*) need not itself be moved."[3] This is a functional, not a mechanical conception: it is what makes possible the notion of an "unmoved mover."

Hence for Aristotle sensing is a being acted upon, a "passion." It is a kind of "alteration" (*alloiōsis tis*), or "qualitative change." But there are two different kinds of "alteration." "Sometimes it means a sort of destruction by the contrary; sometimes it means rather a preservation of what exists as a power by what exists as an operation and is like it, so far as a power can be like an operation."[4] Sensing is an "alteration" or qualitative change in this second sense: as the functioning of a power.

---

[2] "For just as acting and being acted upon are in the thing acted upon and not in the agent, so also the operation of the sensed object (*to aisthēton*) and of the power of sensing (*to aisthētikon*) are in the power of sensing (*to aisthētikon*)." *De Anima* III, ch. 2: 426a 9–11.

[3] *De Anima* III, ch. 2: 426a 4–6.   [4] *De Anima* II, ch. 5: 417b 2–5.

Thus sensing is a becoming like the object sensed. "In one sense what is acted upon is acted upon by what is like it, in another sense by what is unlike it. . . . While being acted upon it is unlike, after it has been acted upon it is like the agent." [5] In these terms Aristotle tries to deal with the problem that has vexed modern philosophy since Galileo, the problem of the subjectivity of sense qualities; it had been posed for him by Democritus.

Now, as the operation of the sense-object and the power of sensing are one and the same, although in their being the two powers are different, hearing and sound thus understood as operations must simultaneously cease to be or simultaneously continue in being, and so also with flavor and taste, and similarly with the other senses and their objects. But when they are understood as powers, there is no such necessity. On this point the earlier natural philosophers spoke unwisely, when they supposed that without seeing there is neither white nor black, and without tasting no flavor. Their statement is in one sense correct, in another incorrect. For sense and what is sensed are said in two ways, as a power and as an operation. In the latter sense, as operations, the statement holds good; in the former, as powers, it does not.[6]

Aristotle's position here is clearly that sense qualities are in bodies as powers, not as operations. Hence Locke is in formal agreement with him in taking secondary qualities as powers of bodies. Where he differs is in his purely mechanical account of the way those powers act.

In sensing the sensible objects (aisthēta), colors, sounds, smells,

[5] De Anima II, ch. 5: 417a 18–20.

[6] De Anima III, ch. 2: 426a 15–25. Compare Metaphysics Gamma, ch. 5: "In general, if only the sensible (to aisthēton) exists, without animate beings there would be nothing; for there would be no sense (aisthēsis). That there would be neither sensible qualities nor sensations (aisthēmata) is probably true. For these are a being acted upon of the senser (ho aisthanomenos). But that the substrates which cause the sensing should not exist even apart from the sensing, is impossible. For sensing is not of itself, but there is something else too besides the sensing which must be prior to the sensing; for the mover is prior by nature to what is moved." (1010b 28–1011a 2)

etc., we get the "sensible forms" of things apart from their matter. "Sense is that which is receptive of sensible forms (*eidē*) apart from their matter, as wax receives the imprint of the signet-ring apart from the iron or gold of which it is made." [7] "Whiteness" operates in the sense, in the seeing of the eye, but not the bricks of which the wall is made. Thus though in sensing we always respond to the stimulus of a particular mover, a particular white wall, the sensing is "of" the universal, "whiteness."

Aristotle is careful to state precisely this view of the relation of the power of sensing to the sense organ:

The primary sense organ (*aisthētērion*) is that in which such a power resides [the power to receive sensible forms]. Thus the sense organ is one and the same thing with the power of sensing, but in their being they are different. For that which senses (*to aisthanomenon*) must be an extended magnitude. But the power of sensing (*to aisthētikon*) and sense are not extended magnitudes: they are rather a certain character (*logos*) and power of the sense organ. [8]

Aristotle is clear that the sense organ which the function of sensing uses as its instrument or means—and this is the way Aristotle always puts it: it is not our eyes that see, or our ears that hear, but we see *with* our eyes and hear *by means of* our ears—is very intimately connected with that function, so intimately that he can say the organ and the power are "one and the same thing." Yet the function and its instrument differ "in their being" (*to d' einai heteron*). He tries to introduce a concept from each of his two sets to state this relation. The power of sensing and the function of sensing are the "logos" of the sense organ: they are not the physical and extended organ

---

[7] *De Anima* II, ch. 12: 423a 18–20.

[8] *De Anima* II, ch. 12: 424a 24–28. Compare: "If an aged man could procure an eye of the right sort, he would see just as well as a young man. Hence old age must be due to an affection or state not of life as such, but of that in which life resides, just as is the case in intoxication or disease." *De Anima* I, ch. 4: 408b 22–24.

itself, but what discourse would *say* makes that organ the kind of sense organ it is. And they are its "power" or *dynamis* of acting in that specific way. Perhaps nothing makes so clear the peculiar force of Aristotle's functionalism as his way of stating this problem and relation.

Turning to the separate senses, Aristotle follows his contextual principle by beginning with the *aisthēta,* the objects in the environment correlative to the power of sensing in the organism. "Sense objects," he points out, are said in three ways, of which two we say are sensed "in themselves" (*kath' hauta*), while the third is sensed "incidentally" (*kata symbebēkos*). Of the first two, the first is the object proper to a particular sense, which cannot be sensed by any other, and about which we cannot be deceived. Thus vision is of color, hearing of sound, etc. These particular senses are never deceived as to whether there is a color, a sound, a flavor, and the rest; though there may easily be error as to what or where the colored or the sounding object is. The second type of sensed object is the "common sensibles."

By common sensibles (*koina pasōn aisthēseōn*) are meant motion, rest, number, figure, size; for such things are not proper to a particular sense, but are common to them all. Thus a particular motion can be sensed by both touch and sight. What is meant by being sensed incidentally is as if the white thing were the son of Diares. He is sensed incidentally, for he is sensed as incidental to the whiteness. Hence you are not acted upon by the incidental sense object itself.[9]

In discussing "imagination" (*phantasia*) Aristotle returns to the common sensibles, and there lists them merely as motions and magnitudes. He qualifies also the possibility of certainty in sensing colors or sounds:

Sensing of the objects of the particular senses is true, or has the least degree of error. Second is the sensing that they are attributes; and at this point error may come in. That it is sensing white, sense

---

[9] *De Anima* II, ch. 6: 418a 17–23.

is not mistaken, but it may be mistaken as to whether the white object is this thing or something else. Thirdly, there is the sensing of the common attributes of the things to which the particular attributes belong: I mean things like motion and magnitude, which are attributes of sensed objects. It is about them that sense is most apt to be deceived. But the motion which comes from actual sensing will be different as it comes from each of these three kinds of sensing. The first kind while the sensing is present is true. The other two kinds may be false, whether the sensing is present or absent, and especially when the sensed object is a long way off.[10]

Like the Greeks in general, and unlike the Newtonians, for whose world of masses it is touch that must be the primary sense, Aristotle regards vision or seeing as the primary sense, and tries to model his analysis of the other senses on that of vision. The function of vision must be understood contextually in terms of the object of vision in the environment that stimulates seeing, to which seeing is a reaction, and toward which it is directed. The object of vision (*opsis*) is what is visible (*horaton*); and what is visible is color: color is on the surface of what is visible in itself, because it contains within itself the cause of being seen, color. But every color has the power of moving the transparent when it has been set in operation; to do so is the very nature of color. Hence color is not seen without light, and every color is seen in light. And at this point Aristotle rather brashly says, "Hence we shall first have to explain what light is."

In view of his total lack of any instruments of exact measurement, Aristotle's theory of color and light is quite a remarkable achievement. It runs: There is a transparent medium, *to diaphanes,* the Diaphanous, which is potentially light, and which becomes actual light when the sun or fire imparts motion to it. This motion of the transparent or diaphanous medium, when actualized as light, in turn actualizes the color of the wall—which is thus a kind of "second light"—in the seeing of the

[10] *De Anima* III, ch. 3: 428b 18–30.

eye. Thus the answer to the question, What makes us see? What is the efficient cause of seeing? is that it is ultimately motion that makes us see, the motion imparted to the transparent medium by the agent of illumination, and transmitted from the colored surface to the eye. For motion is the only agent, the only efficient cause, to be found in Aristotle: only motion can ever "make" things happen for him.

Aristotle attempts to generalize from this example of seeing. The motion of some medium becomes for him the efficient cause of every kind of sensing: the motion of the transparent in seeing, of air or water in hearing, etc. He is generalizing from the distance receptors, and so he naturally gets into trouble when he comes to touch. What he comes out with is that "flesh" seems to be the medium with that kind of sensing! The microscopic discovery of nerves would undoubtedly have delighted him.

What is really surprising is that Aristotle's theory of light should be so much like our own. What he called "the transparent," that could be set in motion by a source of illumination, and could in turn be modified by the colors it itself set in motion, we call the "field of radiation." And though our own knowledge is very much more precise mathematically, it may be doubted whether we have really gotten much further than Aristotle in answering his question, What *is* light?

But whatever detailed analysis of the various complex mechanisms involved in sensing we have managed to achieve, or may still achieve, Aristotle's analysis of the factors involved in the process of sensing remains fundamental. It takes sensing as the vehicle of meaning, as the setting in operation of the "sensible forms" of things; and it views that process of "actualization" as the joint co-operation of powers, involving powers of both the sensing organism to sense, and of the environment to be sensed. In other words, for Aristotle sensing is a "natural" or "physical" process, it is in no sense a "mental" one. For him sensing and sense images, *phantasmata,* are not "mental," they are physical.

In Aristotle and the whole Aristotelian tradition, the line is drawn between sensing and "nousing," between sensing the particular and knowing the universal, not between "body" and "mind." Descartes was thus introducing a genuine and fundamental revolution into the analysis of human nature and human knowledge, when he took sensing and all the other "passions" of the soul out of the physical world, now reduced to extension alone, and put them into "mind," *penser,* a revolution from which we have hardly recovered yet. For Aristotle and the tradition that followed him, images, imagination, pains, and emotions are all particular and corporeal, not "mental" at all. Nor are they in any sense distinctively human. What is so confined to man alone is rather the power of *nous,* of perceiving universals.

Two other points are of general philosophical interest in Aristotle's analysis of sensing. He rejects the notion that there can be any special sense organ (*aisthētērion*) for sensing the common sensibles, here listed as motion, rest, figure, magnitude, number, unity. We sense them by every sense.

All of these we sense by motion, as we sense magnitude by motion, and consequently figure, figure being a kind of magnitude; while that which is at rest we sense by the fact that it is not moved. Number we sense by the negation of continuity, and also by the special sense organs: each sense senses unity. It is clear, then, that it is impossible for there to be a special sense for any one of these, like motion: in that case we should sense them as we now sense sweetness by sight. For we happen to have a sense by which we can know both simultaneously when they occur together. Were it not so, we should never sense them except incidentally, as of the son of Cleon we sense not that he is Cleon's son, but that he is white; that he is Cleon's son is incidental to the whiteness. But of the common sensibles we have already a common sensing, which is not incidental, so that there cannot be a special sense for them. For if there were, we should never sense them otherwise than in the way we said we saw Cleon's son. But the various senses sense incidentally each other's proper objects, not as so many separate senses, but as a single sense, when the two are sensed together, as for instance when we sense that gall is bitter and yellow.[11]

In equal anticipation of Ockham's razor, Aristotle also holds that each sense at the same time senses that it is sensing: there is no need to assume any further sense of "awareness" of sensing.

Since we sense that we are seeing and hearing, it must be either by vision that we sense that we are seeing, or by some other sense. But it may be urged that the same sense that senses vision will also sense the substratum of color. So either there will be two senses to sense the same thing, or vision will sense itself. Again, if the sense sensing vision were really a different sense, either the series would go on to infinity, or some one of the series of senses would sense itself. Therefore this is to be posited of the first sense.[12]

Aristotle thus rules out the many series of awarenesses stretching up to the One or to God, characteristic of Neoplatonic analyses like that of Augustine.

2. Knowing

Thinking and knowing, "nousing," is that activity of "life" that characterizes men alone. Of all animate things, only men possess this power of *nous*. Aristotle takes "nousing" as, like sensing, a being acted upon. There are differences: it is a function not found in other animals, and unlike sensing, which is not mistaken about its immediate objects, colors, sounds, and the rest, "nousing" can be wrong: it can make mistakes. Since "nousing" and the factors involved in it are much less accessible to observation than is sensing, Aristotle tries to push the analogy between the two functions as far as he can.

Just as sensing is a being acted upon by the sensed object, the *aisthēton,* so thinking or "nousing" is a being acted upon by the

[11] *De Anima* III, ch. 1: 425a 16–425b 2.
[12] *De Anima* III, ch. 2: 425b 12–17.

noused object, the *noēton:* this object of thought is the universal. The power of the human organism that is *nous, intellectus,*[13] is nonexistent before it is set in operation, before *nous* thinks, because *nous* is not a "thing," an *ousia,* but a function, an activity or behavior of the human organism, a "part," as Aristotle puts it, of its unified functioning or *psychē. Nous* is essentially a capacity, a *dynamis* or power. Borrowing an analogy from his physics and cosmology with their doctrine of natural place, Aristotle says that *nous* is as it were the "place" (*topos*) of forms, the "place where" universals are actualized, the "natural place" to which universals by nature tend to go.

Nous is thus the power of becoming all things without their matter. Hence *nous is* potentially all *noēta,* all objects of thought, though it is actually nothing at all until it thinks. It is "potentially" all universals, just as on a blank tablet which has

---

[13] There are terminological difficulties of translation here. The traditional Latin term for *nous* is *intellectus,* "intellect." *Intelligentia* is often used interchangeably with *intellectus.* But in accordance with the usage of American culture and American philosophy, "intelligence" is here being reserved for "practical intelligence," what Aristotle calls "practical *nous*" (*ho praktikos nous*), and often more concretely "forechoice" (*proairēsis*). "Mind" is often employed to put into English the Greek *nous.* But since Descartes "mind" has been so definitely and exclusively involved in the mind-body dualism that its connotations are very misleading. It is not with the body that *nous* is to be contrasted, but with particularity. And in English "mind" has come to include both the two levels of "life" that Aristotle distinguishes as "sensitive living" and "rational living."

Conceptions like *nous* which sum up and concentrate the ultimate intellectual aims of an entire culture, are almost impossible to translate into the tongue of a different culture, with different aims. *Nous* meant to the Greek "intellectual vision," and the verbs associated with it, like *theōrein,* or *eidenai,* are sight words, conveying the flavor of "seeing" something. The function of *nous* is to lead to *theōria,* the kind of aesthetic spectacle properly beheld in a "theatre," the natural abode of *theōria.* Ultimately, when Greek culture became very much aware of its central aims, as in Plato, the function of *nous* was seen as leading to a beholding of human life in the world as a transparently intelligible dramatic spectacle. It is such an aesthetic *nous* that Aristotle is trying to bend to his own purposes, more scientific if in the end no less ultimately aesthetic.

The Oxford translation often turns *nous* into "intuition." This is all right in Latin, where *intueor* does mean "intellectual vision." But the cardinal trait of *nous* is clarity, and it can hardly be said that "intuition" has survived the Romantic movement without falling into association with some very shady characters.

nothing actually written on it, all possible writing can be said to be present potentially. The understanding as a blank tablet, a *tabula rasa,* is thus an Aristotelian [14] figure. It has been fundamental for modern empiricism since Locke. But Locke and his successors have had a quite different conception of experience, that is, of the nature of the writing process, from Aristotle, for whom it is not merely mechanical.

Now *nous,* since its function is to think all things, all forms and universals, can have no form of its own, no inherent structure of its own, to keep it rigid and inflexible, and incapable of becoming any form whatsoever that may happen to be the object of its thinking. Its only form or structure is the capacity to become any form or structure whatsoever. Its only "nature" is to be a pure capacity, a pure power, a *dynaton*—that is, an indeterminate power, much less limited and determinate than a *dynamis. Nous* is therefore the nearest thing there is to "pure potentiality," complete formlessness, nothing at all! In this respect, says Aristotle, *nous* is like the "receptacle" (*hē hypodochē*) of the *Timaeus,*[15] which, because it too must receive all forms, can have no form or nature of its own.

If *nous were* something—if it had a definite and determinate structure of its own—then men could not transparently "see" and know what is, without distortion. They could not really "know" things as they are, but only things mixed with the structure of *nous.* Such a *nous* would have turned Kantian: it would have become "constitutive" and creative, it would have ceased to be the Greek *nous* that is intuitive and "sees" directly, that enjoys *theōria.* That we can know things as they are, that such knowledge is possible, is the fact that Aristotle is trying to explain, and not, like Kant and his followers, trying to deny and explain away. Aristotle is here expressing the basic position about human knowledge maintained in the classic tradition that has

---

[14] The figure seems to have originated in the *Theaetetus:* 191 C ff.
[15] *Timaeus* 50 D–51 A.

come down from Greek thought, its fundamental logical "realism," as we call it: that the human mind can grasp the structure of things directly, that, as Spinoza put it, "The human mind has an adequate knowledge of the infinite and eternal essence of nature." [16] This structural realism of the classic tradition has of course been abandoned in nearly all of our critical philosophies of experience since Hume and Kant. That knowledge is not the passive reception of the structure of things, that it is an active process of interpretation and construction, is the biggest difference between our voluntaristic and biological conceptions of knowledge and that of Aristotle.

Nous is thus initially a bare capacity, a *dynaton*. But when it has acquired knowledge, then it is no longer an indeterminate capacity, but a much more determinate power.

When *nous* has become each thought, in the sense in which one who actually is learned is said to be so (which happens so soon as he can exercise his power of himself), even then it is still a kind of power (*dynamei pōs*): not, however, in the same sense as before it had learned or discovered. And then too *nous* can think itself.[17]

Hence *nous,* if it is really to know the object of thought directly, must be, in words Aristotle explicitly borrows from Anaxagoras, who had first made *nous* central in Greek philosophy, *apathēs,* "impassive" or "unaffected," by what acts upon it, universals. "Since it thinks all things, it must needs be *amigēs,* 'unmixed,' as Anaxagoras said, if it is to rule, that is, if it is to know." [18] *Nous* must be "unmixed" with any other structure than that of the object of thought. It must be unmixed with any structure of its own, as we have seen; it must be unmixed with any structure of what it thinks, save that structure it is thinking; and it must be unmixed with any structure of the body, in the way the sense organs are so mixed. It must be mixed with no bodily quality, and with no particular organ (*organon ti*).

---

[16] *Ethics,* Part II, Proposition 47.
[17] *De Anima* III, ch. 4: 429b 5–9.   [18] *De Anima* III, ch. 4: 429a 18–20.

Likewise it must be "unaffected" by what acts upon it, and by the body, in a way that sense is not. Sense is "unaffected" through a certain range, but if the light becomes too bright or the sound too loud, we can no longer see or hear. Sense may even be destroyed by its contrary. *Nous* is not so "affected"; its range is unlimited. The action of the object of *nous* does not really "alter" it, but rather brings what it really is into operation.

The power of sensing (*to aisthētikon*) is thus "not without" the body: it has a definite organ, and definite bodily conditions and limitations. But *nous* is *chōristos*, "separable." It is clear this third term refers to the same problem: its context is very clear in Aristotle's text. He is trying to lay down the conditions under which knowing as a transparent seeing of what is will be possible. *Nous* must be "separable" from the body, apart from the body's qualities and structures, uninfluenced by the body's limitations, in a way in which sensing is not. "Nousing" (*to noein*) is a bodily function capable of rising above the body's limitations, and becoming "unmixed, unaffected, and separable." "Nousing" is self-contained, self-sufficient, insulated from all other functions of living, as no other power of the human organism is.

Just how is "nousing" separable? Spatially (*kata megethos*)? or not spatially, but rather in thought (*kata logon*)? In accordance with his contextual principle, that functions are to be understood in terms of the correlative objects toward which they are directed, Aristotle tries to discriminate the function of "nousing" in terms of its objects, universals. "Nousing" is related to sensing just as the objects of mathematics, forms, are related to sensed existent things: just as the concave mathematical curve is related to the "snubness" of the nose of Socrates. Aristotle's frequent use of this example suggests that he was presumably pointing to a near-by bust in the Lyceum. In his view, such mathematical objects as curves are "abstractions" in discourse (*logos*) from existent substances or things. "When we think of mathematical objects, though they are not in fact separate from matter, we conceive them as separate." [19] So to his question, How is "nousing" separable? his answer is, It is separable, like the objects of mathematics, in *logos*.

This "unmixed" and "separable" character of *nous* and "nousing" was taken, in the Hellenistic commentators, and in the religious Aristotelianisms of the Middle Ages, especially in the Christian form, in Thomas Aquinas, for example, to mean, that *nous* is capable of independent existence: it is the immortal part of the human soul, and is hence capable of going to heaven or to hell. But such a view is clearly remote from Aristotle's problem. He is concerned, not to show that the human "soul" is an independent "substance" that survives the death of the body; that is not his problem at all. He is concerned to show that *nous*, intellect, is a human function capable of knowing truth—of rising above the limitations of a particular animal organism to attain a direct intellectual vision, a *theōria*, of things as they are. The effort of the whole Christian tradition of Aristotelian interpretation has been to confuse these quite distinct problems.

Actual knowledge, then, is identical with the universals and forms, the intelligible structure, of the world, that is known. "Knowing" how heavy bodies gravitate toward the center of the earth, that is, knowing the "nature" of heavy bodies, is the same thing as having their nature in your intellect. But the bodies themselves are not there, their matter is absent. Neither intellect, *nous*, nor the nature of heavy bodies exists by itself. Only human organisms and the heavy bodies thus exist. In actual knowing, the universal, the nature, in *nous*, and in the heavy bodies, is the same. And when that universal is in *nous*, in intellect, it is in the image of the heavy bodies. "Knowing" includes both *phantasia*, "imagination," the power of retaining sense images, *phantasmata*, and *nous*, the power of retaining

[19] *De Anima* III, ch. 7: 431b 15, 16.

intelligible forms. "Knowing" is not the same thing as having images—the *Theaetetus* is right! But knowing cannot dispense with such images: it is "never without images."

This means that for Aristotle there can be no knowledge of the what or the why of things without sensing them, without at least having sensed them, without images, *phantasmata,* persisting in the *phantasia:* that is, there can be no knowledge without sense observation. This *phantasia* or imagination is a kind of motion generated by actual sensing: it is a physical occurrence. And sense images, *phantasmata,* are corporeal, not "mental." Aristotle holds, that is, that there can be no knowing, no "nousing" of universals, without particular physical events in the body. This is the main point made by Pomponazzi in 1516, in insisting that intellect cannot for Aristotle exist "without" images, and hence cannot exist "without body."

This dependence of all knowing on observation constitutes what can be called Aristotle's "empiricism." It is what distinguished medieval "Aristotelianism" from medieval forms of Platonism: the position that intellect cannot know "immaterial substances," completely "intelligible objects" or "pure forms," but only the intelligible aspect of sensible objects, the intelligible forms of what can be observed in sense experience. For Aristotle, knowledge comes from observing the world and reflecting upon what can be observed, not, as the Platonists held, from an immediate inner "intuition" or intellectual vision of a supposed intelligible realm. The objects of knowledge, "intelligible forms" or universals, exist "in" sensible forms, in what is empirically sensed, i.e., in something particular and physical—even, as contrasted with the Platonists, the objects of mathematics. "Without sensation a man would not learn or understand anything: at the very time he is actually thinking he must be seeing a sense image." [20] There can be no "imageless thought." It is surprising that, for a man so wedded to *logos,* to language, as

[20] *De Anima* III, ch. 8: 432a 7–9.

Aristotle, he seems to have been, psychologically, as much of a visualist as the major British empiricists. What he has in mind becomes clear in another passage:

It is impossible even to think without an image. The same process occurs in thinking as in drawing a diagram; for in this case although we make no use of the fact that the magnitude of a triangle is a finite quantity, yet we draw it as having a finite magnitude. In the same way the man who is thinking, though he may not be thinking of a finite magnitude, still puts a finite magnitude before his eyes, though he does not think of it as such. And even if its nature is that of a magnitude, but an unlimited one, he still puts before him a finite magnitude, but thinks of it as a magnitude without limit.[21]

This suggests what is undoubtedly the chief lack in the text of the *De Anima* as it stands. There is to be found in it no treatment of *logos*, of language and communication, in connection with knowing—there is no treatment of *logos* in functional terms. In treating *logos* Aristotle is always the formalist, the *logikos*, never the functionalist, the *physikos*.

In the medieval Christian Aristotelian syntheses, in Thomas Aquinas, for example, this "empiricism" of Aristotle is taken as limiting the scope of knowledge, as leading to an agnosticism: as leaving room for a "realm of truths to be propounded by faith," into which "reason" cannot penetrate unaided. For even Thomas took over from the Platonic tradition the existence of a whole hierarchy of pure forms, "immaterial" and inaccessible to sense observation: the nine celestial hierarchies of the angels. Thomas may have thought well of Aristotle, but after all he is known as "the angelic doctor."

In modern empiricism, the dependence of knowledge on sense likewise led to an agnosticism. Sensations are taken by Locke, for example, as a kind of barrier or screen between the understanding and the "real world" that causes sensations and

[21] *Parva Naturalia: De Memoria* ch. 1: 449b 32–450a 6.

ideas, but does not reveal itself fully in them, and therefore remains itself inherently unknowable.

But as opposed to Thomas, Aristotle was not limiting knowledge. He had no knowledge of the Christian angels or the Christian God, and he came in his maturity to maintain that "pure forms" could not exist. And as opposed to Locke, he held that sensations are not an insurmountable barrier between the intellect and the world, but are rather the natural vehicle by which the intelligible structure of the world is brought into *nous,* and made accessible to it: they furnish a vision, a kind of natural revelation of the world to intellect.

Hence Aristotle's own "sensationalism" and "empiricism" did not lead to agnosticism. Rather, for him man is a rational animal, that is, a living organism, an animal or *empsychon,* endowed with the power of thinking, and hence rational; and the world is a world that can be understood by *nous.* As "rational," man can understand the universe; as "animal," he is limited to that aspect of the universe which such an animal can experience through his senses. On the one hand, man can know of the world only what he can learn from "experience" with it: he is limited by the extent of his rational observation. In Aristotle, this was a protest against those "Platonists" who boasted of a direct and internal vision of truth. On the other hand, the world *is* intelligible to a rational animal with the power of *nous,* for there is nothing in it that cannot enter into man's experience of it. "Experience" is the means whereby the intelligible aspect of the world and things is conveyed to the intellect, *nous.* Whatever exists has a "form" or "essence" by which it can be understood. Whatever occurs has a set of "reasons why" by which it can be rationally grasped. Whatever is experienced has a set of *archai,* in terms of which human thinking can find it intelligible. These "forms," "reasons why," and *archai* are made accessible to *nous* through experience, and man's reflection on it. To find them is the aim of human knowledge: to advance from observation, from sense, to reasons why.

And it can be done! For though all knowledge must "come from" experience, it comes from a rational experience with an intelligible world. What experience conveys can be put into language, *logos:* it can be expressed in words, propositions, and demonstrations. And though man cannot say all that the world is, what he can say is truly said. The world has the power of being understood, and man's understanding, his intellect, *nous,* is the operation of that cosmic power, the expression of the world's intelligibility. In the act of knowing, the power of *nous* to understand, and the power of the world to be understood, receive a common fulfillment, a common operation. Human knowledge becomes one with what the world really is: the intellect, *nous,* becomes itself the intelligible structure of things.

3. What Makes Us Know?

Yet Aristotle recognizes certain difficulties. If *nous* is really so self-contained and insulated from everything else, as it must be if it is to know, "if *nous* is simple and unaffected and as Anaxagoras says has nothing in common with anything else, how will it think, if to think is to be acted upon?" [22] If *nous* has really no form or nature of its own, how can *nous* know itself? Perhaps *nous* is in a sense already all objects of thought potentially, like the wax tablet. Aristotle had already stated, in contrasting "nousing" with sensing: "Actual sensing is always of particulars, while knowledge is of universals; and these universals are, in a manner, in the rational *psyche* or *nous* itself. Hence it is in our power to think whenever we choose; but sensing is not in our power: for the presence of the sensed object is necessary." [23] Why then do we not think all the time? Why do we not think

[22] *De Anima* III, ch. 4: 429b 23–25.   [23] *De Anima* II, ch. 5: 417b 22–26.

all things at once? Why are not all universals continuously present to *nous?*

What "makes" us think and know? What actualizes certain universals at certain times? Is the efficient cause of "nousing" like the efficient cause of sensing? What "makes" us see is light: in seeing, it is light that actualizes particular colors, and light is the outcome of the motion of a medium. Throughout Aristotle, only motion can be an agent, "make" things happen, and serve as an efficient cause. So we should expect Aristotle to answer his question, What makes us know? "Some motion makes us know." So far, the whole consideration has been biological and completely naturalistic: and some motion is the only answer consistent with the rest of the *De Anima.* Perhaps it might be some motion of the nervous system: that was the answer to the same question of the efficient cause of knowing given by Spinoza, who on this point was a consistent Aristotelian. Perhaps it might be some motion of discourse, of language and communication: that is the answer given by moderns like George Herbert Mead and John Dewey. The whole discussion certainly implies an answer in terms of some particular experience—some particular *phantasma,* perhaps: that was the answer of Zabarella, the ablest of all the Aristotelian commentators.

But instead of giving any of these answers, Aristotle turns Platonist in the end, as he so often does. What he actually says is: besides the power of knowing and becoming all universals, *nous* as *pathētikos,* "passive intellect," there must be "another distinction in the *psychē,*" *nous* such that it makes all things, a kind of quality (*hexis*) like light. And it is this *nous* that is, in the words of Anaxagoras, separable (*chōristos*) and unaffected (*apathēs*) and unmixed (*amigēs*). It does not become, but is a deathless and eternal activity, and knows "no intermittence," and without it the *nous* that becomes all things would not think at all. And it is such *nous* that makes us know, just as light makes us see: Aristotle falls back on Plato's metaphor, that knowing is like an illumination by an intelligible light, and resorts to a Platonic myth—he certainly employs in this paragraph the "likely language" of myth.

What on earth does Aristotle mean? The problem of interpreting what came to be called the *poiētikos nous*, the "Active Intellect"—the phrase does not occur in Aristotle himself at all, though *pathētikos nous*, "Passive Intellect," does—has determined men's whole view of Aristotle's thought. The problem really belongs, not to Aristotle himself, but to the history of the Aristotelian tradition in Hellenistic and medieval times; for it became deeply involved in one question clearly not intended in Aristotle himself, religious issues.

Aristotle's pupil and successor, Theophrastos, held that what makes us know is "in the *psychē*," a part of us, one of the human functions of our life, something that man does. It is a spontaneous "active intellect," part of the human *nous*, another function or way of acting of the human organism. The Hellenistic commentator Alexander of Aphrodisias held that it is the same for all men, an eternal activity in the world: it is God himself, the Unmoved Mover. The human intellect, man's "passive intellect," the capacity to know, is illuminated by the cosmic *nous*, by God. This is a Platonizing interpretation; since it was largely adopted by St. Augustine, we can call it an "Augustinian" interpretation. The great Arabic commentator Averroes, living in Spain in the twelfth century, held that man does not really think himself at all. The "passive intellect" is also the same for all men, one and single. Only "intellect" ever thinks—in us! The "rational intellect," *nous*, both active and passive, is not the form of the human body, it is not a human function at all. It is the lowest of the "intelligences" informing the heavenly spheres: its proper "sphere" is the entire human race. Man has a form and function of his own, the "cogitative soul," which is the passive power of the *phantasia* or imagination to serve as the instrument of this single "rational intellect" of all mankind in knowing. Averroes thus construes intellect, *nous,* not as a personal human activity, but as a kind of "realm of truth," in which men "participate," a realm which actualizes itself *in* men as knowledge, but not *by* men. This view strikes the student of modern philosophy as quite Spinozistic: that is, Spinoza is in many respects in the Averroistic tradition, or at least in the tradition common to Averroes and Maimonides, who held rather similar opinions on the unity of the intellect.

At this point Thomas Aquinas and the Christians appeared upon the scene, anxious to combat this Averroistic doctrine of the "unity of the intellect." They were not pantheistic, but fairly humanistic in their emphasis; and they were greatly concerned with the individuality of particular souls. Thomas held that the "active intellect" is the highest "part" or function of the individual human rational soul, and that it requires no bodily organ. We are thus back with Theophrastos once more.

Finally, Pomponazzi and Zabarella, Italian Aristotelians of the beginning and end of the sixteenth century, of all professed Aristotelians probably the closest to the elusive "Aristotelian spirit," held that intellect or *nous* is indissolubly united to the individual body in its existence, and perishes when the body perishes. But in its functioning it can rise above the body's limitations. It needs sense images as its necessary materials, but in knowing *nous* lifts itself to universals, for a mortal intellect can nevertheless know eternal truth. It is in the act of knowing that *nous* is "separable and unaffected and unmixed," but not in its existence. The human or passive intellect is mortal, and dies with the body. The active intellect is alone immortal, for it is the intelligibility of the universe itself, its intelligible structure. So to Aristotle's question, What makes us know? Zabarella answers, It is truth itself, the logical structure of the world, joined to images as their "intelligible form."

The difficulty is that Aristotle's meaning cannot be found in his words alone. He does not press the point: there is a single concise, very elliptical paragraph. He then goes on in a thoroughly naturalistic vein as before. The "active intellect" is thus really the least important or significant part of the *De Anima*. To mix the metaphor, it is a Platonic wild oat coming home to roost: that is, it seems to be all that is left in the present text of the *De Anima* of what had been in his early dialogues a much more important part of Aristotle's youthful Platonism. This is the view of Werner Jaeger, A. E. Taylor, and most present Aristotelian scholars: it is documented in F. Nuyens, *L'Évolution de la Psychologie d'Aristote,* which follows Jaeger's methods.

Perhaps it is best to leave it at that. Such a view of recent scholars transforms the logical problem of harmonizing the active intellect with the rest of Aristotle's thought into the psychological problem of his intellectual "development"; and we moderns somehow feel that when we have abandoned logic for psychology we have "solved" a problem.

Of course, what Aristotle *ought* to have meant by "the *nous* that makes all things," the active intellect, in terms of his own thought, is clear enough. To his question, What makes us know? What actualizes universals? the answer is, it is *logos,* discourse, language and communication. The "active intellect" is actually *logos.* Moderns like Mead and Dewey seem not only to be right—they are also thoroughly Aristotelian. But it is striking that, important as Aristotle makes *logos,* what things can be said to be, he never treats *logos* itself in biological and functional terms, as an activity of organisms with the power of *nous:* he never treats *logos* as a "part" of the *psychē,* as one of the functions making up "life." Such a treatment is not in the *De Anima* at all, but it ought to be.[24]

What Aristotle himself actually meant cannot be learned by torturing this brief paragraph. One can get farthest by noting

[24] The author has sometimes thought he might write out this section himself on papyrus and bury it in Egypt, where a future archaeologist might discover it.

carefully the problems to which it is presented as an answer. My own judgment is that the most probable answer arrived at by such a method is that of Pomponazzi and Zabarella. It seems clear that for Aristotle the "active intellect" must be something that is more than merely human. It may well be "the greater" or the cosmic *"nous"* of Anaxagoras,[25] to whom Aristotle specifically refers throughout. Thus it is likely that as an Aristotelian interpretation Thomas Aquinas' is inaccurate. In any event, the "active intellect" is quite impersonal: Aristotle leaves no doubt on that score. It is immortal and eternal, but has no memory. It is thus of little help to a Christian theologian, but it is very much like Spinoza.

If this really be Aristotle's own view, what can this mean? Accepting the account of Aristotle's intellectual development away from Platonism, we still have to ask, Why did he retain this early Platonic view?

If we know what Santayana has called "The Secret of Aristotle,"[26] that he is a naturalist through and through, we can, I think, see in the "active intellect" a recognition of the cardinal difficulty in any naturalistic theory of knowing and intelligence. If we grant "knowing" to be a fact—if we hold that intelligence is not merely an organ of adjustment and adaptation, but a means of arriving at what may fairly be called "truth"—then mind does seem to rise above the limitations and conditions of its bodily instrument, and to be, as Aristotle puts it, "unmixed and separable," and in its vision "deathless and eternal." This is Plato's insight. It is not so much a theory about the ontological status of *nous,* as an appreciation of what *nous* can do.

Aristotle seems to be pointing, as always, to facts: here, to paradoxical facts. When we think, it is we men who are thinking: this is the individual and creative aspect of human living, in which our minds do seem to be able to lift themselves by

[25] Diels, fragment 12.
[26] See Santayana, *Dialogues in Limbo,* X, "The Secret of Aristotle."

their own bootstraps, and to become at once more self-contained and more self-sufficient, and more universal, more unlimited, more penetrating, than anything connected with a particular animal organism has any right to be. The human mind *is* "unmixed with," "unaffected by," "separable from" its bodily conditions: it does seem to be in some sense "free" to seize on truth. Yet—we could not think at all if the world were not thinkable, if it had no intelligible structure, if it were not, in some sense, the embodiment of "reason," of *logos*—if it were not what can be aptly called a "realm of mind." [27] The hardheaded Spinoza, a consistent naturalist, displays the same "Platonism": "Man thinks, therefore God is." That is, the world is an intelligible system or order, a "realm" of reason and mind. And when we think, in spite of all our limitations, in spite of all the "perturbations" of our individual human minds, it is more than just we men thinking. It is more than just particular animal organisms doing something by themselves. It is the actualization of that system and order, of that "greater and cosmic *nous*," as Anaxagoras calls it.

Thinking and knowing is the "thought" embodied there in the world, "potentially," Aristotle would say, being actually thought by us mortals. It is the world reason or *nous* flowering in our human knowing. The farther you push the human mind, as Aristotle does, to "pure potentiality," to the power to know all truth, the closer you come to "pure actuality," to that perfect truth itself.

In other words, Aristotle seems to be saying something very much like what Spinoza said. The human mind can free itself, is "separable from," *chōristos,* determination by the mere play of the mechanical actions of the body, to be determined by the "reason" of the world-system—by the *"nous* that makes all things," by embodied truth.

It is a metaphor, perhaps, in both cases. But it is a Platonic

[27] See F. J. E. Woodbridge, *The Realm of Mind* (New York, 1926).

metaphor into which all the great "Knowers"—those who make sheer knowing their aim—seem to fall in the end. It is a metaphor that points to facts. The "active intellect" is clearly a Platonic myth, like the very similar Platonic myth of Book Lambda of the *Metaphysics*. It is clothed in the language of Platonic myth, the "likely language" of the *Timaeus,* not in the normal Aristotelian language of exact statement. Such language always points to human experience; and if taken too literally always turns out to be nonsense. But it expresses the "Platonism" in which all sincere naturalisms—like Aristotle's—seem to culminate.

The implication of the myth, the point of the metaphor, is that thinking is not something alien to the universe. "Mind" is not a kind of cosmic accident. It is rather a natural and inevitable development in a universe with the character ours displays, reaching its "highest" actualization in the minds of men.

In conclusion, it is worth stating the significance of Aristotle's functional approach to knowing. He treats knowing as a function of the human organism responding to its environment, as a way of dealing with its world, a way of functioning in a context. He treats it as a natural process: there is no gulf between "mind" and the rest of nature. Mind is an intelligible interaction between a knowing organism and a knowable world. There is no problem of "How knowledge is possible, and why it isn't." For Aristotle, "knowing" is not a problem to be solved, but a natural process to be described and analyzed. In the light of our experience of many other approaches to the construing of the fact of knowledge, the approach of Aristotle, it is here submitted, is the only sensible and intelligible, the only fruitful attitude.

Indeed, any construing of the fact of "knowledge," whether Kantian, Hegelian, Deweyan, Positivistic, or any other, seems to be consistent and fruitful, and to avoid the impasses of barren self-contradiction, and insoluble and meaningless problems, only when it proceeds from the Aristotelian approach, and pushes Aristotle's own analyses farther, as in the light of our scientific knowledge they must be pushed farther today—only, that is, in the measure that it is conducted upon an Aristotelian basis.

Indeed, in some respects Aristotle's functional and contextual behaviorism seems to be superior to our own biological and mechanistic behaviorism, because it views human experience, not as the interaction between a "merely" biological organism and a wholly illogical world, but as a co-operation between an intelligent biological organism and an intelligible world.

Chapter VI

FIRST PHILOSOPHY: THE

ULTIMATE DISTINCTIONS

The Metaphysics is in composition the most complicated and contradictory of the Aristotelian writings. Parts of it seem to belong with the earliest Aristotle we possess, written while he still regarded himself as a follower of Plato, and was still willing to say, "we Platonists." Parts, like the chapter about the fifty-five unmoved movers in Book Lambda, are among the last things Aristotle wrote: chapter 8 was inserted after the astronomical discoveries of Eudoxus and Callippus. Werner Jaeger has managed to distinguish at least ten different layers. Aristotle apparently reworked the themes treated all his life. There are changes in style, as in the Platonic dialogues; there are fundamental changes in the position maintained, there are even changes in the conception of what the science and its object are. Hence, despite the many attempts made over the centuries to extract a consistent body of doctrine from the *Metaphysics,* to modern critical scholarship it seems hopeless to try to "harmonize" everything in these collected papers—there are too many glaring contradictions.

Werner Jaeger's first and best critical analysis of Aristotelian texts is his *Studien zur Entstehungsgeschichte der Aristotelischen Metaphysik,*[1] and his conclusions will in general be stated here.

[1] Berlin, 1912. For a straightforward attempt to find a guiding thread through the text as it has come down to us, see Edith Henry Johnson, *The Argument of Aristotle's Metaphysics* (New York, 1906), a dissertation written under the Aristotelian scholar F. J. E. Woodbridge.

Ta Meta ta Physika is apparently the last of our Aristotelian documents to take its present form. It now consists of fourteen books. It seems likely that no two of them, except Zeta and Eta, which form a unit, originally belonged together as a single work. They are different lectures or "notebooks" dealing with themes connected with what Aristotle came to call "First Philosophy." They seem to have been first brought together into a collection by Andronikos of Rhodes, about 70 B.C., two hundred and fifty years after the death of Aristotle himself. They were then given, for the first time, the colorless title, *Ta Meta ta Physika,* that is, "the Writings that come after those on Physics," in the order of Andronikos' edition. In our own Oxford edition such a title would be "Volume Eight."

Andronikos seems to have drawn on the texts available in several different centers of Aristotelian study, including Rhodes, his native city, as well as Alexandria and Athens.[2] His collection apparently included only ten books, omitting Books Alpha Minor, Delta, Kappa, and Lambda. We do not hear of a fourteen-book collection—our text—until Alexander of Aphrodisias, in the 3d century A.D., five hundred years after Aristotle's death. Not until then, in the full swing of Platonizing religious interests, was it felt that the Unmoved Mover of Book Lambda was the culmination of Aristotle's First Philosophy; not until then, it seems, was Book Lambda even included in Aristotle's "metaphysical" writings. This is a fact worth remembering.

Aristotle set out as a "Platonist," full of religious feeling and aspiration, anxious to make such "Platonism" intelligible. He set out to construct a science of "supersensible being," a science of *noused* or intelligible things—of Plato's "intelligible world." This science he originally called "Theology," the "science of Divine Things," and also the "science to be sought after." This is the

---

[2] See Felix Grayeff, "The Problem of the Genesis of Aristotle's Text," *Phronesis,* I (1956), 105–22. For a full discussion of the problems of Andronikos' edition, see W. D. Ross, *Aristotle's Metaphysics* (Oxford, 1924), pp. xxiv–xxix, xxxi–xxxiii.

aim and view of his inquiry Aristotle states in Books Alpha, Epsilon, and Kappa, and also in Book Lambda, which seems to be a single lecture, written independently, and summarizing the views Aristotle held at the time. It is stated also in Physics II, ch. 2.

But this theology of the Unmoved Mover, the expression of Aristotle's early Platonistic faith, was gradually pushed into the background. There are preserved in the collection several different layers of criticism of the "Platonists." In Book Alpha, in chapters 9 and 10 of Book Mu, and in Book Nu, there is a criticism of Speusippos. In Mu, chapters 1–8, the object of criticism is Xenocrates. Aristotle developed more and more interest in the experienced, sensed world. He was gradually becoming convinced that all things, and especially concrete sense objects in their motions, are intelligible. Hence for him the science that we have come to call "metaphysics" ceased to be the "science of Divine Things," "Theology," and came to be rather the "science of any existent, as existent," "First Philosophy." Books Zeta and Eta, and also Book Theta, were apparently written as independent lectures, with no connection with the earlier lectures. The editor Andronikos of Rhodes interpolated them and made them central in the collection as we have had it ever since.

They contain an analysis of the fundamental characteristics any existent thing must possess, if it is to be and to be known, a set of ultimate distinctions to be used in making any existential subject matter intelligible, including the activities of animate beings, *ta empsycha,* and of rational animate beings, men: living and knowing. What we know as the science of "metaphysics" thus starts for Aristotle as "Theology," the science of Divine Things, but becomes for him "First Philosophy," the science of any existent as existent, what is involved in "being" anything whatsoever. This science emerges as the Aristotelian counterpart of mathematics in our own body of sciences. It can be said that mathematics and mathematical logic are the "metaphysics," in the Aristotelian sense of being the "First Philosophy," growing out of our own physical science, our mechanics and physics. That is, they set forth the formal structure or order in terms of which we find natural processes intelligible, they constitute our instrument of distinguishing, measuring, and relating. In very much the same sense, Aristotle's First Philosophy is the "metaphysics" growing out of his logic and biology: it provides a set of distinctions in terms of which he conducts his formal analysis of things as they lend themselves to discourse and demonstration, and another set he employs in his functional analysis of the way in which they take part in natural processes. It examines the two different sets of ultimate distinctions in terms of which he finds things intelligible as the subjects of discourse, and as the bearers of natural processes; and it considers the relations between the two sets.

1. The Problems of First Philosophy

We have seen that the aim of every science can be stated as the attempt to answer the question, What is it to be a certain kind of thing?—that kind that is the distinctive subject matter of that particular science. We can ask, What is it to be a living being, an *empsychon?* What is it to be a natural process or "motion," a *kinēsis?* What is it to be a good man? a good city? a good poem? a good speech? And so on. That is, we can ask, What properties and characters are involved, and how are they causally related to being that kind of thing?

Now, generalizing, we can drop off the distinctive kind, and ask merely, What is it to be any kind of thing, any subject matter whatsoever? What is it merely "to be"? What properties are involved in "being" anything, in any subject matter that can be investigated, in "being as being"? This general question had been asked in Plato's dialogue of *The Sophist,* where it is pre-

sented as growing out of the problem of non-being raised by
Parmenides and his Eleatic followers.[3]

To this generalized question, Aristotle finds we can give two
kinds of answer:

1) "To be" anything means "to be something that can be stated
in discourse." It means, to be something of which we can ask the
question, "What is it?" *ti esti?* and get the answer, "It is thus
and so"—of which we can state "what it is," its *ti esti*. In this
sense, anything that is, any *ousia,* is anything that can be talked
about, any *subject of discourse.*

2) "To be" anything, in the world of natural processes, means
"to be something that comes into being and passes away," something that is subject to change, that persists throughout a determinate change. In this sense, anything that is, any *ousia,* is
anything that is what it is as the result of a process, a *kinēsis.*
It is any *outcome of a process,* the full functioning or *energeia*
of powers.

Both these simple answers demand further specification and
some qualification. The second represents Aristotle's view when
he is thinking primarily of *ousiai* in the encountered, sublunar
realm of change. When he attempts, as he often does, to extend
his analysis of what is involved in the outcome or full functioning of "natural" processes so that it will apply also to the unchanging stars, he faces the difficulties created by his disruption of the
universe into two realms, and has to modify and enlarge the
meaning of his concepts. *Ousia* as the outcome of a process of
change is then generalized into *ousia* as activity, *energeia.*

These two kinds of answer to the question, What does it mean
to be? reflect Aristotle's double interest, in talking, *logos,* and
in natural processes, *kinēseis.* And when he goes on to examine
what is involved in "being" anything, in these two senses, he is
led to formulate two sets of distinctions: the one set appropriate

[3] *Sophist* 243 C ff.

to understanding any "thing" or *ousia* as a subject of discourse, the other set appropriate to understanding any "thing" or *ousia* as the outcome of a process, as the operation or functioning of powers, and ultimately as sheer functioning, activity.

1) What characteristics must be distinguished in things if they are to be talked about, if "what they are" is to be stated in rational discourse, in words—if they are to be intelligible? This question leads to distinctions appropriate to a logic of discourse, in which a thing, an *ousia* or *res,* is what can be talked about in words, made the subject of propositions. Hence the precise question is, What is involved in being anything that can be made the ultimate subject of a proposition?

2) What characteristics must be distinguished in things if we are to understand how they come into being and change, act and interact in the world of natural processes which experience reveals to us? This question leads to distinctions appropriate to a pattern of motion and change, of processes and activities, in which a thing or *ousia* is what can change, take its part in a process, set its powers in operation. What is involved in being something that can change and achieve a fuller functioning?

It is significant that when Descartes asked, "What is Substance?" he was asking for what persists unchanged throughout change, what it is in change that does not itself change. And in Locke and in Kant, in fact, throughout modern philosophy, "substance" has been taken as the unchanging, the permanent in change, whether Locke's "I know not what," or Kant's "permanent in relation to phenomena." But for Aristotle, who since he gave the technical meaning to the term *ousia* rendered into Latin as *substantia,* ought to know, *ousia* or *substantia* is defined precisely as that which undergoes change in change, what is at the end of any process different from what it was at the outset. And in the most important and fundamental kind of change of all, *genesis kai phthora,* "generation" and "corruption," a new *ousia* or substance is present at the end that was not there at all in the beginning, or a substance has disappeared completely. Thus it is clear, Aristotle's pattern of motion and change is a pattern of novelty that emerges in process.

And it is also significant that the first question is discussed in general terms, in terms of a *logos,* a discourse, isolated from any particular context. But Aristotle's formal analysis always arrives at the point where further questions cannot be answered in that isolation. Then, he always resorts to the second question: to a specific context in the generation of existent things, in some particular process of nature or art.

This procedure followed by Aristotle suggests that while discourse can be analyzed in isolation, "formally," up to a certain point, and certain fundamental distinctions thus brought to light, these distinctions can never be understood, concretely, apart from some specific subject matter. That is, the distinctions made in discourse are relative to a definite functional context, they are not understood when "isolated" from all contexts, when taken as just given, "absolutely" or *haplōs.* For example, what a thing can be said to be, its "form," and what is "essential to" and what is "incidental to" being that kind of thing, cannot be determined in discourse alone. Such questions take one to the context of some specific inquiry into some particular process of nature or of art. This methodological procedure can be stated generally: the *ousia* expressed in statement leads beyond statement to the *ousia* encountered in its natural operations. Starting with the things that are said, *ta legomena,* what things can be said to be, we are led to *ta onta,* to things themselves.

Nota bene: For Aristotle all existence is "determinate" and "individual," and is hence plural: existence forms a many of things and processes, *ousiai* and *kinēseis.* This he takes for granted from common usage: "to be" means "to be some thing," *an ousia.* The question he is examining is, in what sense can other types of being than particular things be also said to be "things" or *ousiai?* Aristotle states his general principle: "To be separate (*to chōriston*) and individual (*to tode ti*) belongs above all to any *ousia.*" [4] He criticizes and reformulates other views in the light of this controlling assumption.

Aristotle's own way of stating the aim of his inquiry runs:

There is a certain science which investigates being taken as being, and what "to be" means, taken by itself. It is identical with none of the sciences whose objects are defined less generally. For none of them looks upon being on the whole or generally, but each, isolating some part, gets a view of the whole only incidentally, as do the mathematical sciences. But since it is the *archai* and the highest causes we are seeking, these must clearly be distinctive traits of some nature. If those who have sought the elements of things were also engaged in this same search, we must interpret their "elements," too, as intrinsic and not merely incidental aspects of being itself. Accordingly, we too must grasp the first causes of being taken as being. [5]

Now "to be" is said in many ways; Aristotle lists various of his categories. But they all have a central reference to one *archē, ousia* or primary being. Even process can be said "to be" as the way to becoming an *ousia* (*hodos eis ousian*). Knowledge is chiefly concerned with what is primary, that upon which the rest depend and from which they are derived. If *ousia* is this primary nature, the philosopher must grasp the *archai* and causes of such primary things or *ousiai*. Hence the inquiry into the factors involved in every case of what can be said "to be" becomes the inquiry into the factors involved in understanding and grasping primary things or *ousiai*.

These factors Aristotle proceeds to list as a number of ultimate distinctions. Since being and unity are the same, and there are as many kinds of unity as of being—for to be and to be one are the same—the first philosopher must investigate the kinds of unity. And since the same science deals with opposites (*ta*

---

[4] *Metaphysics* Zeta, ch. 3: 1029a 27, 28.
[5] *Metaphysics* Gamma, ch. 1: 1003a 21–32. By "elements" and "first causes of being," Aristotle does not mean efficient causes, but formal causes, primary factors and traits found in everything that can be said "to be."

antikeimena), he must also investigate plurality. Sameness and otherness, similarity and dissimilarity, equality and inequality, identity and difference are some of the polar concepts set forth: metaphysics must examine all the various ways in which they are said.

For just as number taken as number has its own peculiar modifications (*idia pathē*), such as oddness and evenness, commensurability and equality, excess and defect, and these things are inherent in numbers both considered in themselves and in relation to other members, . . . so being taken as being has certain peculiar modifications of its own, and it is about these that it is the function of the first philosopher to discover the truth.[6]

Does it belong to the first philosopher to study the axioms of mathematics and of substance, taken for granted without question in the special sciences? Yes, for they apply to all existing things: "But since there is some one higher than the *physikos,* the natural philosopher, since nature is only one genus of being, the investigation of these axioms will belong to him whose investigation is most inclusive and concerns primary being. Physics is a kind of wisdom, but not primary." [7] First Philosophy will also examine the *archai* of the syllogism itself, of analytics or logic. The first philosopher will thus examine the most certain *archē* of all, about which we cannot be mistaken, the Law of Contradiction.

In conducting all these examinations, the first philosopher will distinguish carefully the various ways in which these concepts and distinctions are said: for this procedure, Book Delta, Aristotle's philosophical lexicon, is exemplary. In considering the truth of axioms, he can employ only what Aristotle has distinguished as dialectic: he can develop the consequences of denying them.

His treatment of the Law of Contradiction is a case in point.

[6] *Metaphysics* Gamma, ch. 2: 1004b 11–17.
[7] *Metaphysics* Gamma, ch. 3: 1005a 34–1005b 2.

Heraclitus is supposed to have denied it—"but what a man says does not necessarily represent what he believes," Aristotle skeptically remarks.

All men who are demonstrating anything refer back to this as an ultimate belief; for it is by nature the *archē* of all other axioms as well. . . . Some indeed demand to have the law demonstrated, but this is because they lack education. . . . For it is quite impossible to prove everything and of no *archē* is this more true. . . . In the case of this law we can demonstrate the impossibility of denying it by refutation, if only our opponent makes some statement. If he makes none, it is absurd to seek for an argument against one who has no arguments of his own about anything; for such a person is really no better than a vegetable.[8]

That is, he has literally no sense, no "sensitive life." Aristotle's dialectical refutation establishes the Law of Contradiction as the condition of intelligible discourse.

If it be said that "man" has an infinite number of meanings, obviously there can be no discourse; for not to have one meaning is to have no meaning, and if words have no meaning there is an end of discourse with others, and even, strictly speaking, with oneself; because it is impossible to think of anything if we do not think of one thing.[9]

2. *Ousia as a Subject of Discourse*

Being, *to on,* is said in many ways, as is set forth in detail in the *Categories.* Now of all these senses which the term "being" has, it is clear that "first being is the 'what' (*to ti estin*) which denotes the *ousia,* and all other things are said to 'be' because they are either quantities or qualities or affections or some other such thing, of such a being." [10] For when we describe the quality of a particular thing, we say that it is good or bad, and not five feet

[8] *Metaphysics* Gamma, ch. 3: 1005b 23–1006a 18.
[9] *Metaphysics* Gamma, ch. 4: 1006b 6–10.
[10] *Metaphysics* Zeta, ch. 1: 1028a 14–20.

high, or a man; but when we describe "what" it is, we say not that it is white or hot or five feet high, but that it is "a man" or "a god." None of these other things that can be said about a thing has by nature an independent existence, or can be separated from the thing it is said about. But the thing they are said about can be said to "be" in its own right (*kath' hauto*); and such things seem to "be" more truly, because as subjects of discourse (*to hypokeimenon*) they provide something definite (*horismenon*) and determinate. "Hence that which 'is' primarily, not in a qualified sense but just as 'being' (*on haplōs*), will be *ousia.*"[11]

"First" or "primary" is said in many ways. But *ousia* is first in all these senses, in definition, in knowledge, and in time. Hence for Aristotle the inquiry into the criteria of what it means to "be" anything is transformed into the inquiry into the character possessed by *ousia.* "Indeed, the question which was raised long ago, is still raised today and always will be asked, and which always baffles us, What is being? (*ti to on?*) is the same as the question, What is *ousia? (tis hē ousia?*)."[12]

Ousia is said in four main senses, as the essence (*to ti ēn einai*), the universal (*to katholou*), the genus (*to genos*), and the subject (*to hypokeimenon*). The subject, or the subject matter, is that of which the other three, like all predicates, are said, while it is not itself said of anything else. Hence the primary subject matter or subject seems to be *ousia* in the truest sense. *Ousia* Aristotle thus defines in his First Philosophy, as in the *Categories*, as the subject of discourse.

What, then, is involved in *ousia* as a subject of discourse? I ask, "What is this thing, this *ousia?" (ti esti?*). The answer will be "what it is": "This thing is a table." But just what is it that is a "table"? What is the "what it is," the *ti esti,* of this thing?

1) Is "what this thing is" to be identified with "what it is made out of"? Is it enough to say, "It is wood"? Is the thing to

[11] *Metaphysics* Zeta, ch. 1: 1028a 30, 31.
[12] *Metaphysics* Zeta, ch. 1: 1028b 2–4.

be identified with its "material," its *hylē?* Is it just "wood"? No; for this thing is clearly more than just "wood"—it is "this here wood," to indicate which we can only point. The material of this thing alone has no individual character, and is ultimately unstatable in words, and thus unintelligible. This thing is, to be sure, "this here wood," a *tode ti,* a "this here thing." But to say that alone is not an adequate statement of what it is. Well, then,

2) Is "what the thing is" its "form," its *eidos?* Is it a "classroom table," something to put books and papers and watches upon? Is it a "such," a *toionde?* No; "form" or "character" alone does not tell us what this individual thing really is. "Classroom table" is what we can truly *say* this thing is. But "this thing" is not merely "classroom table," it is not merely "such," *toionde;* that alone is not an adequate statement of "what it is." "Classroom table" in general does not exist, "such's" do not exist. We can say and think "such's"; but no "such's" exist as individual, concrete things we can point to and talk about. You cannot point to, look at, observe, experiment with, "such's," with "classroom table." What exists is always "this here thing," "this here classroom table."

In the discussion in Book Zeta so far paraphrased and illustrated, Aristotle has clearly a twofold interest. On the one hand, he wants to take account of the insights of the Platonists. What *logos* grasps and states really "is"—it is *ousia.* We have a genuine knowledge of the real structure of things, and its formulation in scientific statements, like the definition of the essence (*to ti ēn einai*) of a thing, in which, as set forth in the *Posterior Analytics,* science culminates, does give us an intellectual grasp of that structure. Things are what they can be said to be.

On the other hand, the formulations of discourse are not themselves "what is," they are not *ousiai,* they are not "separate" and "individual." The Platonists fell into confusion in hypostatizing forms, objects of mathematics, universals, genera, and such other formulations of *logos.* They are not "things," *ousiai.* Neither the universal nor the genus is an *ousia*. They are not concrete, particular things: they are predicates common to many things. The same holds of the Platonic forms.

But the "essence" of a thing, what it is to be that thing (*to ti ēn einai*), since it is not common to anything else, and since in a sense it is identical with the thing itself, can be said to be the *ousia* of that thing. The *ousia* of an individual thing is peculiar to it and belongs to nothing else.[13] And it is just this character we mean by "what it is to be that thing" (*to ti ēn einai*), and call its "essence." It is this "essence" we express in a formula (*logos*) when we state what that thing is. The "essence" of each thing is that which it is said to be in itself (*kath' hauto*) and in accordance with its own nature (*kata physin*).[14] Hence the essence is one and the same thing with the particular thing,

for it is when we know its essence that we have knowledge of a thing. . . . It follows that each individual thing is one and the same with its essence, and not merely incidentally, because to have knowledge of the individual is to have knowledge of its essence; so that it is evident that both must be identical.[15]

"Essence" is thus defined as what is knowable and statable about an *ousia*, what the definition of a kind will formulate. It is not the formula (*logos*) or the definition (*horismos*) that is identical with the concrete thing, or can properly be said to be an *ousia*, it is what the *logos* formulates, the intelligible structure or make-up of the thing, what we know and state when we know the thing.

Aristotle is wrestling with the attempt to state the same problem as Spinoza, who tries to maintain that the "idea" of the circle is one and the same thing with the circle itself.[16] In an obvious sense, the geometrical circle is different from its algebraic formula

---

[13] *Metaphysics* Zeta, ch. 13: 1038b 10–12.
[14] *Metaphysics* Zeta, ch. 4: 1029b 14–17.
[15] *Metaphysics* Zeta, ch. 6: 1031b 7, 8; 19–23.
[16] *Ethics*, Part II, Proposition 7, Note.

or "idea," $a^2 + b^2 = r^2$. Yet in another sense they are two alternative expressions of the same thing. In Spinoza's language, it is possible for him to say, it is the same circle conceived under two different "attributes." Aristotle puts it: in one sense the essence is identical with the individual, in another it is obviously not.

For Aristotle, the difficulty arises because so far he has been dealing with the questions *logikōs,*[17] confining himself within the circle of linguistic analysis. He has raised the question, What is the relation between what language formulates, and that of which it is the formulable aspect? What is the relation of the "such's" we can truly say things are, to the things themselves, that actually exist to point to and look at? Such questions, of the relation between discourse and its subject matter, cannot be answered in terms of the distinctions we can draw within discourse alone. We must have some other way of getting at the subject matter besides talking about it: we must look at it and do things with it. We are taken beyond discourse itself, beyond talking, beyond the talking of the *logikos,* who, to judge by the long and very painstaking analysis of his problems and mistakes in Book Zeta, must have been talking for quite a while and to no very good purpose before Aristotle came upon the scene to set him straight.

Aristotle takes us to the functional setting of discourse, to the processes by which things are produced and brought into existence, whether they be processes occurring "by nature," or, as in the case of our table, occurring "by art." At this point we are forced to ask, "Just how did this here thing come into existence?" Well, a cabinetmaker took some oak planks, and made them into a "classroom table." He took a this here stuff, a *tode ti,* "some oak wood," and made it into a "such," a *toionde:* he made "some oak wood" into a "classroom table."

3) So this thing, this *ousia,* is really a "this here such." It is a *tode toionde,* "this here classroom table." It is a union of a "this here stuff," of "this here wood," which is its material (*hylē*), and

[17] *Metaphysics* Zeta, ch. 4: 1029b 13.

of a "such," a *toionde,* its "form" or *eidos.* It is a "from both" (*to ek toutōn*), a "composite" (*synolon*).

An individual *ousia,* the particular thing we have been talking about, is the object itself in its "intelligible make-up" or "essence." This *ousia* is not adequately stated as just "some wood," nor yet as merely "something to put books, papers, and watches upon." It is "this here wooden classroom table."

This particular thing *is* of course what it can be correctly defined to be, what it can be truly said to be, a "wooden classroom table." But it is really more than that. It is "this here wooden classroom table." And to be precise, we cannot omit the "thisness." That is, existing things, *ousiai,* are clearly more than their definitions alone, they are more than what they can be truly said to be. Such concrete things can never be exhausted by what we can say about them. We can never exhaustively "define" any particular and individual *ousia,* we can never say everything that is true about it.

What is involved in *ousia* expressed in discourse, can be stated in another way. Things "are" what they can be said to be, if the saying, the definition, is the outcome of successful inquiry. But *being* what they are is clearly not the same as *saying* what they are. Discourse can state what things are. But things are not discourse. Things can be said to possess a "discursive" or "logical" character or aspect, and this is precisely what we state and express, when we state what they are. This logical or discursive character of things, which Dewey preferred to call their "logiscible" character, is precisely what we state and express when we say what things are, when we state their *"ousia,"* their structure or "essence." [18] But things are not their character, their "essence,"

---

[18] It must be realized that no single term corresponding to the Latin *essentia,* "essence," occurs in Aristotle. Aristotle uses at least half a dozen terms which can all be translated, in some contexts, as "essence." What complicates the matter is that they can all be translated in certain other contexts as definitely not meaning "essence." *Ousia* is the most troublesome and misleading of these ambiguous terms.

alone. They are not exhausted by discourse. Discourse can truly state that "essence" or character: it can state what is "essential" to being that specific kind of thing. But discourse cannot say or state the concrete thing itself. This can be put into Latin: "We can state in words the 'essence' of things, but we cannot state in words their 'existence.'"

These concrete things, that cannot be stated about anything else, that are always subjects of discourse, always what we are talking about, but never predicates, never what we are saying, are things or existences, *ousiai,* in "the first and best sense." They are primary things, primary *ousiai,* "primary substances," the ultimate subject matter of discourse. Their character, what they can be said to be, is their *ousia* put into words. It is what we call *the ousia, the* "substance," or *the* "essence" *of* that kind of thing. Such an *"ousia* expressed" is *ousia* as a predicate, not a subject. Thus when we say 1) "This table is thus and so," we are using "table" to designate a subject, a primary *ousia,* a primary substance. When we say 2) "This is a table," we are using "table" to designate a predicate, a secondary *ousia,* a secondary substance or essence. This distinction between "primary" and "secondary *ousiai"* or "substances" occurs only in the *Categories,*[19] but it clarifies Aristotle's pretty consistent usage of the same term to denote two quite different notions. *Ousia* as subject matter, "primary *ousia,"* exhibits something that cannot be stated in words, but only denoted by pointing: *ho tis anthropos,* "this here man." This is its material or *hylē,* its "matter": what makes it a *tode ti.*

Aristotle's conclusion may be stated: Whatever is can be expressed in words and discourse. There is nothing that cannot be talked about, nothing wholly inaccessible to discourse, nothing "ineffable." But discourse is not its own subject matter—unless the talking is about language itself. Discourse is "about" something that is not itself discourse; though what it is about—its subject matter—has a discursive or logical character, and that

[19] *Categories* ch. 5: 2a 11–16.

character, that intelligible structure, is just what discourse can express and state. Whatever is can be known. There is nothing that is unknowable. But knowledge is of and about something that is not itself knowledge, it is of *ta onta,* the things that are; though what *ta onta* are is precisely what *nous* grasps in its knowing: their *ti esti,* their "what," their "form" or "essence," their knowable aspect.

Aristotle's careful distinctions so painstakingly—and so painfully—worked out in Books Zeta and Eta were necessary to clarify the confusions about talking and its relations to what is talked about into which several generations of Greek garrulity seem to have gotten the Greeks. They are still pertinent today: they could, for example, have saved F. H. Bradley several decades of a futile attempt to get literally everything into words.

3. Ousia as the Outcome of a Process

What is involved in *ousia* as something that changes, that is the outcome of a process? What is involved in the classroom table that was once part of a tree, and that will end in a bonfire? Change in the most general sense, becoming, *metabolē,* and process, "movement" or *kinēsis,* is a fundamental fact of our experienced world, the world "we see." "Only a vegetable would try to deny it," Aristotle remarks rather scornfully of the Eleatics. How is this fact to be expressed, understood, and made intelligible? Things, *ousiai,* are always changing into something else. Materials are always taking on new forms. "This such's" are always becoming "other such's." Of things taken as undergoing such change, as subjects of processes, *kinēseis,* we can ask four different kinds of questions, and get four different kinds of answer, four kinds of *aitia. Aition* means literally the answer or response to a question; it meant in Greek what could be held "answerable" or "responsible" in a law court. Aristotle's four *aitia* are the four different factors "responsible" for a process, the four "necessary conditions" of any process, four *dioti*'s or "reasons why," four "wherefores." Since Cicero translated them into Latin as the four *causae,* they have been known in the Western tradition as the "four causes."

1) What is it?	*ti esti?*	*to ti esti*	The What	*Formal Cause*
2) Out of what is it made?	*ex hou?*	*to ex hou*	The From What	*Material Cause*
3) By what agent?	*hypo tinos?*	*to hypo tinos*	The By What	*Efficient Cause*
4) For what end?	*hou heneka?*	*to hou heneka*	The For What	*Final Cause*

Thus we can ask, What is it? It is a flag. Out of what is it made? Bunting. By what was it made? The firm of Rosenkranz and Guildenstern. For what was it made? To serve as a patriotic symbol.

These are four kinds of reason, four kinds of answer, four necessary conditions—necessary for understanding the process: we need to know all four if we are to find it intelligible. Only one of the four, the By What, the agent, the efficient cause, is a "cause" in the popular sense today—if "cause" have any clear meaning in our ordinary language. The unfortunate neglect of the other three has been due to the dominance of mechanical thinking since the day of Newton, complicated by the popular heritage of Hume and John Stuart Mill. It is worth noting, incidentally, that the empiricist notion of causation as constant succession, of "cause" as the invariable antecedent of its effect, is wholly lacking in Aristotle. Cause and effect are always for him simultaneous, *hama.*

All four are factors discoverable in any process. Every process or *kinēsis* is something being made out of some material by some agent or mechanism for some end. This is obvious in processes that take place "by art," *apo technēs,* in human production. But in natural production, processes that take place "by nature," *physei,* or "in accordance with nature," *kata physin,* the situation seems different. And such processes are significantly different. In the first place, in them there is no intelligent maker or craftsman. Secondly, in them there is no "purpose," no consciously foreseen end. Aristotle's "For What," *to hou heneka,* is "end," *telos,* or "final cause"; it is incorrect and very misleading to translate it as "purpose," which in English means "foresight" and "intention." For Aristotle, human purposes do display foresight and intention, and they do form one subdivision of "final causes" or "ends." But whatever may have happened later in the religious adaptations of Aristotelian thought in the Middle Ages, when the operations of nature were identified with the Divine Providence, Aristotle himself finds such "purposes" and "intentions" only in the processes by art, in human production. For Aristotle, there are no purposes in the world outside human actions and makings. Final causes, *telē,* are for him a much broader class than the subclass of "purposes." That broad class includes not only human purposes, but also all natural ends and outcomes in the processes that take place by nature.

For although for Aristotle nature, apart from human arts, exhibits no discoverable purposes, it *does* exhibit natural ends or *telē.* Nature is the scene of productive enterprises, that are not to be understood as mere mixings and unmixings of elements. Events do not merely "happen," they have consequences, they achieve results, they exhibit a pattern of reaching outcomes that is repeated over and over again, that is "always or for the most part." Clouds form, rain falls, seeds sprout, plants grow, with a structure of natural teleology, a fixed order of stages of development. Nature is indisputably teleological; its processes are full of ends, *telē,* that are achieved, of conclusions that are reached over and over. Only in human life are these ends and conclusions consciously intended, only in men are purposes found. For Aristotle, even God has no purpose, only man!

In a genuine sense, nature is a "life," and not a mere mixing and unmixing of elements, as was held by Empedocles, Democritus, and the atomists. In sharp contrast to Plato, Aristotle took these atomists very seriously, for they were real *physikoi,* genuine students of natural processes. He directs his main efforts to supplement their correct but incomplete analysis. For nature, to be sure, is a mixing and unmixing of elements. But it is a mixing and unmixing that reaches outcomes and ends; and natural processes are not adequately understood unless these outcomes and ends are understood.

We ask, for example, "What is an egg?" Democritus can tell us, it is a chemical process. But it is clearly not a "mere" chemical process: it is a chemical process that grows into a chicken. We can go back, find the elements out of which the egg is made up, either Aristotle's elements or our own, we can find the material of the egg, its From What. We can find the hen and her reproductive system, the cock and his, we can find the agents that generated the egg, the efficient cause of the egg, the "By What." Both material and agent are necessary and important. But we clearly do not understand what an egg really is, unless we recognize the egg as a possible chicken. So to the old question, which comes first, the chicken or the egg? Aristotle has a clear answer: the chicken comes first—in understanding eggs, the chicken that is to be.

Aristotle's viewpoint and approach are, as we often say, biological, rather than "merely" mechanical. They spring out of the experience of the biologist that Aristotle was. He takes biological examples, living processes, as revealing most fully and clearly what natural processes are like. He analyzes the behavior of eggs, not of billiard balls. He seems to have spent much time with the chickens, while the seventeenth-century founders of modern dynamics seem to have spent their lives, like Pascal, at the billiard and the gaming table.

But Aristotle expands his essentially biological approach into a generalized functional conception and analysis for understanding any natural process. He takes motion in place—the billiard ball behavior from which modern dynamics started—as a limiting instance of more complex "motions" or processes. In this respect, his procedure is not without analogy to that of our own physics, which has likewise passed beyond billiard balls and the motions of masses to the more complex processes of the field of radiation. Aristotle puts the emphasis, not on beginnings, but on outcomes, not on initiating efficient causes, or By Whats, but on results achieved, ends, For Whats. For him, real understanding of processes comes not primarily from past efficient causes, but from present and future activities and operations. Our own physics is likewise subordinating efficient causes to formal or mathematical causes and to operations.

For Aristotle, the world is a great spectacle and panorama of processes, of things with powers, *dynameis,* putting those powers to work, *energeia*—in Latin, into "operation"—passing from the mere power to the working, the operation of that power, from potentiality to actuality. Everything in the world has the power to operate in a distinctive, characteristic way, the way of the kind of thing it is. And everything has also a drive, an impulse, a tendency—Aristotle calls it a *hormē*—to put its powers into operation, a *hormē* "implanted" in each thing to become the kind of thing it can become. The verb, *oregetai,* for this impulse or drive is often translated "strives": acorns "strive" to become oak trees, eggs "strive" to become chickens, heavy bodies "strive" to reach the center of the earth. Occasionally Aristotle even says, the stone "strives" to become a doorstep. With reservations as to the doorstep, this is true. Types do persist, and acorns never do become pine trees or elephants.

This Aristotelian *hormē* was translated in the seventeenth century as *"conatus,"* "endeavor." It is the counterpart in Aristotle's vision of the world of the "inertia" of seventeenth-century mechanics. The major difference is that inertia is a *conatus sese conservandi,* an endeavor to remain in the same state; while Aristotle's *hormē* is an endeavor to become different, to fulfill all a thing's powers. This is fundamental in Aristotle's vision of the world: nature is "dynamic," the scene of fruitful productivity. This *hormē* appears in animals as desire, *orexis* (in Latin, *appe-*

titus) in response to the stimulus of the desired, *to orekton;* and in rational animals, in men, as the distinctive power all men "strive" to realize, the desire to know. Book Alpha opens with the sentence, "All men by nature desire to know." The fundamental drive in mankind is to set its distinctive power of *nous* in operation, and thus to become the kind of thing truly which men alone can become, "knowers." Thus man fits into the panorama.

Hence, the world being this great complex of processes, each directed toward its own distinctive end, and each having a drive implanted to realize that end, to understand any process we need to find out its end, the results, the outcome it achieves. To understand man, for instance, we need to find, not merely impulses, reflexes, habits, but what man can do, his powers and possibilities, his end: the good life, living well. And to understand the world as a whole, we need to find what it can do. For man, this means that we need to find how it can make living, moral action, and knowledge possible.

What "makes" all these processes happen? What they do? their ends, their possibilities, their powers, their outcomes? the good each achieves? Not at all! If potentiality, the power to do something, were itself an efficient cause, says Aristotle, if it were an agent, a By What, then everything that can happen would have happened already. For Aristotle, the only agent is motion, ultimately, the eternal motions of the heavens acting on the earth. Aristotle himself is a naturalist, not an idealist, though he was so taken in the Middle Ages. For Aristotle, ends, final causes, outcomes are fundamental in understanding processes; but they never "do" anything. Ends do not act or operate, they are never efficient causes. Only motion can "do" anything, or "make" anything take place.

The world is a great complex of processes, which can be ordered roughly into a kind of loose hierarchy, in terms of man's distinctive function of knowing. We can arrive at "higher" or more inclusive processes, on which more and more lower processes depend, until we come ultimately to the eternal circular motions of the heavens, which in the last analysis "make" the whole cosmic panorama of processes endlessly unroll.

It is to be noted that for Aristotle the world is not a process of processes, it is not an "evolution." Aristotle is not thoroughgoing enough, he does not exhibit enough "natural teleology" in his conception of the world, to satisfy our own present-day evolutionary thinking. Far from being too much of a teleologist, to a post-Darwinian Aristotle does not seem to have been enough of a teleologist.

4. Ousia as Activity

So far we have been considering an *ousia* as the outcome of a process of change, as the operation or functioning of the powers of certain materials. By far the greater part of Aristotle's examples are drawn either from natural processes or from the processes of human art. But in the world that Aristotle can see there are clearly existences that do not appear to change, like the stars. Nor in the ordinary sense is a star the outcome of a process; its only motion is motion in place. Are not such unchanging existences also *ousiai?* And how about those existences that are in a sense functionings, but seem to call for no antecedent powers, no passage to their functioning? The Unmoved Mover is clearly described as such an *ousia.* And even *psychē,* life, is on occasion called an *ousia.*

In Book Theta of the *Metaphysics* Aristotle attempts to give complete generality to the distinction he has arrived at in the analysis of motion or process. He pushes the meaning of *energeia,* which for him begins as the operation or functioning of powers (*dynameis*) in a process of change, to apply to those cases in which there is no process of change. The distinction that arises in the physical world between what things actually are and what they can become, is adapted to those things that always are what they can become, and hence strictly speaking exhibit no change or motion. Such *ousiai* are not "outcomes of processes," they are just "outcomes." They are *energeiai,* activities or functionings. And the most general notion of *ousia,* that will apply to and include all cases, will thus be *energeia* or "activity."

Aristotle points out that the primary meaning of *energeia* applies to motion or process; the other meanings are derived from this one. "The word *energeia,* which is associated with the word *entelecheia,* has been transferred to other things from motions, to which it is especially applicable. For motion above all things seems to be *energeia.*" [20] In this derived sense sitting, or even just being, though they are not changes or motions, are called "activities," *energeiai.*

Aristotle explains this extension of the meaning of the term "activity."

The actual is to the potential as a man building is to a man who can build, as waking to sleeping, as one who is seeing to one who possesses sight but has his eyes closed, as that which has been separated out of the matter is to the matter, and as the accomplished to the unaccomplished. To one of the terms in each case let us assign operation or functioning (*energeia*), to the other power (*dynamis*). Not all things are said to be functioning in the same way, but only by analogy: as that is in that or to that, so this is in this or to this. For some are as motion is to power, others as *ousia* is to some matter.[21]

Thus in the last sentence *ousia* is to matter as activity (*energeia*), even when that activity is not strictly the outcome of a motion or process of change, but is only the functioning—perhaps, as in the case of the stars, the eternal and unchanging functioning—of the powers of that matter.

Aristotle goes on to distinguish between two kinds of activities,

---

[20] *Metaphysics* Theta, ch. 5: 1047a 30–32. In this section, the author is greatly indebted to the thorough doctoral thesis of Emerson Buchanan, *Aristotle's Theory of Being* (1959), ch. 6, "Being as Activity."

[21] *Metaphysics* Theta, ch. 6: 1048b 4–9.

those which do not have their end or goal in themselves and those
which do, that is, those which are directed toward an external end
and those which are their own end. Thus reducing is undertaken
not for its own sake but in order to become slender. As long as
the motion or process of reducing is going on, the end has not
been reached. In contrast, there are activities like seeing, thinking,
living, and living well. As Aristotle puts it, in them a man at
the same time sees and has seen, thinks and has thought, lives
and has lived. The first sort of activity is motion; it is not an end
in itself, but is "without end" (*ateles*). The second sort of activity is its own end; it is self-contained and aims at no external
work or product. In a literal sense, activities of this latter type
can be designated by the portmanteau word, "entelechy" (*entelecheia*): they have their end in themselves. "Entelechy" is made
up of the three elements, *en,* in; *telos,* end; and *echein,* to have.

Thus there is one kind of activity that is a process of change,
resulting in a further product: the functioning of the power to
build a house results not only in the building, but also in the
house, and the house as an *ousia* is the outcome of the process of
building. But there is also a second kind of activity that is not
strictly a process, motion or change, in which there is no further
external product beyond the exercise or functioning of the power
itself. The functioning is itself the end, as seeing is the end of the
power of seeing, or vision. Such an activity is in the most precise
sense an "entelechy," a complete, self-inclosed functioning, a "consummation." From the notion of such an activity there has vanished all the temporal sense of motion, change, or process. There
has vanished also all sense of relatedness to a further objective.
Where the product is an outcome beyond the functioning itself,
the activity is located by Aristotle in that which is being acted
upon: building is in that which is being built, cutting is in the
tree, and in general, as we have seen, motion is in that which is
being moved, not in the mover. But in the second kind of activity,
both goal and activity are in the actor: seeing is in the seer, think-

ing in the thinker, living and living well in the *psyche*. "So that," Aristotle concludes this discussion, "it is evident that the *ousia* and the form are *energeia, activity*." [22]

Aristotle has thus achieved the generality he has been seeking. He has pushed further his usual notion that *ousia* is *energeia* in the primary sense of being the outcome of a motion or process, an activity which is the fulfillment of the powers of motion. He has arrived at the more basic conception that *ousia* is an activity which is in its own right a fulfillment or consummation, with no necessary reference to motion, process, or powers to change. In this most generalized sense, what can be said to be, *ousia*, is activity. This is the point Aristotle finally reaches when he universalizes what we have here been distinguishing as his second or functional analysis of what it means to be, or to be an *ousia*. "Activity (*energeia*) is the thing's being there otherwise than potentially, or as a power." [23]

Ousia as activity will apply to those cases which are not strictly the outcome of a process. In this sense, those eternal activities that are the stars are *ousiai*. The "pure activity" that is found to characterize the Unmoved Mover can be said to be an *ousia*. And in the realm of natural processes the *psyche* or life of a living being, as the complete functioning or consummation, the entelechy of that living being's powers, the comprehensive activity for the sake of which it exists, can likewise be identified as an *ousia*.

How does Aristotle's conclusion, that being is activity, compare with Plato's? We have seen that Aristotle's First Philosophy seems to take its start from the question raised in the *Sophist*, What does it mean to be anything? During the course of the discussion in that dialogue, the most general definition of being suggested is that being is power, *dynamis*—the power either to act on or be acted on by something else.[24] Aristotle seems to be recon-

---

[22] *Metaphysics* Theta, ch. 6: 1050b 2.
[23] *Metaphysics* Theta, ch. 6: 1048a 30.   [24] *Sophist* 247 D–E.

structing this dynamic conception of being. Being is not something static: Plato is right. But being is not power, *dynamis*, it is activity, *energeia*. Ultimately it is the kind of activity that has its end in itself and needs nothing else to act upon. It is difficult, especially in the light of the arguments for the priority of activity in Book Theta, chapter 8, not to think that Aristotle has this suggestion of the *Sophist* in mind, and that in his own conclusion he is correcting and reformulating Plato's dynamic conception of being.

In generalizing the notion of *ousia* which serves him well in the analysis of natural changes—*ousia* as the outcome of a process, the full functioning of the determinate powers involved in a change—into the conception of *ousia* as activity, a conception that would apply also to the unchanging and eternal, Aristotle persists in rejecting any purely static conception of being, of what is. Even in those cases in which no change or motion seemed to him to be involved, even in those elements in his thought which are usually judged to be reminiscent of "Platonic" conceptions, being, what is, *ousia,* is still a doing and an acting, an activity and a functioning. In his First Philosophy Aristotle extended and universalized but did not desert the dynamism of his analysis of the world of natural processes, the functionalism of his physics.

5. The Archē of Motion Itself

It is change, *metabolē,* and motion, *kinēsis,* that "make" every process happen. The only agent, the only "cause," in the conventional modern sense, the only efficient cause, is motion. How are we to understand this fundamental fact of motion itself?

This does not mean that we are asking the question, What is the "cause" of motion? Motion has no efficient cause. Nothing "makes" motion in general take place. Motion in general is uncaused and eternal. Each particular motion is "caused," "made to occur," by another particular motion. And no matter how far back in time we may go, we never find any motion not itself "caused" by a previous motion. Efficient causes, like material causes, must form an endless chain.

Motion in general has no efficient cause. But if it is to be intelligible, motion must have a "reason why," a *dioti*. To understand motion in general, we must find and know the "reason why" there is motion at all. This does not mean what "caused" motion, for nothing ever "caused" it, but rather, what it does, the function it performs, its excuse for being.

There was never a time when motion "began"; motion, like time itself, never had a beginning—Aristotle specifically denies any creation of motion. Men beget sons, those sons grow to manhood and beget further sons in turn, in a continuous unending chain, with neither beginning nor end. If we ask, what causes or produces the begetting? the answer is, a man: a man is the only cause of begetting, some man is the cause of every particular begetting. But if we ask, Why do men beget sons? Why does this endless chain of begettings take place, involving agents or causes, physical materials, and the preservation of types? the answer to this question is not, some man; it is not in terms of production, of efficient causes—such considerations are clearly irrelevant. We ask, Why do men beget sons? It is irrelevant to answer with the perfectly true fact, that men, and only men, do beget sons. What is the "reason why"? How are we to understand the fact of motion itself?

How are we to understand the fact that it is motion, and only motion, that "causes" motion, world without end? The answer to this question will be a principle of intelligibility: it will be the *archē* of motion. In our own physics, motion is understood in terms of the "laws of motion," Newtonian or Einsteinian. Aristotle's answer, the Unmoved Mover, is just such an answer to just such a question: it is the Aristotelian counterpart of Newton's *principia mathematica* of motion, the laws of motion of the science of dynamics.

The Unmoved Mover has nothing whatever to do with any "creator" of motion, any "beginner" or "initiator" of motion—with any "first cause" in any temporal sense of "first." It is a logical explanation, not a physical cause, a natural law, not a force. It renders the great world-complex of natural processes intelligible, it does not "make" those processes occur, any more than a natural law "makes" anything happen. It is an *archē*, a principle of intelligibility, a "reason why."

In modern dynamics, the *archē* of motion is its mathematical structure or formula, its formal cause or reason why, the factor expressing its formal or mathematical relations. For Aristotle, the *archē* of motion is its final cause or reason why, the factor expressing what it is directed toward, the fullest expression of what it can do. Now since for Aristotle what a thing can do is identical with what it fundamentally is, since its fullest functioning, its culminating activity, its entelechy, is its intelligible structure, the final cause and the formal cause of a process are in the last analysis identical. The Unmoved Mover is hence both the final and the formal cause of motion.

Final causes and formal causes are alike also, in that in both no infinite regress is possible, or else they would not be *archai*, genuine "beginnings" of understanding: while both material and efficient causes not only can, but must form an infinite series, with no temporal starting point or "beginning." For Aristotle there is a "first efficient cause" only in the nontemporal sense that the circular motions of the outermost heavenly sphere, the round and round business in the sky, is the ultimate spring, as it were, of the great cosmic clockwork. With regard to efficient causes Aristotle is a thoroughgoing mechanist: there must always be direct physical contact between what is acting and what is being acted upon—there can be no action at a distance.

The Unmoved Mover belongs, strictly speaking, to physics and astronomy, not to First Philosophy at all. The fullest treatment is to be found in Books VII and VIII of the *Physics*. Book

Lambda thus has no real place in Aristotle's metaphysics, taken as his mature First Philosophy. It does not even belong to "theology" in any religious sense: it is not for Aristotle the *archē* of religion. That is, the Unmoved Mover is not to be identified with "God," in any Moslem, Jewish, or Christian sense: it has nothing to do with the God of Moses and the Prophets, or with the God of Jesus or of the Church—to say nothing of the God of Mohammed. It is not the "creator" of anything, for the world is eternal, and motion and time are eternal. It is not even the eternal "sustainer" of the world, in a Neoplatonic sense: for to Aristotle, the world does not need to be sustained, it needs rather to be explained and understood. The Unmoved Mover exercises no providence, it has no "will" and no "purpose." It does not "know" the world: it does not "know" anything, any more than the laws of nature can be said to "know" anything. It is not "intelligent," as man has the power of intelligence; it does not "think," as man can be said to think at times. It can be called *nous* or intellect only in the sense in which Spinoza's Order of Nature or Substance can be said to be "intellect." And Aristotle could even say, with Spinoza—with some exaggeration in both cases—that there is no more in common between this Cosmic *Nous* and human *nous* than there is between the Dog, the constellation in the heavens, and the dog, the animal that barks. It is an intelligible structure or order, a principle of intelligibility. Hence Avicenna, Maimonides, Thomas Aquinas, and the rest, in identifying the Unmoved Mover of Aristotle with the "God" of the religious traditions, were, like all rational or natural theologians, indulging in double talk. The technical theological term is, they were speaking not univocally but "equivocally"—they were equivocating.

The clearest indication of the irrelevance of the Unmoved Mover to later religious concerns is to be found in the fact that when Callippus, the astronomer, showed that the motions of the heavenly bodies were independent, and not to be explained by a single *archē*, but required rather a number of independent *archai* for their understanding, Aristotle inserted chapter 8 into Book Lambda. There are really fifty-five Unmoved Movers, because there are fifty-five independent heavenly motions to be explained. There must be fifty-five separate cosmological postulates, or *archai*, as an empirical fact—fifty-five *theoi*, fifty-five "gods."

Aristotle's Unmoved Mover has no power, no knowledge, no moral or religious relevance: it is a purely intellectual ideal. Its only value is to give understanding. And therefore, for Aristotle the Knower, it is the source of the greatest of all goods, and is *theios*, Divine. Of course, it appears that the early, Platonistic Aristotle, who presumably set down Book Lambda, did attach religious feeling to the ultimate postulate of his cosmological theory, to his ultimate principle of explanation for the world of processes. We need hardly wonder that he did so, since we have seen more recent physicists falling over themselves to do the same incomprehensible thing. If Aristotle be blasphemous, so are the long line from Newton down to Millikan, Whitehead, and Montague. The one thing the mature Aristotle did not understand, and apparently had no interest in investigating, was religion. This makes the use of his thought by the great medieval traditions as a religious apologetic seem a colossal irony.

6. *The Unmoved Mover*

Motion fulfills all processes: they are all moving toward a completed and perfected functioning, they are aiming at the perfect oak tree, the perfect chicken, perfect moral excellence, perfect knowledge—at a state in which all possibilities would be realized, and nothing would be left to be achieved, a kind of being and doing in perfection, an eternal activity. That would be the complete working-out of what motion has the power to effect. And motion in general is to be understood as aiming at it, as directed toward that end. That is what motion is "for"—its For What, its final cause. It is not, of course, a state ever to be achieved, but rather a continuous achieving.

The nineteenth century put some such end in future time, and saw the world as moving toward it. There is no such cosmic evolution in Aristotle: for him, nothing new or different ever actually happens. It has been well said that for him nature is like an army forever marking time, but never marching anywhere. The army is, to be sure, the scene of a continuous process of promotion: privates are becoming corporals; corporals, sergeants; sergeants, lieutenants; lieutenants, captains; and so on. All these promotions are aiming at the General, and the whole army is kept going by the promotions that have actually been made. Nature is kept operating by the ends already realized, and their motions: by men begetting, hens laying, acorns oaking, and the rest. There must clearly be a General, an End toward which all the processes are directed, and in terms of which the complex "life" of nature can alone be truly understood. There must be a perfected functioning of the world's highest possibilities.

It is possible to interpret Book Lambda as a complete naturalism; see Santayana's "Secret of Aristotle," in which he concludes, "Nature is an automaton, and does not work by magic." [25] For Aristotle's thought is thoroughly naturalistic. But his feelings and emotions in Book Lambda are clearly not. The language, the metaphors, the religious exaltation, are all theistic, and have been so interpreted for centuries. As Dante put it, 'Tis Love that makes the world go round! Not the blind forces of nature, not Newtonian inertia, the sheer continuance in motion—to Aristotle, this would have seemed unintelligible; and in Newtonian physics it *is* unintelligible, and has to be accepted as a brute fact. This is not enough for "rationalists" like Aristotle—or Whitehead. For them, there must be a force like "love"—desire, aspiration, the striving toward perfection. That is what makes men go round;

[25] Santayana, *Dialogues in Limbo*, X, "The Secret of Aristotle."

and if men are a fair sampling of nature, that may be what makes nature go round too. For Aristotle, such a force, such a drive or *hormē,* is "implanted" in every natural process: the urge to perfect one's own being.

If the world as a whole has a single ultimate "reason why"— and chapter 8 gives us reason to doubt whether in the end Aristotle maintained that Platonic conviction—it must be that kind of a "reason why." It must be the ultimate focus toward which all processes are impelled by their drives, their *hormai,* to direct themselves. If there be a God who is the authentic Ruler of heaven and earth, he must be a God standing to the world as the Beloved stands to the Lover. He must "move" the world, not by any force of his own, not as an efficient cause, but by his attractive power.

In other words, Aristotle's Unmoved Mover is an ideal. It is what Arthur O. Lovejoy calls "Self-Sufficing Perfection," the Platonic "Idea of the Good," and contrasts sharply with the Demiurge of the *Timaeus,* which he calls "Self-Transcending Fecundity," a creator of being and good.[26] Mr. Lovejoy points out that the Western religious tradition has tried to combine these two ideas of God, which he himself finds incompatible, and logically inconsistent; as though the lover of God needs to have a single, logically consistent idea of God, any more than the earthly lover needs a logically consistent idea of his beloved! For the logic of theology is after all far closer to the logic of the lover's discourse than it is to the professed logic of rational metaphysics.[27]

It is precisely Aristotle's problem in Book Lambda, how to unite the two different logics. The Unmoved Mover is an ideal: it is the object of what Santayana calls "spirituality," defines as "devotion to ideal ends," and makes one half of religion; the other

[26] Arthur O. Lovejoy, *The Great Chain of Being* (Cambridge, Mass., 1936), Lecture II.

[27] See the author's "The Theology of Arthur O. Lovejoy," *The Review of Religion,* 2 (1938), 343–53.

half being "piety toward the sources of our being." [28] In Aristotle, the two are sharply divided: piety is directed toward nature, but spirituality is directed toward the Ideal, the Unmoved Mover.

It is true of human life: man does serve such a God, such an ideal, such an envisaged perfection. It can be said to be true of the world also by metaphor. Does Aristotle think it true of the world literally as well? Was he a "Platonist," an "idealist," when he wrote Book Lambda? If the answer must be, yes, it was because he made a "science" out of Plato's poetry, because he followed the "logic of perfection," the "logic of the lover's discourse," and not the "logic of existence," the logic of physics, of natural processes. It was because he allowed his Platonic feeling for "the Good" to carry him away, to lead him to commit the same fallacy, of which he constantly—and, if Jaeger be right, later—accuses the Platonists. It is the fallacy of taking an intelligible structure distinguished in experience, and feeling so intensely toward it as a human ideal, that he makes it into an independent, self-existing *ousia* or substance. It is the fallacy of hypostatizing an ideal.

But—*is* the Unmoved Mover more than the sum total of all possible fulfillments of the world's processes, of all the realizations constantly occurring, of all the ends continually being reached by its processes? Is the Unmoved Mover not merely the Aristotelian "form" of the world, the ordered structure of all the particular ends at which individual processes aim, and toward which their *hormai* are directed, but in addition the Platonic "Idea of the Good," and the "Good," not only of Plato's own aspiration and *Eros,* but also of the cosmological theories of the Platonistic tradition and of scholastic theology? Does Aristotle, in Book Lambda, really forsake his basic convictions, as expressed in the *Organon* and in the main body of his First Philosophy, Books Zeta, Eta, and Theta, that such an "independent immaterial *ousia*" is quite unintelligible? Is Aristotle in Book Lambda a literal-

---

[28] Santayana, *Reason in Religion,* ch. X and XI.

minded Neoplatonist, and not a naturalist at all? Has he suc-
cumbed to the very "Platonism" he attacks so devastatingly in
the last two books of our *Metaphysics,* Mu and Nu? Perhaps
we should ask, if Jaeger is right, Was Aristotle still a "Platonist"
in Book Lambda, before he outgrew his youthful folly? Would
the mature Aristotle have repudiated Book Lambda, as Bertrand
Russell has repudiated his youthful "Free Man's Worship," as
an adolescent aberration?

The answer is clear: none of this is true for Aristotle's thought,
whatever his feeling or language. The language of Book Lambda
is the language of the Platonic myths, the "likely language" of
which the *Timaeus* speaks. And much in Book Lambda can be
interpreted as "Platonism," if you have the will, and can forget
Aristotle's thought and its content. In the thought of Aristotle,
God stands to the world as form to substance, as the end at which
processes aim to the process within which that end is discriminated, as possibilities completely fulfilled to the present partial
achievement. The Unmoved Mover may well be called a
Platonic myth, like the "Active Intellect" of the *De Anima.*
If so, the "mythical" element is not the manifold specific "unmoved movers" to be found in every process, for they are literal
enough. It is rather the generalization and the unification into
a single Cosmic Unmoved Mover. But then, the unification of
the Divine by means of myth is common enough in philosophical
theology.

Aristotle argues that the perfected functioning of the highest
activity in the world is the only justification, the only "reason
why" for the world's existence. From man's point of view, for a
human philosophy, this is clearly true. And neither eggs, nor
stars, seem to create or require philosophies. Nor have angels,
those beings said to be higher than men, to whom everything is
transparently clear, admirable creatures that they doubtless are,
left us any accessible records of their philosophical achievements.

Now, if God must be the highest activity in the world, the

ideal fulfillment of the world's best possibility—an activity functioning at the highest level conceivable—then God must be pure *nous*, pure understanding. We can understand the world only as making possible the most perfect functioning of *nous*, of "understanding," of the direct intellectual vision of "why." For Aristotle, there is no slightest doubt that *nous*, the power to know and understand, is the "highest" power in the world. At the same time, with fitting humility, he also insists that man is by no means the highest embodiment of the power of *nous:* he thinks the stars are much better at it than men! This humility distinguishes Aristotle among the small band of "Knowers" in our Western tradition. Spinoza holds that man is that part of God by which God knows himself; and Hegel is convinced that man "understands" better than anything else in the universe, certainly better than the stars, and that he, Hegel, understands better than any other man. Hegel was not only a German, to whom such *hybris* comes naturally, but also a German Romanticist, in whom it is perfected.

For Aristotle, indeed for any Greek, the perfected functioning of *nous* must be a "life." It is "the life of *nous*," the "life of reason": that is, *nous* eternally present to the highest object it can conceive, itself. It is *nous*, "reason," the rational and intelligible structure of the world's possibilities and powers, existing not merely as the potentially discernible order of natural ends, but as realized actually, in the most vivid and concrete way possible. Such a "life" would be the highest functioning of the world's powers, the highest ideal conceivable to men. It would lend value to and confer significance and intelligibility on everything else in the world.

Therefore *nous* thinks itself, if it is that which is best, and its thinking is a thinking of thinking (*estin hē noēsis noēseōs noēsis*). . . . Just as is the state of the human *nous* for a certain time (for it does not possess the good at this or that moment, but attains the best which is other than itself for a certain entire period), such is the state of the thinking that thinks itself throughout all eternity.[29]

Following Aristotle's thought, rather than his feelings, which in Book Lambda are clearly Platonistic, "developing his meaning," as T. H. Green used to put it; quite possibly, as Santayana phrases it frankly, stating "what he ought to have meant," we can ask:

1) Does God exist "apart from" the world? Aristotle's answer, to be consistent, would have to run, No, God could not possibly exist apart from the world. God is the form of the world's matter, the *energeia* and *entelecheia* of its *dynameis,* and he would be nothing without the world in which he is an essential factor. God is discriminated in the world as one of its aspects or dimensions. He must be in the world as the harmony of its natural ends.

Aristotle raises this question himself.

We must also consider in which of two ways the nature of the universe contains the good or the highest good, whether as something separate and independent (*kechōrismenon ti kai auto kath' auto*), or as the orderly arrangement of its parts (*hē taxis*). Probably in both ways, as an army does. For well being is found both in the order and in the general, and more in the latter: for he does not depend upon the order, but the order depends upon him.[30]

Just so, for Aristotle God is immanent in the world as its intelligible order, and transcends the world as its ideal end: God is both formal and final cause. In generalizing the notion of an unmoved mover, discriminated as a factor found in every process, Aristotle retains its characteristic relation to the process in which it is discriminated, of being in one sense essential to the process, and in another sense external to it: the relation is that which Whitehead has called "internal-external." [31] For Aristotle,

---

[29] *Metaphysics* Lambda, ch. 9: 1074b 34–1075a 11.
[30] *Metaphysics* Lambda, ch. 10: 1075a 12–17.   [31] See page 73, footnote 9.

this is a combination of Platonic feeling and Aristotelian logic.

2) Where is *nous* actualized? Where does *nous* think itself? in things? in a separate ideal existence? To be consistent, Aristotle must answer, No, in the minds of men. So interpreted, Aristotle's natural theology would be sound, probably the only sound natural theology in the Western tradition. For it would be maintaining that the only "reason" for the existence of the world as a whole, the only fact that makes it more than a sheer occurrence, and renders it intelligible, the only fact that justifies nature to man, is that the world exists to make life possible, and at its fullest, to make possible the best life, which for Aristotle is the life of sheer knowing, *"Nous* nousing *nous."*

Chapter VII

THE HEAVENS

The treatise known as the *De Caelo* (*Peri Ouranou*), *On the Heavens,* sets forth a cosmology, a scheme of the universe, with special reference to the nature and properties of the various bodies contained in it. Aristotle's cosmology proved to be of momentous historical significance. It came to play a central part in the later Aristotelian and Neoplatonic traditions. From the thirteenth until well into the seventeenth century, it provided the main outlines of the universe educated Europeans conceived themselves to be living in. Hence it colored the way men felt as well as thought about the cosmic scene of human life; it was reflected in their common way of speaking, and embodied in their highest imaginative achievements. For anyone who wants to understand the long history of thought and feeling in the Western tradition, a knowledge of Aristotle's cosmology is indispensable.

It was also this cosmology of Aristotle's that became the acceptable formulation of the closed world of ancient and medieval thinking, whose destruction was necessarily involved in the birth of modern science and philosophy. The intellectual revolution of the seventeenth century was a direct attack on the two central ideas that dominate the *De Caelo*. M. Koyré even states that whole "crisis of European consciousness" in terms of this specific conflict. Speaking of the changes in the very framework and patterns of men's thinking, he says:

They seemed to me to be reducible to two fundamental and closely connected actions that I characterised as the destruction of the cosmos,

and the geometrization of space, that is, the substitution for the conception of the world as a finite and well-ordered whole, in which
the spatial structure embodied a hierarchy of perfection and value,
that of an indefinite or even infinite universe no longer united by
natural subordination, but unified only by the identity of its ultimate
and basic components and laws; and the replacement of the Aristotelian conception of space—a differentiated set of inner-worldly places
—by that of Euclidean geometry—an essentially infinite and homo-
geneous extension—from now on considered as identical with the
real space of the world.[1]

Much of Aristotle's natural philosophy can take its place in the
not too orderly but still cumulative working out of scientific
ideas. Even his dynamics stated hypotheses which in the course
of three or four centuries were finally reconstructed into the
principles of Galileo. And though in fact his functional and
contextual concepts, and with them most of his carefully worked
out ideas for the understanding of motion, were abandoned in
disdain by the pioneers of Newtonian science and philosophy,
in our present wisdom we see that logically this need not have
occurred, and that Leibniz's attempt to combine them with the
new mathematical interpretation of nature was not wrongheaded
but merely premature.

None of this applies to the *De Caelo,* or to Aristotle's cosmology
in general. This bandbox universe of natural places could not,
like Ptolemy's excellent geometrical construction designed to save
the appearances, lead to more adequate hypotheses. Its disruption
of the universe into two quite different systems of dynamics was
a major disaster. No one need regret for a moment that the
revolutionaries from Cusanus to Newton rejected it completely,
or expect that our thinking will ever return to its central ideas.
From the seventeenth century on, the *De Caelo* has been viewed
as the repository of many of Aristotle's most curious ideas. Even
today, one can be quite sure that anyone criticizing Aristotle as

[1] Alexandre Koyré, *From the Closed World to the Infinite Universe* (Baltimore, 1957), p. viii.

a scientist, from George Henry Lewes to Bertrand Russell, will cite abundantly from it.

1. The Imaginative Temper of the De Caelo

Yet what gives even the most sympathetic reader pause in the *De Caelo* is not merely or wholly the fact that here Aristotle has clearly come out with what is hardly even antiquated science, but rather outgrown speculation. One who comes to the *De Caelo* from the careful analysis of concepts in the *Physics,* or from the combination of close observation with clear functional reasoning in the biological writings, cannot but be impressed by the great difference in temper and indeed of fundamental aim. Like the *Timaeus,* which it greatly resembles, and which it devotes whole chapters to criticizing in detail, taking that imaginative dialogue throughout as the literal setting forth of a cosmology, the *De Caelo* seems to move in the atmosphere of myth. If the *Timaeus* be a creation myth, the *De Caelo* can be called an uncreation or eternal myth. Both glorify the Divine by showing what it makes possible in the Whole.

Aristotle clearly realizes what he is doing. In answering his question, "For what cause does the universe move in one direction and not the other?" he remarks, "It may be objected that the attempt to furnish proof of everything indiscriminately, omitting nothing, may seem to be the sign either of great simple-mindedness or of great zeal." [2] But this is just what he is here trying to do throughout. Despite the fact that he must constantly complain of our meager opportunities for observing the farther reaches of the heavens, he manages to set forth why the whole universe is as it is and why it could not be otherwise. And while wherever possible he reinforces his conclusions by appealing to observation, to what "we see," he reverses his normal order of arguing. Both in his theory of science and in his usual practice,

[2] *De Caelo* II, ch. 5: 287b 29–32.

he begins with establishing the fact that things are so, and then shows why they have to be so. Here the necessity is first shown, and then observation brought in, to confirm the fact.

In all these ways the *De Caelo* strikes the reader as clearly the most imaginative of all the major Aristotelian writings, and the least distinctively "Aristotelian." Its subject matter, the different kinds of bodies in the universe, and their distinctive properties, natures, and motions, seems to follow logically after the consideration of nature and motion in general in the *Physics;* and there are in fact some ten cross references in the *De Caelo* to conclusions arrived at in the *Physics* But these may well have been added later, while everything about the *De Caelo* gives the impression of its being an early and quite "Platonic" work. In his early dialogue *On Philosophy* Aristotle took the Platonic position that the stars must move by voluntary motion, as *empsycha* or living. Here in the *De Caelo* the First Heaven moves eternally by a purely natural circular motion, and the stars are carried around with it mechanically. There is no clear trace of the immaterial First Mover of Book VIII of the *Physics* or Book Lambda of the *Metaphysics*. The *De Caelo* thus seems to represent a first breaking away from the Platonic theology of souls or *psychai*. All in all, it is not too much to see the *De Caelo* as Aristotle's Ph.D. thesis, with rather more of the cocksure and the bumptious about it than the later writings.

2. *Empirical Natural Theology*

Moreover, here is no mere sober account of the structure of the Whole. Central in the *De Caelo* is the religious interest we find in the early Platonizing dialogues like the *De Philosophia*. What fascinates Aristotle is clearly the heaven of the fixed stars, about whose divinity he grows lyrical. He begins with it, instead of with the more accessible elements; and more than half the treatise is devoted to it. The further details of planetary motion he dismisses in a brief chapter; he is content to leave them to the astronomers. Indeed, however far his indefatigable curiosity ultimately took him in debating the details of the cosmos with his predecessors, in the *De Caelo* Aristotle's controlling concern seems to be to reconcile science and religion. He is trying to work out what in the most literal sense will be a "natural" theology. In a universe dominated by a scheme of "natural" places, discriminated and defined in terms of the observable natural motions of the elements toward them, he will find also a natural place and a natural motion for the Divine. The deathless and eternal will not be located in another "realm," as the Platonists would have it. It will be a natural and observable part of an orderly universe. Aristotle is not merely trying to formulate a scheme of the heavens; he is trying to naturalize the Platonic Heaven, a heaven that is genuinely "heavenly" and divine. He is not only convinced that observation tells us that above the moon motion is different; if we will but lift our eyes beyond the scene of generation and corruption, we can actually see the deathless and eternal, and see that it is perfect and complete.

The natural theology of the *De Caelo,* perhaps in sharp reaction against the Platonists, is an empirical theology: the Divine can be seen literally, and its eternal activity is one natural motion among others. Aristotle did not rest content with this rather crude though emphatic way of naturalizing the Divine. But in becoming in the *Physics* and in Book Lambda of the *Metaphysics* rational rather than empirical, his theology remains no less natural. The Divine is no longer a physical body, however exalted, that moves naturally; it is the intelligible *archē* of natural motion. Where the First Heaven of the *De Caelo* can be seen, the Unmoved Mover must be known and understood. Where the eternal activity of the former is circular motion, that of the latter is knowing—*nous* nousing itself, Aristotle puts it. The Divine no longer needs to be assigned its own distinctive natural place, because it is now conceived rather as a natural function, to which all considerations of place are ultimately irrelevant. Its activity is no longer taken as the most "complete" motion, involving Pythagorean overtones. It has become the most perfect function, knowing.

But if the Divine is now naturalized by identifying it with knowing, this means that knowing has itself become a thoroughly natural activity. Man, even in his most exalted function, has found his own natural status in the Whole: by nature he desires to know, he is the living being that knows. In generalizing that factor to be found in every process, its unmoved mover, and unifying it into a single cosmic Unmoved Mover—in instituting what to our prejudices appears a metaphysical myth—Aristotle may have arrived at no better reason for the motions of the heavens than he had found when he set down the *De Caelo*. But he has certainly arrived at a better reason for the motions of man. In going on from the empirical natural theology of the *De Caelo* to the rational natural theology of the Unmoved Mover, he was advancing from a merely cosmological theology to a human theology—a natural theology that provides a place for man in the Whole because it construes the Divine in terms of human experience.

And, ironically enough, with that change there remains no further religious reason for Aristotle's disruption of the universe. The question becomes purely empirical, to be decided on the basis of observed differences. Closer observation and a more sophisticated scheme of motions need have no repercussion on religious emotions. Indeed, though there is no evidence that Aristotle ever modified the cosmology based largely on the theology he had come to discard, his rational theology of the Unmoved Mover, with its combination of immanence and transcendence—of the order of the army and the general—would seem to accord rather better with the abandonment of his early dualism. For it suggests a cosmic and universal order that is both teleological and mechanical. There is certainly irony in the endorsement of that dualism by the great medieval religions.

It is Aristotle's theological interest as well as his passion for intelligibility that dictates the characteristic temper of the *De Caelo*. In no other writing is his reasoning so concerned to show that it is necessary for things to be as they are, and impossible for them to be otherwise. In no other is the early and Platonic program and ideal of science of the *Posterior Analytics* so closely approached. And this is in spite of the fact that with the heavens we have so little to go upon. "We are far removed from the objects of our attempted inquiry, not in the obvious sense of distance in space, but rather because very few of their attributes are perceptible to our senses." [3] Hence we must make the most of the motions and activities we can observe.

Aristotle states the characteristic principle that controls his reasoning about them: "If we are to grasp their cause, we must start from this, that everything which has a function exists for the sake of that function." [4] The activities that we observe are the ways of operating for which things exist. We can understand many of the other observable features of the Whole as the necessary conditions of those activities. Now, the supreme function of the Whole is the eternal motion of the First Heaven. For this to take place, the entire universe has to be as it is. "The activity of a god is immortality, that is, eternal life. Necessarily, therefore, the Divine must be in eternal motion. And since the heaven is of this nature (a kind of divine body), that is why it has its circular body, which by nature moves forever in a circle." [5] Aristotle then proceeds to offer an ingenious argument [6] demonstrating how this eternal motion requires as its necessary conditions the perplexing motions of the planets, and even the whole realm of mutability and corruption, of coming into being and passing away. Thus the entire panorama of ceaseless change on earth is necessarily entailed by the highest activity of the

---

[3] *De Caelo* II, ch. 3: 286a 6–8.　　[4] *De Caelo* II, ch. 3: 286a 8, 9.
[5] *De Caelo* II, ch. 3: 286a 9–13.　　[6] In *De Caelo* II, ch. 3.

Divine heavens. Aristotle has achieved no mere astronomical system; he has set forth a theodicy.

Thus much that is most distinctive about the cosmology of the *De Caelo* is reinforced if not actually dominated by Aristotle's desire to bring together his religious feeling and his scientific understanding. The careful mathematical astronomers of the later Hellenistic age were doubtless quite sound in disregarding what is clearly a contribution to natural theology rather than to their own sober discipline. It might well help in the understanding of a puzzling and uncharacteristic work to take the *De Caelo* as we have come to take the *Timaeus,* as more of a myth than a scientific inquiry. To be sure, as in the early dialogues that are close to the Platonic writings, Aristotle doubtless believes he is rationalizing Plato's imaginative vision, and correcting it where observation demands. He is doing what he did in the *Eudemus* to the vision of the *Phaedo.* But his too facile explanations for everything have not always gotten far beyond the naive teleology of the less critical parts of the *Timaeus.* He even offers his own version of Plato's "language of probability."

One must see what is the reason for speaking, and what sort of conviction the speaker is aiming at, whether merely human or something more unassailable. Whenever anyone hits upon proofs of a more strictly compelling nature, then we must show due gratitude to the discoverer, but for the present we must state whatever seems plausible.[7]

But a natural theology, especially a radically empirical natural theology, cannot be confined within the strict limits of myth. If Aristotle is trying to bring together his religious feeling and his scientific understanding, to his enterprise that understanding is essential. Within the framework set by his larger problem he tries to employ the rigorous methods demanded by science. As in all his scientific writings, his arguments are conducted with a careful consideration of all the major views or hypotheses that had

[7] *De Caelo* II, ch. 5: 287b 32–288a 3.

already been advanced. As befits their concern, the Pythagoreans
and the *Timaeus* figure prominently; with a view perhaps to the
early Academy, he delights in pointing out at length their
mathematical mistakes. Democritus, who strictly speaking had
no cosmos, is not so central a foil as in the other physical writings.
These other views are not set forth so sympathetically as is
Aristotle's general wont; there is little concern to point out the
considerations that made them seem plausible. He is apt to in-
sist brusquely that his own conclusion is necessary, and that
others are simply impossible. But in the midst of all this dialectical examination and all the emphasis on the necessity of the
arrangements that in fact obtain, what is most impressive is the
controlling authority of observation. If ever an empirical attempt
was made to save the phenomena, it is to be found in the *De
Caelo*. In no other Aristotelian writing is it more true that the
"mistakes" come from this implicit reliance on what "we see"
as beyond question.

3. The Cosmology of Natural Motions

At the outset the *De Caelo* makes it clear that this is an inquiry
belonging to the science of nature. It is concerned, that is, not
primarily with the mathematical positions of the heavenly bodies,
like astronomy; but with those bodies themselves, their properties,
motions, and nature, and the *archai* in terms of which they are
to be understood. Now all natural bodies can move of themselves
in place; nature is by definition an *archē* of motion. There are
two kinds of simple motion, straight and circular; corresponding
to them are two kinds of simple body, as determined by their
observed natural motions or operations. There are the four earthly
kinds, which we can see move naturally in straight lines, either
down to the center of the Whole, like earth and water, or up
away from the center, like air and fire. But as we can also observe,
the body that constitutes the substance of the heavens has by

nature a circular motion. Hence, since it thus possesses a different nature, it must be a different kind, and exhibit different properties.

If there is simple motion, and if circular motion is simple, and if the motion of a simple body is simple and simple motion is the motion of a simple body, then there will necessarily be a kind of simple body so constituted naturally as to move in a circle in accordance with its own nature.[8]

Now, circular motion is "first," for that which is complete (*teleion*) is prior in nature to the incomplete, like motion in a straight line, which has no limit or end.

From this it is clear that there is to be found a kind of bodily substance besides the four in our sublunary world, more divine than and prior to these. . . . Thus the reasoning from all our premises goes to make us believe that there is another kind of body separate from those around us here, and of a nobler nature as it is removed from the sublunary world.[9]

This first body whose natural motion is circular can be neither heavy nor light, since those are properties which imply the rectilinear natural motions of the elements. It will be subject to neither generation nor corruption, for those are from contrary to contrary, and circular motion has no contrary. It cannot grow or diminish, for those are but special cases of coming into being and passing away. Nor can it change its qualities, for such change depends on being acted upon, and occurs only in bodies susceptible to growth. Circular motion will be the only one of the different kinds of change it can exhibit.

From what has been said it is clear why, if our hypotheses are to be trusted, the first of bodies is eternal, suffers neither growth nor diminution, but is ageless, immutable and unaffected. I think too that the argument bears out what we see and is borne out by it. All

[8] *De Caelo* I, ch. 2: 269a 3–7.
[9] *De Caelo* I, ch. 2: 269a 30–33; 269b 14–17.

men have a conception of gods, and all assign the highest place to
the divine, both barbarians and Hellenes, as many as believe in gods,
supposing clearly that immortal is closely linked with immortal. For
it could not be otherwise. If then there is something divine, as there
is, what we have said about the first substance among bodies is well
said. It is equally clear also from the evidence of the senses, enough
at least to warrant the assent of human faith. For throughout all
past time, according to the records handed down from generation
to generation, we find no trace of change either in the whole of the
outermost heaven or in any one of its proper parts.[10]

The ancients also have handed down the name; for believing
that the first body was something different from earth, air, fire,
and water, they called the uppermost place "aither" or "ever
running." [11]

Thus to the First Heaven Aristotle assigns all the traditional
attributes of divinity, trying to enlist the support of the ancients
and the "ancient beliefs of our fathers," for which there was
something deathless and divine among moving things, and for
which the gods belonged to the imperishable heaven and upper
place. He even identifies it with the Platonic region "outside
the heavens" where there is neither place nor void nor time, of
which he had written in his "popular philosophical writings"
like the dialogue De Philosophia; though he now insists that all
divinity has its seat in the outermost and uppermost heaven itself,
the natural body which is in the outermost periphery of the
Whole.[12]

Yet Aristotle can claim that his natural theology is thoroughly
empirical. The existence of the two radically different kinds of
simple motion, straight and circular, is obviously an observed
fact; and what is a more immediate generalization from ex-

[10] De Caelo I, ch. 3: 270b 1–17.
[11] Aristotle very rarely calls this fifth simple body "aither"; normally it is "the
first body" or "the body of the heavens." In the medieval Latin it became quinta
essentia or "Quintessence."
[12] De Caelo I, ch. 9: 278b 10–16.

perience than that bodies whose natural motions are different, like earth and fire, are of different kinds? Even the immutable and unchanging character of the heavens rested on Babylonian and Egyptian records whose antiquity, to be sure, the Greeks grossly exaggerated. It is no wonder that it was so difficult a job for Galileo to argue against observation, and that it required a quite new evaluation of the relation of mathematics to experience.

Two properties especially Aristotle is anxious to defend against other views. The Whole is eternal, ungenerated and indestructible; and it is finite and limited spatially. The deathlessness and eternity of the world he calls a "belief of great strength," though he does not claim to have demonstrated its necessity. It is reinforced by the inability of those maintaining the contrary opinion to offer any account of its generation that is logically possible.

Trusting, then, to the foregoing arguments, we may assume the belief that the whole heaven was not generated and cannot be destroyed, as some allege, but is single and eternal, having no beginning and no end of its whole existence, containing and embracing in itself infinite time.[13]

Aristotle's arguments are dialectical; he spends most time refuting those views like that of the *Timaeus* that the world can be without end and also have come into being. It is not hard to suspect that his insistence on the eternity of the heavens springs here primarily from a religious faith in their divine character. The arguments from the necessary infinity of time and motion are not formulated.

The finite and limited character of the world has more empirical support. An infinite heaven could not revolve, and we clearly see that ours does. The mathematical difficulties of infinite motion are pointed out, and it is shown that an infinite body is impossible. Not even place or void can exist outside the heavens, since they entail the possibility that body might fill

---

[13] *De Caelo* II, ch. 1: 283b 26–31.

them, additional reason why the heavens must be spherical with
no protruding corners. Aristotle has to argue more seriously
against the Democritean notion of an infinite number of worlds.
There can be, he holds, only one universe, one system of nature.
For every observable kind of motion and body is included in
ours. If there were unobserved bodies, they would be parts of
the same system of natural places as ours, and would display
the same natures and act in the same way.

All the worlds must be composed of the same bodies, being similar
in nature. But at the same time each of these bodies must have the
same power, fire, that is to say, and earth, and the bodies intermediate between them. For if these bodies resemble our own in name only,
and not by having the same form, then it would be in name only
that the whole they make up could be called a "world" (*kosmos*).
. . . Either we must deny that the simple bodies of the several worlds
have the same nature, or if we admit it we must make the center
and the circumference the same for all. And this means that it is
impossible for there to be more than one cosmos.[14]

In contrast to the First Heaven itself, which Aristotle takes as
divine, the fixed stars are treated purely mechanically. They are
not self-moved, but are fixed in the heaven, as we can see by their
orbits, which are not independent. It is "most logical and consistent" to take them as made of the same body in which they
have their movement. They are certainly not made of fire,
which is confined to a lower sphere. Aristotle suggests the not
very happy hypothesis that the stars emit heat and light because
of their friction with the air, which they set on fire. They are
spherical, since we can see the moon and the sun are, and all
the heavenly bodies are alike. Moreover, they are carried along
without action on their part, and the sphere is least adapted to
independent motion.

Aristotle has most trouble trying to explain why the planets
move as they do. He is hard put to find any good reason for their

[14] *De Caelo* I, ch. 8: 276a 31–276b 4, 18–22.

complicated courses. Aside from the sun, whose motion along the ecliptic causes the seasons, and thus the entire panorama of generation and corruption, their motions seem to have no discoverable function. Aristotle is committed to a mechanical theory, in which the First Heaven moves the others by contact, like clockwork. Hence he needs actual bodily spheres to cause the planetary motions, and to carry the planets around with them. He took over the excellent geometrical construction of epicycles of the astronomers, and tried to construe it as a physical fact. In this insistence on an explanation through mechanical contact, he is, like the later seventeenth-century pioneer astronomers, far too much of a mechanist.

But it is striking, in view of the way later medieval Aristotelians wrestled seriously with this theory, that the *De Caelo* shows no interest at all in working out its details; it does not face the difficulties of conceiving the mathematical epicycles as bodily spheres. The questions it does raise are not specific but general, and they soon abandon astronomy for theology. Why is it the intermediate planets that exhibit the most complicated movements? Why does the First Heaven carry innumerable stars, while the systems of epicycles bear only one? To these challenges Aristotle replies:

These are questions on which it is worth while seeking boldly to extend our understanding. It is true that we have very little to start from, and that we are situated at a great distance from the phenomena we are trying to investigate. Nevertheless if we base our inquiry on what we know, the present difficulty will not appear as something without reason.[15]

The mechanical reason offered is that the arrangement of epicyclical spheres takes so much work that it can carry only a single planet.

This is why the other motions carry one body; the motions before the last one, which carries the one star, move many bodies, for the last sphere moves round embedded in a number of spheres, and each

[15] *De Caelo* II, ch. 12: 292a 15–19.

sphere is a body. The work of the last one, therefore, will be shared by the others. Each one has its own proper and natural motion, and this one is, as it were, added. But every limited body has a limited power.[16]

But this mechanical explanation is prefaced by the earlier and Platonic view that the stars and planets are alive and have "souls": "We are inclined to think of the stars as mere bodies or units having a certain order but completely lifeless (*apsychon*), whereas we ought to conceive them as partaking of action and life." [17] We must take the action of the planets rather as analogous to that of animals and plants. To achieve the best state, which lies above them, the intermediate planets have to strive much harder than the First Heaven, which is already in that state by nature. The sun, moon, and earth are so far from it that they hardly make the attempt.

To attain the end would be best for all; but if that is impossible, a thing gets better and better the nearer it is to the best. This then is the reason why the earth does not move at all, and the bodies near it have only a few motions. They do not arrive at the highest, but reach only as far as it is in their power to obtain a share in the divine principle. But the First Heaven reaches it immediately by one movement, and the stars that are between the First Heaven and the bodies farthest from it reach it indeed, but reach it through a number of movements.[18]

Such a discussion makes it clear that the interest of the *De Caelo* hardly lies in advancing the science of astronomy. We are therefore scarcely surprised that the problem of saving the appearances of the planetary movements, which so exercised the Greeks, is dismissed in a brief paragraph: "The questions of their order, their relative positions before or behind each other, and their distance from one another, may best be studied in the writings on astronomy, where they are adequately discussed. . . . How this occurs is demonstrated by the mathematicians." [19]

[16] *De Caelo* II, ch. 12: 293a 5–12.
[17] *De Caelo* II, ch. 12: 292a 19–22. [18] *De Caelo* II, ch. 12: 292b 18–25.
[19] *De Caelo* II, ch. 10: 291a 29–33; 291b 10.

The Pythagorean theory of the harmony produced by the revolving stars is discussed seriously and sympathetically, but rejected, not only because no such harmony is heard, but more especially because such sound would be of insupportable force and violence, and would shatter the earth. The discussion is introduced so that Aristotle may use the observed fact that the heavenly movements are noiseless to reinforce his view that the stars are not moving in a stationary medium, but are carried along by their spheres. Yet he is also capable of a long discussion of the Pythagorean position that the Whole has a top and bottom, and a right and a left side. And he answers his question, Why do the heavens move one way rather than the other? by replying, Because it is obviously better to move forward rather than to move backward.[20]

With the earth and the elements Aristotle has regained the firm ground of observation. The earth is at rest in the center of the Whole, because no parallaxes of the stars are observed, and because bodies fall straight back when thrown directly upward. It is spherical, as we can observe from its shadow during eclipses, and from the different positions of the stars in different latitudes. It is of no great size in comparison with the other stars, for a small northward or southward change of our position causes a considerable shift in the position of the stars.

For this reason those who imagine that the region around the Pillars of Hercules joins on to the regions of India, and that in this way the ocean is one, are not, it would seem, suggesting anything utterly incredible. . . . Mathematicians who try to calculate the circumference put it at 400,000 stades.[21]

---

[20] For Aristotle, since the heaven is alive and contains an *archē* of motion, like all living things it possesses these directions. "Right" is that side from which motion in place starts, i.e., from which the stars rise. Hence "top" is the south pole, and "bottom" the north. "Front" is that toward which sensations are directed, i.e., toward which the animal looks.

[21] *De Caelo* II, ch. 14: 298a 9–17. This comes to 9,987 geographical miles. This passage was the basis of Columbus' confidence that he could reach the Indies by sailing westward.

The last two books of the *De Caelo* deal with genesis or coming into being, in a way preliminary to the more thorough discussion in the *De Generatione*. They include the treatment of the elements and their natural motions to their natural places. The natural motion of the elements is in straight lines, earth and water moving down, air and fire up. These observed motions of gravitation and levitation define the heavy and the light. "Down" means toward the center of the Whole, "up" means away from it. These motions of the elements also define their natural places in the four concentric circles between the earth and the moon, which constitute the structure of the sublunar region. Motion of a body toward its proper place is motion toward its proper form as heavy or light. The characteristic operation of bodies as light or heavy is to be in their proper position in the system, and to pass from being potentially light or heavy to that actualized form. In this whole discussion Aristotle exhibits, within the limits of his uncritical observation, much of his customary acuteness, and much penetrating criticism of the Pythagoreans and of the *Timaeus,* on whose mathematical atomism he is very severe.

A large part of the fascination of the *De Caelo* lies in the juxtaposition of imaginative Platonic speculation with downright empiricism. It is the former which gave the treatise and its neatly structured universe its strong hold on the religious imagination in the later traditions of religious Aristotelianism. Men could take their mathematical astronomy from Ptolemy, but it was Aristotle who showed them how to transform that astronomy into a natural theology. Yet even in the *De Caelo,* for all its youthful brashness and self-confidence, Aristotle is hardly the dogmatist of the Schoolmen's closed system. He is with great assurance offering "explanations" for the observed facts that are far too facile. But Galileo—who was not wholly without self-confidence himself—could maintain, and that not merely for polemical purposes, that Aristotle would have been convinced by him if that doughty fighter had only been able to get hold of him. For the Aristotle who had passed beyond the strain of immaturity that used to irritate and now merely amuses moderns in the *De Caelo,* Galileo's insistence is doubtless just. But the reader will still suspect that Aristotle would have been convinced, not by Galileo's mathematics, but by his telescope.

Chapter VIII

THE UNDERSTANDING OF

NATURAL PROCESSES

Physics or Natural Philosophy is for Aristotle one of three "theoretical" sciences. These sciences satisfy and fulfill man's distinctive desire to know, to know the ways of things that are followed "always or for the most part," and not merely, like the practical sciences, to know the variable, contingent, and relative goods involved in living well, or, like the productive sciences, to know how to make things, equally a knowledge of the variable, contingent, and relative. These three theoretical sciences are First Philosophy, Mathematics, and Physics.

First Philosophy or Theology is defined in the *Physics* as the science of changeless things existing by themselves, that is, of intelligible or divine things. This clearly reflects Aristotle's earlier or Platonistic conception of First Philosophy, before it had been abandoned in Books Zeta, Eta, and Theta.

Mathematics is defined as the science of changeless things existing only by abstraction from changing things, or as the science of changing sense objects in their unchanging aspect. For Aristotle, mathematics is not a study of detached essences and postulate systems. This was the Platonic view, and is also for the most part the modern view. As Aristotle considers the matter, mathematics studies the same objects as physics, but studies them from a different point of view. It disregards the sensible qualities of things, and deals only with the quantitative and the continuous. The subject matter of mathematics consists of surfaces, solids, magnitudes, lines, and points. Physical bodies can be said to "have" these aspects. But the mathematician does not study them as the limits of natural bodies, he "separates" them from such physical bodies; they are all separable in thought (*chōrista tē noēsei*) from motion. The partisans of Ideas (the Platonists), indeed, separate physical things (*ta physika*) themselves from motion, which are much less separable. Aristotle's favorite example is the concave curve "separated" from the snubness of Socrates' nose.

The "more physical parts of mathematics," optics, harmonics, astronomy, and mechanics, are really parts of physics. Geometry studies the physical line, not as physical, but as separated by thought from movement; optics studies the mathematical line, as physical and in movement.[1]

Thus for Aristotle physics is not applied mathematics; rather, mathematics is "separated" or abstracted physics. Hence there arises no problem of the relation between mathematics and nature, or why mathematics "applies" so successfully to natural bodies. For mathematics is taken as isolating certain characteristics of natural bodies, and then manipulating those isolated characters. This Aristotelian philosophy of mathematics prevailed throughout the classic tradition, down through Newton. It avoids a host of difficulties that have created great philosophical perplexity: those of Kant, for example, to say nothing of those implicit in our own view of mathematics as a pure postulate system.

Physics itself is defined as the science of things that change, that come into being and pass away, the science of becoming, of *kinēsis,* that is, of motion or process. Physics will thus include biology, dealing with the special kinds of change and motion peculiar to living organisms, to animate things, *ta empsycha.* And biology will in turn include the special kinds of change and motion peculiar to living things with the power of *nous,*

[1] *Physics* II, ch. 2.

rational animals or men. This is important, since for Aristotle living and knowing are the most complex and developed forms of change and motion. Hence change in general, *metabolē,* must be understood in terms that will make intelligible "living" and "knowing," and not merely explain the simplest form of change, motion in place, *phora,* the "motion" of Galileo and Newton. If the more complex forms of change are not understood, change in general is not really understood at all.

Nature is a kind of "life" of things in process of change; and change is fundamentally not a mere "event," an observed temporal difference, but a "process" resulting in the generation of novelty. It is not a mere quantitative rearrangement of elements, as Empedocles and Democritus held, though they were quite right in insisting that such a rearrangement of elements is always involved in any change. In other words, Aristotle is convinced that any science of change or process must explain the egg-chicken "motion," and not merely the behavior of billiard balls.

1. The Significance of Aristotle's Natural Philosophy

From the limited point of view of early modern physics, seventeenth-century and Newtonian mechanics, Aristotle's physics, and especially his astronomy, in the *De Caelo,* seemed perverse and barren. Aristotle was judged by those pioneers as far behind his contemporaries. His physics was qualitative, not mathematical; it was teleological and functional, not exclusively mechanical. The Pythagoreans and the Platonists had developed a mathematical physics and astronomy, which were judged in the seventeenth century to be "real science," a combination of atomism and mathematics. Out of their activities there developed Alexandrian mathematical physics. In later antiquity Aristotle's physics enjoyed in fact little influence outside the Aristotelian school, and was hardly known except in the Lyceum. It came to be enormously influential during the Middle Ages; and during the modern era since the seventeenth century this influence has been judged to have been very unfortunate. It has been assumed that when the moderns, first in the thirteenth century, and then again in the sixteenth, turned from Aristotle to Platonic and Pythagorean ideas, they immediately began to secure fruitful results.

In the nineteenth century the attitude toward Aristotle as a scientist began to change. As biology came to the fore, it was realized that Aristotle was the greatest biologist until the eighteenth century. Darwin made the enthusiastic remark, "Linnaeus and Cuvier have been my two gods; but they were mere schoolboys compared to old Aristotle." In biology, Aristotle's mistakes and failures come from his lack of detailed observation, his lack of a microscope, his trust in common opinion; all these things could be easily remedied by time. But in physics and astronomy it was Aristotle's aim itself that was "unfruitful." His method was "wrong," his direction "barren"—judged, that is, by the modern aim of seeking practical techniques for the control of nature.

Hence while he was an object of execration to the early modern scientists who were concerned exclusively with mathematics and mechanics, Aristotle's greatness as a scientific observer and theorist began to be appreciated as biology felt the impact of Darwin and Wallace; for the central Aristotelian ideas of process and function are fundamental in biology. But during the whole nineteenth century it was still held that as a physicist Aristotle was a first-rate biologist. This view prevailed, despite the fact that Aristotle maintains that any science of nature that fails to explain the most complex natural processes, living and knowing, is wholly inadequate; and that nineteenth-century physics, face to face with the problems of dealing with living and knowing, broke down miserably.

Then, in the twentieth century, the physicists themselves found their billiard balls, the Newtonian mass-particles following the simple laws of motion of molar masses, dissolving into complex functional systems of radiant energy. They discovered that the subject matter of physics itself must be treated in functional and contextual terms, in terms of concepts appropriate to "the field." And what this means is that in his basic concepts the physicist himself must think like the biologist.

Today, the concepts of Aristotle's physics, those notions involved in his analysis of process, have been driving those of Newton out of our theory. That our revolution in physical theory can be so stated is mostly unrealized; but it is often explicitly recognized that the ideas of Aristotle's physics are far closer to present-day physical theory than are the ideas of the nineteenth century. Thirty years ago it was still possible to regard Aristotle's physics as the least valuable part of his thought, and as of mere historical interest.[2] Today, his analysis of the factors and concepts involved in process strikes us as one of the most valuable parts of his whole philosophy, one of his most illuminating and suggestive inquiries. Far from being obviously "wrong," it seems today far truer and sounder than the basic concepts of Newton, And it is fascinating to speculate how, had it been possible in the seventeenth century to reconstruct rather than abandon Aristotle, we might have been saved several centuries of gross confusion and error.

The exclusively mechanical emphasis during early modern science, from the age of Newton through the end of the nineteenth century, is now beginning to seem a kind of transitory interlude in scientific thought. The functional concepts of Aristotle were not necessary for the simple molar mechanics of the seventeenth and eighteenth centuries; they were discarded in

[2] Even in 1952 Mr. D. J. Allan, in his *The Philosophy of Aristotle,* could say: "His principles were well adapted to historical and biological inquiry, but extremely ill suited to other departments of the study of nature," and could call his physics "a sterile system of physical science." *The Philosophy of Aristotle* (Oxford, 1952), pp. 206–7.

But compare Kurt Riezler, *Physics and Reality: Lectures of Aristotle on Modern Physics* (New Haven, 1940), especially ch. 5, "Concreteness."

large part because they were not manageable by the available mathematical techniques. With the advance of mathematical methods themselves, and above all with the carrying of scientific methods into the much more concrete, rich, and less abstract fields, like radiant energy, we have been forced to return to Aristotle's functional and contextual concepts—this time, of course, in exact, analytical and mathematical formulation.

Thus the temporary eclipse of Aristotle's physics is emerging as a kind of adolescent stage in the development of our own physical theory, a mere passing blindness. Today it is Aristotle who often seems strikingly modern, and Newton who appears "of mere historical interest." Newton, despite his epoch-making contributions to "natural philosophy," that is, to the science of dynamics, seems in the notions and concepts of his more general "philosophy of nature" to have been confused, in many of his ideas barren, and even wrong in his aim. It is Aristotle who strikes the present-day student as suggestive, enlightening, and sound.

Hence Aristotle's philosophy of nature, his analysis of the factors involved in process, and of the concepts of physical theory by which they can be rendered intelligible, as contrasted, of course, with his antiquated cosmology and astronomy, deserves the most careful study. And he is to be studied in the light of our own enterprise of revising and reconstructing the confused concepts we have inherited from Newton's "philosophy of nature." Where we are often still groping, Aristotle is frequently clear, suggestive, and fruitful. This holds true of many of his analyses: his doctrine of natural teleology; his view of natural necessity as not simple and mechanical but hypothetical; his conception of the infinite as potential, not actual; his notion of a finite universe; his doctrine of natural place; his conception of time as not absolute, but rather a dimension, a system of measurement; his conception that place is a coordinate system, and hence relative. On countless problems, from the standpoint of our present theory, Aristotle was right, where the nineteenth-century Newtonian physicists were wrong.

Aristotle has various physical writings, dealing with the analysis of natural processes. The *archai* of all natural change and process, *metabolē*, are considered in the first two books of our *Physics*, which the other texts usually refer to as "the books on Nature." The analysis of the factors and concepts involved in "motion," *kinēsis*, which includes not only motion in place, *phora*, but also growth or quantitative change and alteration or qualitative change, is carried on in our *Physics*, Books III to VIII, usually referred to as the "Books on Motion." The analysis of the most fundamental change of all, substantial change, "coming into being and passing away," is undertaken in the *De Generatione et Corruptione*. A description of the order and movements of the heavens occupies the *De Caelo*, Books I and II. The analysis of the elements and of chemical change is found in *De Caelo*, Books III and IV, and in the *Meteorologica*, Book IV.

The *Physics* is really a philosophical introduction to the concepts of natural science. As such, it is directly relevant to the criticisms we have now been making for a generation of the concepts of our inherited Newtonian philosophy of nature. For Aristotle is a thoroughgoing functionalist, operationalist, and contextualist, criticizing the views of those whom in our day we call the reductive mechanists. He is trying to reinstate, reconstruct, and defend the ancient Ionian conception of "Nature," *physis*, and of natural career or process, against the critics who had discredited it, Parmenides and the Eleatics, whose criticism had culminated in the mechanistic views of Empedocles and the atomists. These critics had used Parmenides' test of thinkability to conclude that there is no "nature," no *physis*, no process in the world: there is no genuine coming into being, no genesis. For it is not thinkable that anything should come to be out of what is not. There is only a mixing and unmixing of elements which themselves do not change. There are no "powers" in things coming into "operation," but only a sheer succession of actual states and their rearrangement.

As against this view, Aristotle insists that the world displays real geneses, real comings into being, with a fundamental unity and continuity, a basic temporal pattern or structure. Wherever we cut into these processes, we find them, in the words of Leibniz, the seventeenth-century Aristotelian, "heavy with the past and big with the future." We find that in a significant sense, every process *is* now what it will be. It has genuine temporal parts and relations which are essential to its being that process, and not merely incidental to it. The process cannot be adequately understood apart from this temporal character and pattern.

Now this, as Whitehead has made clear, is precisely our own criticism of the Newtonian philosophy of nature. That philosophy makes time an accident, we say; it does not take time seriously. It regards motion as a succession of instantaneous states, as just one state after another. This view, as Whitehead pointed out, culminates in the structureless world of Hume, in which "anything may be followed by anything."

To such a view, which he found maintained by the Megarians, Aristotle answers, No! Every process involves the operation of determinate powers. There is nothing that can become anything else whatsoever. A thing can become only what it has the specific power to become, only what it already *is,* in a sense, potentially. And a thing can be understood only as that kind of thing that has that kind of a specific power; while the process can be understood only as the operation, the actualization, the functioning of the powers of its subject or bearer. Aristotle generalizes: even local motion, motion in place, *phora,* the "motion" of Galileo and Newton, is the operation of a power, a genuine process: it is a passing from one position to another. Such motion in place is not to be understood in the terms in which the structuralists try to understand it, the Eleatics, the Newtonians, in our day

Bertrand Russell, as a "distance traversed," a succession of successive points occupied at successive instants of time. It is rather "the traversing of a distance." It is not a succession of determinations, but the determining of a succession, a continuous operation or process. This is the view in terms of which Aristotle deals with and solves Zeno's puzzles.

It is in *Metaphysics,* Book Theta, chapter 3, that Aristotle defends his conception of the operation of powers in the only way in which such an ultimate distinction can be defended, by a dialectical development of the consequences of denying it.

There are some, for example, like the Megarians, who say that a thing has a power only when it is functioning, and that when it is not functioning it has no power. For instance, they say that a man who is not building cannot build, but only the man who is building, and at the very moment when he is building; and similarly in the other cases. It is not hard to see the absurd consequences of this theory. Obviously a man will not be a builder if he never builds, because "to be a builder" is "to be capable of building"; and the same will be true of the other arts. Now if it is impossible to have such arts unless at some time the art is learned and acquired, it is also impossible to cease to have them unless at some time they are lost, either by forgetfulness or by some misfortune or by the passage of time; but they never can be lost by the destruction of the thing itself, since this remains always. Hence, when a man ceases to practice his art and is supposed no longer to have it, how can he have acquired the art anew when he subsequently readily knows how to build?

Likewise in the case of inanimate objects that are cold or hot or sweet or in any way sensible: they will not be anything at all when they are not being sensed; so that those who maintain this position will have to affirm the doctrine of Protagoras. Indeed, nothing will have the power of sensing unless it is actually sensing. If, then, one who has normal organs of vision, but is not using them, is blind even though he has eyes and is normal, then one will be blind many times a day, and deaf too.

Also, if what has been deprived of a power can do nothing, then whatever has not yet come into being cannot possibly come into being. Now, of what cannot possibly come into being it can never be truly said that it is or that it will be, for not having the power means just that. Consequently, these doctrines take away all possibility of change or coming into being. Accordingly, whoever is standing must always have been standing, and whoever is seated must remain seated, since if he is seated, he has no power of rising; for it would be impossible for anything to rise which has not the power to rise. Since, then, we cannot say these things, it is clear that power and operation are different. But these doctrines make power and operation the same; hence it is no small thing they are trying to do away with.[3]

2. Nature and By Nature

Aristotle announces his inquiry as "the science *Peri Physeōs*," *Concerning Nature*. It was a familiar title, reminiscent of the Ionians and those who had written before Parmenides. He soon identifies "whatever exists by nature" (*ta physei*) with anything that is in motion (*ta kinoumena*), and he proceeds to examine previous opinions as to the *archai* of movement (*kinēsis*) and of every kind of change, becoming and process.

In other words, movement and process is what he is trying to understand in terms of "nature" (*physis*). Nature indicates and delimits a certain subject matter of inquiry, "natural bodies" (*ta physika*) or the things that exist by nature (*ta physei*). In just the same way, "life" (*psychē*) indicates and delimits a certain subject matter, "animate" or "organic things" (*ta empsycha*), which form a large and distinctive class among *ta physika*. Thus "nature" (*physis*) is, like "life" (*psychē*), an *archē*: it is that in terms of which a specific subject matter or field of inquiry is set off and distinguished, and then analyzed and understood.

In *Metaphysics,* Book Epsilon, Aristotle defines physics as "the science of that kind of being that has the power (*dynaton*)

---

[3] *Metaphysics* Theta, ch. 3: 1046b 29–1047a 21.

of being moved."[4] In *Meteors* physics is defined as "about the first causes of nature," and its subject matter is stated as being "all natural motion."[5] Just as the *De Anima* is really examining the functions and operations of living bodies, the way they behave, so the *Physics* is examining the functions and operations of natural bodies in general, the way they act and behave. And "nature" (*physis*) means for Aristotle the powers and functions of natural bodies, just as "life" (*psyché*) means the powers and functions of living bodies, and is in fact the "nature" of such living bodies.

It is to be noted that if the subject matter of physics is thus defined as "motion," Aristotle means something much broader than the "motion" that has been the subject matter of dynamics since Galileo and Descartes. This latter kind of motion, "motion in place," though fundamental for Aristotle, in the sense that there can be no other form of motion which does not involve it, is only one of six different kinds of "motion." It is because of this broader meaning of the term that it is preferable to translate Aristotle's *kinēsis* as "change" or "process."

It is to be noted also, that the familiar title Aristotle chooses, *Peri Physeōs, Concerning Nature,* is designedly polemic. He is proposing to defend motion and change against the denial of the intelligibility of all change by the Eleatics. And he is proposing to defend "nature" and "natural motion" against the denial of "nature" by Empedocles and Democritus.

"Nature" (*physis*) thus starts for Aristotle as a means of distinguishing among three different ways of acting or kinds of process. It is basically an adverb, *physei,* "by nature," or *kata physin,* "according to nature."

Now, some processes occur "by nature," *physei.* Some take place "by art," *apo technēs.* And some are caused "by violence" or "constraint," *bia:* that is, some other process impinges upon them.

---

[4] *Metaphysics* Epsilon, ch. 1: 1025b 19–29.
[5] *Meteorologica* I, ch. 1: 338a 20.

In the latter two cases, the process is to be understood in terms of an *archē* "external" to the subject of the process. In the processes that occur "by art," something is made by an external artist or maker. In the processes that take place "by violence," the occurrence is to be understood in terms of the external impinging process.

Natural bodies, *ta physei,* which include animals, their parts, plants, and the simple bodies earth, air, fire, and water, display a different way of acting. In their case, there is no discoverable artist or conscious maker. And their behavior does not spring from any external impingement from without. Their motions are to be understood rather in terms of a tendency, a *hormē,* "implanted" in them, a tendency to change in a specific way, a way "according to their nature" (*kata physin*): to grow, to alter, to move up or to move down in place, until they reach their form. This *hormē* is a kind of inertia: it keeps them going, or rather, it keeps them pointed in a certain direction. Products of art do not act that way, nor do the processes that occur "by violence."

This specific way of acting which natural bodies, *ta physei,* display, is called their "nature" or *physis.* It might equally be called, as it came to be in early modern times, the "law" of their operating.[6] "Nature" is for Aristotle not an efficient cause: the "nature" of a thing never itself does anything, any more than a physical "law" of nature ever does anything. The "nature" of a thing is its power of acting in a specific determinate way. This way is called "the nature of" that thing. That is, like every power, it is determinate: it implies a certain structure or pattern of acting, a structure to be investigated in the operating and functioning of that power. Thus a man begets a son, because of his "nature"; and the begetting is to be understood in terms of the "nature" of man. But it is the individual man, and not his "nature," that does the begetting. It is the nature of a stone, as a

<hr/>

[6] See Edgar Zilsel, "The Genesis of the Concept of Physical Law," *The Philosophical Review,* 51 (1942), 245–79.

heavy body, to fall: the stone exhibits a passive power of falling, and the stone could never fall if it did not have that nature. But the nature of the stone does not "make" the stone fall. For it to start falling, it needs some agent: another stone striking it, a boy kicking it off, etc. Then, if there be no obstacle, the stone will fall in a determinate way toward the center of the earth, according to its nature as "heavy," according to its "gravity." Thus "nature," *physis,* does nothing at all. But without such determinate natures, no agent, no motion, could ever do anything whatever.

As a generic term, "nature" in general means for Aristotle the totality of nature, or of natures in the plural: the sum of the determinate powers possessed by things, what everything has the power to do, the concrete order or pattern of the processes that are taking place "by themselves." Nature is thus an intelligible, teleological, or functional order of motions, a system of natural "laws" in terms of which all natural motions or processes are to be understood. As a specific nature, the nature of a stone to fall, the nature of a dog to bark, the nature of a man to seek knowledge, a "nature" is a specific passive power of being moved or acted upon, set in operation or actualized by some external motion or agent, or some unmoved mover, and of then moving in a determinate way.

Now, since the specific way in which anything operates is identical with what that thing is, is the same as its "essence" or "form," the "nature" of anything is the same thing as its "essence." The subject of any process is said to "have" a certain nature, just as it can be said to "have" an "essence" or "form." This is the sense in which "nature" or *physis* is used as a noun, as in speaking of "the nature of" anything. "Nature" as a noun is thus derived from "nature" as an adverb or way of acting. When "nature" is thus used as equivalent to "essence," it always indicates a power or tendency to act in a certain way. Normally in Aristotle, the nature of anything is expressed as a verb. Thus, the "essence" of man, as expressed in a definition of "what it means to be a man," is to be a rational animal: the essence will be expressed in terms of a noun modified by an adjective, expressing the genus and differentia. But the "nature" of man will be, "to desire with intelligence," "to respond intelligently to the object of desire"; the nature will be expressed in terms of a verb modified by an adverb. Aristotle is not always completely consistent in following this usage. But the two different contexts of discourse and of natural process from which the two different terms come usually make themselves felt in some way.

It is to be noted, that a "nature," like an "essence," belongs not to an individual as such, but to individuals as members of a certain kind or species. Any individual, any *tode ti,* possesses an inexhaustible number of powers. Those powers that can be said to be "natural" to it are those powers that can be said to be "essential" to its being the determinate kind of thing it is: it is that kind that possesses a certain "nature." Thus "human nature," as we still use the phrase, is not a private and individual possession, though a man can acquire by practice a set of habits (*hexeis*) which will become a kind of "second nature" for him, as Aristotle calls it, and these may well be distinctive and personal.

Thus, an individual acorn can do an indefinite number of things. It can serve as a missile in a boy's slingshot; or it can become a squirrel's breakfast. But only certain of these powers are "essential" to its being an acorn: those, namely, involved in the power to grow into an oak tree. It is such powers that form the "nature" of the acorn. It may be poisonous, and hence shunned by all right-minded squirrels; but so long as it can grow into an oak tree, it will be an acorn. But if it does not have that power under the right circumstances to become a mature oak, it will not be an acorn, even if squirrels love it.

These powers that form the "nature" of the acorn are the object of any science of acorns, that is, of that kind of thing. There can be no science of all the many things an individual acorn can do, only of those that are "natural" to the acorn, that belong to the nature of that kind, of the powers any acorn possesses "by nature." The rest are contingent, accidental, incidental to being an acorn. They are facts, but of them there can be no science, no prediction, no necessity. But there could be no science at all if different kinds of things did not exhibit different determinate natures, specific modes of behaving that are predictable. Of course, it may well be the nature of squirrels to eat acorns. But it is not the nature of acorns to grow into squirrels' breakfasts. They would never do that "of themselves": they would grow into oak trees. We may put Aristotle's relativism, or his immanent teleology, however we care to label it, by saying: from the acorn's point of view, being eaten by a squirrel is a process "by violence," *bia;* from the squirrel's point of view, eating acorns is a natural process. Both are quite compatible. For as Aristotle puts it, natural bodies, *ta physika,* have the *archē* of their motion in themselves: they are to be understood in their own terms, in terms of their own ways of acting when left to themselves, the way they act of their own nature, when that is not interfered with either by some process by violence or by art.

That there are such processes "by nature," and that "nature" is hence an *archē,* Aristotle accepts from experience.

As for trying to show that there is such a thing as nature, that would be ridiculous; it is clear that there are many such natural beings. To demonstrate what is clear by what is obscure is the act of a man who cannot distinguish what is self-evident from what is not. That such a state is possible is plain: one blind from birth can indeed argue about colors, and such men must needs talk about words, since they have no knowledge.[7]

There are, indeed, several senses in which we can talk about the "nature" of a thing. In one sense, particularly in the case of the products of art, we can say that their nature is the material they are made out of. Thus Antiphon pointed out, that if we planted a wooden bed, and it took roots and sent out shoots, it

[7] *Physics* II, ch. 1: 193a 4–10.

would grow, not into a bed, but into a tree (he was contrasting art and law with nature). Or if we drop a statue, it will fall according to the nature of bronze as heavy, not according to the form of Apollo. In another sense, however, the nature of a thing will be its form. For in natural bodies, the form is the specific power of operating in a determinate way, just what the definition of the form will seize upon; and the body does not possess or exhibit its own proper nature until it is actually functioning that way. In a third sense, *physis,* in its root meaning of "growth," signifies the process itself, the passage to the full functioning (*hodos eis physin*): this is nature as genesis. But nature as the process is itself understood in terms of the goal, the nature that is the operation or form.[8]

3. What Constitutes a Process?

Aristotle sets out to render change and motion, and genesis, the emergence of novelty, intelligible, as against the Eleatics and the atomists, by means of his functional concepts. His formal definition runs: "Motion (*kinēsis*) is a process in which something which has the power to become a definite something else, becomes that something else. . . . It is thus the continuous actualization of what is potential, taken as being potential."[9] Motion is thus the present tense of the verb, not the past participle: it is an incompleted operation (*energeia atelēs*), a process going on, partaking of the character of both a power and an operation.

And fundamental is the fact that all processes are determinate. Contradicting Hume in anticipation, Aristotle insists that there is nothing that has the power to become anything else whatever. "We must first admit that of all beings there is none whose nature permits it to act on another or be acted on by another

---

[8] *Physics* II, ch. 1: *passim.* In *Metaphysics* Delta Aristotle lists the root meaning of *"physis"* as "the genesis of growing things, as though the 'y' were pronounced long," as in *phyesthai,* "to grow." *Metaphysics* Delta, ch. 4: 1014b 16, 17.

[9] *Physics* III, ch. 1: 201a 10–11.

in any chance way whatsover, nor is there any coming into being of any kind of being from any other kind." [10]

Aristotle's whole argument is directed, first, against the Eleatics who denied the intelligibility of any kind of change or motion; and secondly, against Empedocles and the atomists, who denied "nature" (*physis*) and coming into being (*genesis*). The first group, Parmenides and his followers, he cannot take very seriously. They have no *archē,* for an *archē* is relative to a subject matter, and they deny the subject matter of motions. They are "talking for the sake of mere talk" (*dialegesthai tōn logou heneka legomenōn*), and they rely on eristic reasoning (*logon eristikon*). Aristotle's own position he states: "For ourselves, we take for granted that natural things (*ta physei*), either in whole or in part, are in motion (*kinoumena*). This is clear from induction." [11] And he is equally clear that experience reveals things that can be understood only in terms of their "nature": "There are *ta physei."* He answers Empedocles and the atomistic critics of *genesis* and *physis* by admitting that they are right in holding there can be no coming into being from non-being as such. But there can be genesis from "not being such." His answer depends on his introducing his functional distinction between powers and their operation.

Aristotle tries to establish what are the minimum conditions of such a determinate process, what is the smallest number of factors needed for delimiting a process. First, there must be a pair of contraries: any process is a passage from "this state" to "that," from the absence of certain characters to their achievement. But not from the mere absence: that absence must be coupled with the specific power to acquire what is acquired. The contraries are thus two limits marking off the process from other processes, two points of reference on a scale defining and delimiting that

[10] *Physics* I, ch. 5: 188a 32–34. Carteron rightly points out, "This principle of intelligibility dominates the whole Aristotelian theory of change." H. Carteron, *Aristote Physique* (Paris, 1926), p. 39, n. 2.

[11] *Physics* I, ch. 2: 185a 12–14.

particular process. But there is needed also a third factor, "that which passes from one contrary to the other"; that which originally is not in the final state, but achieves it at the end; a bearer of the process, a "subject" or "substrate" which "underlies" the change (*to hypokeimenon*), and "in which" the change takes place. There is the change from one contrary to the other, and there is also that which changes during the process.

Thus in any process there are involved three *archai* or factors: a pair of contraries, and a subject matter. There is 1) the subject, what changes; 2) what it is changed from; and 3) what it is changed to. The first is the material (*hē hylē*) of the process, something which is changed. The third is the form (*eidos*), the specific character the subject acquires. The second Aristotle calls the *sterēsis,* traditionally translated into Latin as the "privation" of being. It means the initial absence of the form which the subject has the specific power to acquire.

Thus, in the process "The uneducated man becomes an educated man," "man" is the subject, the material of the process; "educated" is the form he acquires; "uneducated" is the *sterēsis* or privation, the potential existence of the form "educated," a kind of "not yet." Only a man can be "uneducated," never a table—for the table has no power to acquire an education.

It must be noted that these three *archai* are all relative concepts, depending on the particular process; they are not elements to be fitted together. They are the product of a factorial, not a reductive analysis. Hence they will bear different relations to each other, depending on the standpoint from which we are analyzing the process.

It is significant also that no one of these three factors employed to identify and define the particular process "makes" that process occur: no one of them is an efficient cause. That is due to some cause external to the process itself, an "external" mover, the motion of some agent: in the illustration, it is the activity of the teacher. 1) The agent is not "matter," the power to become educated. Potentiality is never an efficient cause. It is never, we can say, a sufficient condition, though it is always a necessary condition. 2) The efficient cause is not the *sterēsis* or privation: you are not made educated by being "not yet educated"—at least outside progressive schools. 3) The efficient cause is not even the form: you are not made educated by the college graduate you are to be. Yet there is a sense in which "form" can be said to be the agent: you are made educated, not by your ability to learn, but by the educated character of your teacher. He already "actually" possesses the trait you will acquire. The child is generated as a "man" because of the actualized form of "man," not in the child himself, but in the father. This is the sense in which Aristotle holds that actualized form is always the efficient cause or agent, when realized in the agent as his "form" or "nature." Hence Aristotle can say, "the final cause is the same as the efficient cause." For you are begotten as a man by a man, and are made an educated man by an educated man. His formula runs: the outcome or final cause is "the same in form" as the agent, but not "in number." That is, the efficient cause and the final cause will have the same form, but will never be the same individual. It is important to note these distinctions carefully, for this is the only sense in which Aristotle ever admits that a final cause can be an efficient cause.

4. The Four "Causes" and Contingency

Since we are studying knowing, Aristotle remarks, and we do not judge that we know anything before we have grasped for each thing its reason why (*to dia ti*), and that means to grasp its first cause (*prōtē aitia*), we must clearly consider the reasons why and the causes of generation and corruption and of all physical change. Now "reason why," "through what," or "cause" are used in four senses. He lists the From What, the Form, the Whence of the Beginning of Change, and the End or For What.

These four reasons why are involved in any process, and are essential to it; the natural philosopher or *physikos* must know them all. Aristotle tries to explore their relations to each other. One can be the cause of another: walking is the efficient cause of health, and health is the final cause of walking. One cause can be the cause of contraries: the pilot by his presence can ensure the safety of the ship, and by his absence, its doom.

Moreover, the Form and the For What are often the same factor or thing, and the mover or efficient cause is the same in kind as the form, though never in number, never the same individual: it is man that begets man, Aristotle never tires of emphasizing. On the other hand, two of the causes, the form and the end, are not strictly "physical," they are not strictly parts of the process, for they are themselves not processes, like the mover and the material.

Aristotle has distinguished four different kinds of cause or reason why, four forms of *to dia ti*. Is there a fifth kind of cause? Is chance a "reason why"? For we say, so and so happened "by chance," "by accident," *dia to automaton*. Chance thus seems, verbally at least, to be an additional reason why, or *dia ti*. In what sense is this the case? For in so speaking men certainly mean something, they are making a genuine distinction.

There are some who deny chance entirely, and say that everything we say occurs "by chance" is really due to a determinate cause. Thus we go to the agora to buy some oil, and "by chance" meet a man who repays the loan we had made him. There were determinate causes for both of us going to the agora. Yet even if everything said to occur "by chance" really takes place by some determinate cause, it remains a distinction we all make: we should say by good fortune (*tyche*) we met the borrower. The distinction between what occurs by chance and what does not is not a distinction between what has a cause and what has no cause; it is rather a distinction between two kinds of events, all of which have determinate causes.

To occur "by chance" means, not that there is no reason for the accident, but that factors, themselves determined by their own specific causes, do impinge on other processes, and alter and perhaps even destroy them, without being an essential part of those other processes, without belonging to their distinctive nature. For example, some events occur "for some end" (*hou heneka*). Now when such events are effected incidentally, that is called, in human affairs, "luck" or "fortune" (*tychē*); and more generally, it is called "chance" (*to automaton*). The man who went to the agora to buy oil met the borrower "by chance," that is, the encounter was incidental to buying the oil. Events that occur "by chance" are thus unpredictable, but not inexplicable.

When something that would be the object of forethought, like getting the loan repaid, happens without such forethought, the event is called "luck" or "fortune" (*tychē*). More generally, when any natural end is accomplished incidentally or accidentally, or "by accident" fails to be achieved, this is called "chance" (*to automaton*). For instance, a rock falls on the acorn and distorts its growth, or a squirrel eats it, and it never sprouts. These events have no relevance to the process of growing into an oak tree, they are "chance" events, an instance of a process "by violence" (*bia*) from the outside.

Chance is the name given to all events caused by factors that are not relevant to the ends of natural processes, by all the non-teleological factors, the brute events interfering with the natural working out of a process, or achieving a quite different end incidentally, causing the acorn to become a squirrel's breakfast, impinging in the process "by violence" from without. Chance is any event having no end, no For What, "itself in vain," *auto matēn,* says Aristotle with a dubious etymology.

Chance hence presupposes an order of natural teleology, and is posterior to that order. It is said to be "against nature," or "contrary to nature," like the birth of distorted monsters. Chance thus represents a limit set to science: it stands for all those events for which no scientific prediction is possible. It is what the scientist disregards when he says, "Other things being equal, such and such will take place." Chance is what in individual cases is never equal—the particular, the contingent, the variable, the unpredictable about specific events—what is logically incidental (*to symbebēkos*), what science dealing with general rules and universals can never foresee about individual cases.

Aristotle is keenly aware that science deals with regularities, "always or for the most part," in a much more complex world, which also reveals precariousness, contingency as well as stability, order, and regularity. That is why outside mathematics he says things happen in certain ways, "always or for the most part," except in the heavens, where there is no observable chance or contingency. This is Aristotle's way of recognizing the facts the modern scientist expresses by saying that his laws are statistical averages. We often think this is a recent modern discovery, because it was forgotten in the seventeenth century.

5. Natural Necessity

Is the necessity that obtains in natural things and natural processes simple, inexorable, and mechanical, as it seems to be in the heavens, in astronomy? Or is it "hypothetical," "from hypothesis" (*ex hypotheseōs*)? Do the stones have to become a wall? Does the iron have to become a saw? Does the acorn have to grow into an oak tree? These would all be cases of "simple" necessity (*haplōs*).

Aristotle's answer is of course, no. Rather, *if* there is to be a wall, *then* the stones have to be put on each other in a certain way. *If* there is to be a saw, then teeth of hard iron, or some similar material, are necessary. *If* there is to be an oak tree, *then* there must be a proper acorn, and the conditions necessary for its growth. This is what Aristotle calls "hypothetical" necessity. Such natural necessity is teleological. If they are to be attained, the ends of processes impose their necessary conditions. Such natural necessity is always relative: certain conditions are "necessary for" the achievement of the end. If there is to be an oak tree, then there must be the right seed, the right amount of moisture, the right amount of sunlight, and the rest. If those necessary conditions are not present, then there will develop no oak tree. But there is no necessity whatever that there should be an oak tree. The attainment of ends is not necessary by any kind of simple necessity.

Necessity is "almost the same," Aristotle remarks, in mathematics and in physical science—for both are instances of hypothetical necessity. Only the order is different. In mathematics, if the axioms are true, then the conclusions are necessary; if the conclusions are not necessary, then the axioms are not true. In physics, if the end is to be attained, then the conditions are necessary; if the conditions are not present, then the end will not be attained.

In a sense, says Aristotle, the necessity is in the materials or means, for it is they that are "necessary for" the end. But in another sense, the necessity is to be located "in the *logos*," for it is the function of sawing that dictates the kind of saw that is necessary, and that function is expressed in the definition.

Aristotle thus offers an alternative to the kind of natural necessity against which Hume's famous critique is directed. Hume is talking about "necessary connection" between cause and effect: he is thinking in typical empiricist fashion of the causal relation as one of temporal antecedence and consequences, and obviously can observe no "necessary connection" there. Aristotle does not view the causal relation temporally: for him it is not a matter of "necessary connection," but of "necessary conditions." And such necessary conditions can only be discovered experimentally, by manipulation, not by mere observation of sequences. Aristotle is much closer to the present-day notion of a manipulative and experimental science, and of a corresponding and appropriate conception of causation and of natural necessity, than is Hume.

There is also for Aristotle a certain brute "necessity" in matter, in the materials needed in any process. This may result in the birth of monsters that are "contrary to nature"—that is, contrary to the nature or teleological pattern of that kind of thing. Again, he points out, in order to see, eyes are necessary. But their color is due to "chance," that is, to the "necessity of their matter." Their color bears no relation to the seeing, it is not capable of being made the object of a science, it is not predictable, and with respect to our knowledge is contingent. To be sure, there *is* a reason for the color; and interestingly enough, our own science of genetics has extended predictability to this field also, though so far as individuals go, the color of their eyes is still due to what Aristotle calls "chance." This is a further illustration of the fact that science cannot exhaust individuality, that there can be no science of particulars.

6. Natural Teleology

Since he is arguing primarily against the mechanistic views of Empedocles and the atomists, Aristotle thinks it well to offer a special defense with appropriate arguments for his basic *archē* of process, the "end" or "For What." Why is it not enough to say, he asks, that nature acts always by necessity, and that the ends that are achieved by natural processes are purely "incidental," just as Zeus makes it rain not to increase the crops, but by exhalation, when the clouds can no longer contain their moisture? The rain falls "by necessity," and the irrigation of plant life is purely incidental. Evidently for Aristotle there was no teleology about the weather! Why can we not say that most things in nature take place that way? Why can we not say that the teeth meet in a way suitable for biting and chewing incidentally? Empedocles in fact generalized from cases like the rain, and applied necessity to living things also, with a rather crude doctrine of the survival of the fittest. "It is the beings in which everything was produced as though for an end that have been preserved, having been suitably formed by chance; the others have perished and perish, as Empedocles says of his cattle with human faces." [12]

But, says Aristotle, such an exclusively mechanistic view is impossible. Empedocles overlooked certain important facts and differences. Aristotle is arguing for a teleological order in certain types of natural process, against the unsatisfactory reliance of Empedocles and the atomists on "chance," "violence" or *bia*. And in anticipation he is arguing against the seventeenth-century anti-teleologists like Descartes and Spinoza.

In the first place, in many natural processes, in living processes in particular, the achievement of ends occurs "always or for the most part." There is no such regularity discoverable in the processes that take place by chance, in the casual intersections of unrelated causal series. The achievement of ends cannot be a mere coincidence.

Wherever ends are achieved with regularity, we discover a fixed order of means, that has to be followed one after the other, a functional or teleological order, and the following of this order of means is a necessary condition of the achievement of the end. For any living thing, there must be first a seed, of a specific character, then a specific process and order of development and growth. Thus Empedocles was quite wrong in thinking that in vertebrates, the vertebrae of the spine get broken "by accident." This temporal order or structure of means and ends is in each case a fact to be discovered; and it must be followed.

If a house were a thing generated by nature—if it grew—it would be produced in the same way in which art now produces it. If natural things were not produced by nature alone, but by art also, they would be produced by art in the same way that they are produced by nature. Each stage leads to the next. [13]

[12] *Physics* II, ch. 8: 198b 29–32. Aristotle himself gives considerable prominence to survival value, and explains the distance receptors and indeed all the senses in such terms, though of course without placing his argument in an evolutionary context. Compare *De Anima* III, chs. 12, 13.

[13] *Physics* II, ch. 8: 199a 12–15.

The house would have to grow its foundations first, then its walls, and finally its roof.

In general, art "imitates" nature, even when it goes beyond the ends that nature unaided can attain—when it builds a ship or writes a poem. Hence if art is for an end, so is the nature it imitates.

There is the case of animal instinct: bees, ants, and spiders achieve ends without any conscious deliberation.

Natural processes are in fact understood and distinguished by the different ends they attain, and without reference to those ends would be incapable of being distinguished or described.

Hence the teleology found in processes that take place by art is not radically different from the teleological order found in processes that take place by nature. There is no gulf between natural processes and processes of human production, but rather a continuity. Art is actually a cardinal illustration of natural processes, one in which the different factors involved, the understanding of which is necessary to the understanding of the process, are spread out clearly for us to distinguish, and not telescoped as they often are in natural processes. Nor is deliberation, conscious intent, conscious purpose, at all necessary for the achievement of ends. Art, says Aristotle, does not deliberate. And if the art of shipbuilding were in the wood—instead of being in the shipbuilder, who is external to the wood and the ship—then it would act just like "nature." Hence the best example of "nature" is a man who cures himself, that is, whose organism heals him by doing quite unconsciously and without deliberation the same necessary things the physician would prescribe by art.

Aristotle's thoroughgoing functionalism comes out most clearly of all in several of his biological writings, and we shall return to it in that connection.

Chapter IX

THE ANALYSIS OF MOTION

Since nature is the *archē* of motion and change, in the "Books on Motion," the *Physics,* Books III to VIII, Aristotle is led to ask, after stating his formal definition of motion, What factors are involved in motion, and what concepts are needed to understand it adequately?

It seems that motion belongs to the things that are continuous, and in the continuous the infinite appears in the first place; that is why the definitions given of the continuous often employ the notion of the infinite, the continuous being infinitely divisible. In addition, without place, the void, and time motion is impossible.[1]

Aristotle distinguishes four different kinds of motion (*kinēsis*) or change (*metabolē*); since two of them can move in either of two directions, he recognizes six kinds in all. They are change of:

1) The What (*to ti*)	Coming into being and passing away	(*genesis*) (*phthora*)	Substantial change
2) The How Much (*to poson*)	Increase and decrease	(*auxēsis*) (*phthisis*)	Quantitative change
3) The What Kind (*to poion*)	Alteration	(*alloiōsis*)	Qualitative change
4) The Where (*to pou*)	Motion in place	(*phora*)	Local change

The last three involve no change of substance (*ousia*) itself; in them the same *ousia* persists throughout the process, merely changing its size, its qualities, or its position. Aristotle treats these three less fundamental kinds of change in *Physics,* Books III to VIII. He then tries to generalize his analysis to deal with the most fundamental kind of change or process, in which a new

[1] *Physics* III, ch. 1: 200b 16–21.

substance or *ousia* is created, or an old one destroyed. This he deals with in a separate work, known as the *De Generatione et Corruptione*. His analysis starts from qualitative change, alteration, of which the example in Book I, "The uneducated man becomes an educated man," is an instance. He tries to deal with motion in place, "motion" in the narrow modern sense, as a limiting case of alteration. It is significant that he takes over the ordinary term for such local motion, *phora:* it is the brute encountered fact. For the others he employs technical terms taken mainly from Plato.

Two preliminary points deserve comment. They both hinge on peculiarities of Aristotle's terminology, and of the structure of the Greek language he is employing. The first point is that in Greek one does not say, a thing "moves," rather, one says, the thing "is moved." This holds likewise of the Latin and the German languages, which also do not say, a thing "moves." But in them it is usual to employ the reflexive: *se movet, il se meut, es bewegt sich*. This makes it possible to develop and express the notion of "inertia" formulated in Newton's First Law of dynamics. The Greek is restricted to the passive voice, "is moved," which seems to call at once for a By Which, an efficient cause or mover, in all cases of motion. It is this fact of language that gets Aristotle into trouble when he is dealing with "violent" motion, and considering the motion of projectiles. What is it that moves them? Historically it was puzzles about this question that led in the fourteenth and again in the sixteenth century toward the formulation of the Galilean principles of dynamics. Aristotle's own tentative suggestion was clearly unacceptable.

The second point is Aristotle's usage as to the locus of motion and the action of the mover. As already emphasized on page 82, it is fundamental for Aristotle that the motion is in the thing moved, the action has its locus in the thing acted upon. The motion is the actualization of the thing moved (*to kinēton*) under the influence of the mover (*hypo tou kinētikou*). But the actualization of the mover's power to move is the same actualization: there are not two operations, but only a single operation, with its locus in the thing moved.

But this seems to raise a logical difficulty. Are not the operations of the thing acting and the thing being acted upon different operations? Is not there a difference between acting (*poiēsis*) and being acted upon (*pathēsis*)? Certainly there seems to be a difference of *logos,* of terms. But, says Aristotle, in what do they both take place? "Teaching" and "being taught" are one and the same process, with its locus in the person being taught. The operation has its locus in what is being operated on. "Action" and "passion" will be defined differently, but in any concrete case they will be the same process. The active power of the mover to move, and the passive power of the moved object to be moved, are two different powers. But there is only one motion, one operation, one actualization of the two powers.

If we admit that to act and to be acted upon are the same thing, it is not because the two have an identical definition, which formulates what makes them what they are (*to ti ēn einai*), like dress and clothes, but like the way in which the road from Thebes to Athens is the same road as the road from Athens to Thebes.[2]

Aristotle is here making a fundamental point about the difference between a motion or process, and *logos* and discourse. A process has an identity that remains compatible with stating the process in various ways. Like the road from Thebes to Athens, we can look at it from either end; and our position and perspective will determine how we shall get it stated in words. But it remains the same road, no matter how we are looking at it and stating it.

There is also a second fundamental point involved in this discussion. Every operation is really a cooperation of two different powers, a joint operation of the power of acting and the power of being acted upon. It is the peculiarity of Aristotle's

[2] *Physics* III, ch. 3: 202b 12–15.

usage that he assigns the locus of this cooperation to the thing being acted upon. A modern would probably deal more pragmatically with the question of locus, and assign it in terms of where the process could most effectively be controlled.

1. The Infinite

The infinite (*to apeiron*) has the form of an adjective. Magnitudes, motion, and time can all be either "limited" or "unlimited," finite or infinite. But under Aristotle's analysis, the infinite turns out to be an adverb, "infinitely." Continuities can be said to be infinitely divisible, or infinitely extensible.

The ancients, Aristotle points out, all took the infinite as an *archē*. The non-physical philosophers all made it a noun, an *ousia;* the *physikoi* made it an attribute of the continuous. Belief in the infinite comes from the unlimited character of time, the infinite divisibility of magnitudes, the unlimited character of the source of generation, the inconceivability of any limit, and, the strongest reason of all, because thinking cannot exhaust number, magnitude, nor what is outside the heavens. But the inexhaustibility of matter in generation does not demand an actually existent infinite amount of matter, as it is possible for the generation of a new *ousia* to mean the destruction of another, the whole remaining finite. And what thinking can and cannot conceive is a mere accident, with no bearing on what exists.

Aristotle concludes, there can be no actual infinite: nothing that is actually infinite can exist, and nothing that exists can be actually infinite. There can be no infinite apart from sensible things; the infinite is not an *ousia*, for it is a mode of number or magnitude, and they are not *ousiai*. Nor can there exist an infinite body. Speaking as a *logikos*, Aristotle points out that body is defined as "that which is *limited* by a surface." Speaking as a *physikos*, he adds, an infinite body could be neither composite nor simple. If the elements of a composite body were finite, they would never add up to an infinite body; if they were infinite, each would be a simple infinite. If the infinite body were simple, it would display no quantity and thus be wholly indeterminate. Again, every body is some "where," and has a determinate motion, up or down. Bodies and places must be treated alike: you cannot assume an infinite body and retain a determinate scheme of places and natural motions, such as experience reveals. An infinite universe would have no center, and no determinate motions toward or away from a center: there would be no physical system and no fields of force, such as our universe displays. There could be no determinate system of positions, not merely in relation to us and our position, but in the whole itself. It is impossible for position to be infinite, since position is defined by its limits. And since every body is in some position, no body can be infinite. In the light of these dialectical arguments, it is clear why when Cusanus and later Bruno took seriously the notion that the universe is actually infinite, it meant the immediate destruction of the whole Aristotelian physical system and cosmology.

But while nothing can exist as actually infinite, it is impossible to deny the infinite entirely. The infinite, says Aristotle, is rather a power, not in the sense that it ever will be actually, but a potential operation of certain processes. Thus the number series is potentially infinite by addition: the series is infinitely addible, you can always add more numbers. And anything continuous, like a magnitude, is infinitely divisible: you can always subdivide further. Time is potentially infinite both by addition and division. But the existent cosmos is not infinite, it is finite. Beyond its limits there is literally nothing. It is interesting that our own astronomical theory has been playing with the same idea.

Hence Aristotle defines the infinite as:

Not that beyond which there is nothing, but that beyond which there is always something more. . . . The infinite is hence that beyond which one can always go on taking something more, with respect to quantity. What has nothing outside itself is complete (*to teleion*) and whole (*holon*), for we define a whole as that from which nothing is left out, like a man or a chest.[3]

This definition also throws light on what Aristotle means by *teleios,* conventionally translated "perfect," as when he says the circle is the "perfect" figure, and circular motion the "perfect" motion. In contrast, the infinite as infinite is unknowable: it is matter, not form. It is not graspable by *nous.* And hence for Aristotle, as for the Greek mind in general, the infinite is at the opposite pole from the complete, the knowable, the graspable, the divine.

2. Place and the System of Natural Places

As we shall see, Aristotle specifically denies that there is any such thing as "space," the "space" (*chōra*) of Plato's *Timaeus,* or the "void" (*to kenon*) of Democritus and the atomists. As against this notion of a space in itself or existing by itself, on which both the Platonic and the atomistic traditions were in agreement, and which was consecrated for modern thought by the "absolute space" of Newton's scholium, Aristotle develops and defends the relativistic conception of "place" or "position" (*topos*) —in Latin, *locus*—the position of a body in a system of bodies, which is essential as a point of reference in describing the motion of a body from one position to another.

Aristotle asks first, Is there such a thing as place? If so, how does it exist? These are important questions, for everything that is, is somewhere (*pou*). And the most universal and most controlling form of motion is motion in place, *phora.* That place exists is clear from the phenomenon of replacement: place (*topos*) or extension (*chōra*) clearly differs from the bodies in it, for you can take them out of that place, and the place itself stays

[3] *Physics* III, ch. 6: 206b 35–207a 10.

put. Still more important, the motions of the simple natural bodies "up" or "down" not only indicate that there is such a thing as place, but also that place has "a certain power" (*echei tina dynamin*). Such bodies move to their own "proper places," the heavy toward the center of the cosmos, the light away from it. These proper places are parts and kinds of a system of places, which is fixed in relation to our system of bodies; not merely in relation to us, but in itself apart from us (*chōris*). This system of natural places is defined operationally: it is the system of the different "whithers" of the different natural motions. " 'Up' is not any direction whatever, but whither fire and the light are moved; 'down' likewise is not any direction whatever, but whither heavy and earthy bodies are moved, since the two differ not only in their position but also in their power." This system of natural positions differs from the equally objective determinations of mathematical place: "It is also clear of mathematical objects: they are not in place, but in accordance with their position in relation to us, they have a right and a left, though their position is only thought by us, and they do not have any of these determinations by nature." [4]

Hesiod (and Plato) went further: for he said that Chaos was the first of all beings, and then came earth:

as if there must have first existed a place for beings; because he thought like everybody that everything is somewhere, that is, in a place. But if that is so, then the power of place is marvelous and first of all: for that without which nothing else can exist and which exists without anything else, is necessarily first: for place is not destroyed when what is in it is destroyed.[5]

Aristotle is clearly referring to the "receptacle" (*hypodochē*) of the *Timaeus:* this is the Platonic notion of "space."

Now, place cannot be body, for then there would be two bodies in the same place. Nor can it be either form or matter. The

[4] *Physics* IV, ch. 1: 208b 19–25.   [5] *Physics* IV, ch. 1: 208b 31–209a 1.

"proper place" of each body is its first container (*to prōton periechon*), that is, it is a limit (*peras ti*). Does that mean that it is the body's form? But if the place be taken rather as the interval of the magnitude (*to diastēma tou megethous*), then place would be rather matter: not the container, but what is contained, that is, something material and hence indeterminate. The *Timaeus* thus held that matter and space are the same thing, the Receptacle. Plato, Aristotle remarks, in reluctant admiration, is the only thinker who has tried to tell what place is.

But place can be neither form nor matter, for neither is separable from a body in the way that place clearly is. Place is indeed something like a pail, and a pail is a kind of movable place. You can put things into a pail and take them out again; the pail stays put. Again, being "in" a place implies that something else is outside it. Further, if place were either matter or form, it would not be the "whither" of natural motions. And if place were "in" things, then place would be "in" place itself. And in this sense of "in," things cannot be said to be "in" themselves.

There are four possibilities: place can be either form, or matter, or the interval, or the extremities. Place seems to be a form, for it is a "limit" (*peras*). But it is not the limit of the thing itself, it is the limit of the surrounding bodies (*to periechon*). It is not the interval, for that is nothing. It is not matter, for that is not separable from a body, as place is. Therefore place must be the limit of the surrounding body (*to peras tou periechontos sōmatos*). Place, says Aristotle, continuing his analogy, is an immovable pail.

Hence when a thing that is inside another thing that is being moved, is moved and changes its place, like a ship on a river, it is in relation to the surrounding body more as if in a pail than in a place. Place means something unmoved; hence it is rather the river as a whole that is the place, for as a whole it is unmoved.[6]

[6] *Physics* IV, ch. 4: 212a 16–20.

Thus Aristotle's formal definition of place (*topos*) runs: "Hence the immediate unmoved limit of the surrounding body is place." [7] Place is "unmoved," because you can take a body out of its place, and the place does not move.

Place is hence relative to a whole system of bodies.

If a body has outside itself a body which contains it, it is in place; if it has not, it has no place. . . . Hence the whole universe is nowhere. For a thing which is somewhere is first of all a thing in itself, and it then presupposes something else next to it which contains it. But next to the universe, there is nothing outside the whole, rather, everything that is, is in the heavens; for it is clear that the heavens are the whole. Now, place is not the heavens, it is the extremity of the heavens which is in contact with the moving body as an unmoved limit. Hence earth is in water, water is in air, air is in ether, ether is in the heavens, but the heavens are not in anything else.[8]

Every body in the universe is always in some place, in some determinate position. But the universe as a whole cannot be said to be in any place: it is literally nowhere. For it is not related to anything else, and hence has no position or *topos*.

Aristotle's analysis of "place" is obviously limited by his own cosmology, and his doctrine of the natural places to which heavy and light bodies tend to move by nature. But it is a relativistic view, like our own: "place" or "space" is a system of reference, not an independent existence. There is no empty "space" which existed before bodies came into existence, and which continues to exist as the absolute container of all bodies. There is nothing like Newton's "absolute space," which he could identify, following Henry More, with the mind of God. Aristotle examines and rejects the notion of such a "space"—the "chaos" of Hesiod, the *chōra* of the *Timaeus*—in favor of the alternative notion of "place"—a relation between bodies in a common system.

[7] *Physics* IV, ch. 4: 212a 21–22. [8] *Physics* IV, ch. 5: 212b 14–22.

3. The Void

About the void (*to kenon*) the natural philosopher must also inquire whether there is such a thing, and how and what it is. Its partisans, the atomists, make it a kind of place or pail; those who deny that there is such a thing criticize the popular view that it is an interval in which there is no sensible body, and show that air is really a body by pointing to the clepsydra and to the air confined in wineskins. But this fails to meet the real point, which is not whether there is an interval in which there is no body, but one in which there is no continuity.

What needs to be demonstrated is not that air is something, but that there is no interval different from bodies, either separable or realized actually, extending through the whole of bodily nature so that it is not continuous, as say Democritus and Leucippus and many other natural philosophers, or outside the continuous bodily whole.[9]

The arguments for the existence of such a void are, first, that without such a void no motion could take place; secondly, the fact of contraction seems to prove the existence of an internal void: casks can receive their full complement of wine and the wineskins as well; the fact of growth proves that nutriment can be added to the same body, which must have an internal void to be filled; and fourthly, the Pythagoreans take the void as limiting things, including numbers.

Those who maintain a void take it as a place where there is nothing, that is, no tangible body, no light or heavy. This makes the void equivalent to the indeterminate Platonic matter of bodies, which they identify wrongly with place, in which there is nothing individual and no kind of particular bodily substance. But it is at least clear that the fact of motion does not necessitate a void, for a plenum (*to plēres*) can be altered. Motion in a plenum is possible, since one body can take the place of another.

[9] *Physics* IV, ch. 6: 213a 31–213b 2.

Thus a wheel can revolve, and vortices occur in liquids. Hence in his theory of *tourbillons* Descartes was actually following Aristotle.

It is clear, says Aristotle, that there can be no separated void (*kenon kechōrismenon*), no place or "space" in which there is absolutely nothing at all, without structure or determination. How, for instance, could light be transmitted if there were no medium, no diaphanous or transparent? When a void was made a part of the physical theory in the seventeenth century, it had to be filled immediately with a medium, the "aether." And our own theory holds that there is continuous structure everywhere, with no breaks or empty holes in it: "the field," of radiation, we used to say. There is no interval between bodies where there is absolutely nothing, no "void" in the sense Aristotle is criticizing.

Such a void could not be the cause of the determinate natural motions. Why should bodies move determinately in it one way rather than another? No motion would in fact be possible in a complete void. For natural motion demands a determinate character. In modern terms, how could there be gravitation without a "field" of gravity? Why should motion ever stop in such a void? And violent motion demands a vehicle, a mover; projectiles need some medium to push them. Aristotle here commits himself to no detailed theory, suggesting either that the air keeps the bodies that are thrown in motion, or a theory of what was called *antiperistasis*. He cannot escape the notion that a moving body "is moved" by something.

Aristotle advances very interesting, and historically significant, dialectical arguments against a void, that rest on his principles of dynamics. We see that differences in velocity depend on two factors, the density of the medium traversed, and the excess of heaviness or lightness in the body. The velocity will be proportional to the density of the medium, and the consequent resistance it will offer. But in a void there can be no proportion:

motion in a void would hence be instantaneous, and we see that it is never so. Moreover, the velocity will be proportional to the magnitude of the force (*ropē*) with which a projectile is hurled. In a plenum, a greater force can divide the medium more quickly. But in a void there would be no reason for this; in a void all velocities would be equal. But we see that this is never the case.

Here Aristotle is appealing to experience, and correctly reporting its deliverances. He develops hypothetically or "dialectically" what would happen under "ideal conditions," and uses experience to show that those "ideal conditions" do not obtain. This development of what would happen under such ideal conditions is precisely the method followed by Galileo, where it has become the fashion to call it his "Platonism."

Finally, the rare and the dense are advanced as arguments for an internal void. But this would mean either the presence of many small separated voids, subject to all the objections already made, or else a diffused void, which presents many difficulties of its own, and to which Aristotle opposes his own theory of a single matter for all bodies.

4. Time as a Dimension of Motion

Does time belong to the things that are or to those that are not? And what is its nature? It might seem that time does not really exist at all. For it has been, but it no longer is. And it is going to be, but it is not yet. Its parts either have been, or are not yet; how can the whole of time be, if its parts do not exist? Moreover, what is the instant, the now (*to nun*)?

The instant is not a part, for the part is a measure of the whole and the whole must be composed of parts. But time, it seems, is not composed of instants. Again, is the instant which seems to mark the past off from the future always one and the same, or is it always a different one? This is not easy to see.[10]

[10] *Physics* IV, ch. 10: 218a 7–10.

The ancients identified time with the motion of the whole, or even with the sphere itself. But if time be the motion of the whole, if there be many heavens, there will be many times simultanously (*hama*). The simple identification of time with the sphere comes from the fact that everything is both in time and in the sphere. Time seems above all to be a kind of motion and change. But the change and motion of anything are uniquely in that thing, while time is everywhere and in all things equally. Again, motions are faster and slower, but not time: time defines velocity.

But if time cannot be motion itself, it is never found without change: when we are aware of no change in our thinking (*dianoia*) it seems that no time has elapsed. Hence it is clear that "time is neither itself motion, nor without motion." [11]

What aspect then of motion is time? We say that time has elapsed when we have a sense of earlier and later in motion. Hence the definition of time will be: "Time is the number of motion with respect to earlier and later" (*arithmos kineseōs kata to proteron kai hysteron*).[12] That is, time is that aspect of motion which permits the enumeration of successive states. It is not the number which is itself a means of numbering, but the number which is itself numbered and enumerated. Aristotle also calls time the "measure" of motion, the measurable aspect of motion, literally, a certain "dimension" of motion, its temporal dimension. That is, time is an aspect of motion itself, it is not something else measured by motion, like Newton's "river flowing ever equably."

As for the instant (*to nun*) or the now, in one sense it is always the same, in another, always different. It is related to time as the moved is related to motion: motion is known by means of the moved, and time is known by means of the instant, since time is the number of instants that is counted. As a limit, the instant is an accident of time. "The instant, as has been said, is the continuity of time, for it unites past to future time. In general, it

[11] *Physics* IV, ch. 11: 219a 1.   [12] *Physics* IV, ch. 11: 219b 1–2.

is the limit of time. For it is the beginning of one part, and the end of another." [13]

As a continuous magnitude, time is uniform: time is never slower or faster, rather, there is more or less of it. And it is the same everywhere simultaneously (*hama*). Time and motion are measured reciprocally. "We measure not only motion by time, but also time by motion, because they are determined reciprocally. For time determines the motion of which it is the number, and motion, time." [14] Aristotle analyzes what "being in time" means: it means a thing's being measured in its existence by time. Thus though not itself a motion, rest is said to be "in time": time is thus the measure of rest incidentally. Eternal things are not said to be "in time," since they are not acted upon by anything temporal. Nor is non-being "in time." Things are said to be acted upon by time, or to be destroyed by time, because they are acted upon and destroyed by the motion of which time is the measure. Thus time is not the efficient cause, but rather the incidental cause of the destruction and corruption of things.

It is not until the very end of his discussion that Aristotle raises the question of the relation of time to the rational "soul."

One may doubt whether if there were no rational "soul" there would be time or not. For if there cannot be anything that numbers, there cannot be anything that is numbered, and hence any number. But if by nature nothing can enumerate except the "soul," and in the soul, *nous,* it would be impossible for there to be time if the soul did not exist, unless it were the subject of which time is an aspect, as though we should say that motion can exist without the soul. Earlier and later are in motion, and as enumerable constitute time.[15]

Yes, there would be time without a system of measurement. There would not be time actually measured, but the aspect, the power of being measured, the temporal dimension of motion, would still be there in the motion.

[13] *Physics* IV, ch. 13: 222a 10–12.
[14] *Physics* IV, ch. 12: 220b 15–18.   [15] *Physics* IV, ch. 14: 223a 11–28.

Finally, of what motion is time the measure? Are there different times, and can two equal times exist simultaneously (*hama*)? Since Aristotle is not confronted by our present-day problems of measurement, and has no use for the employment of different schemes of measurement at the same time, his answer is, no. Motions are different and separate, but time is everywhere the same. It is the measure of the eternal circular motion of the sphere, which provides the common frame of reference for all temporal measurement, since its number is best known.

In contrast to the notions of an absolute time and an absolute space that have come down in both the Platonic and the atomistic traditions, Aristotle presents what we should call a relativistic notion of both time and space. They are systems of measurement, ways of determining certain dimensions of motion. Time is a temporal dimension of motion, place is relative position within a system of bodies. Both provide an easily measurable system of reference. Aristotle's conceptions avoid all the Platonic and Newtonian difficulties, to say nothing of the subjectivism of the Kantian version of Newton.

5. *The Unity, Continuity, and Divisibility of Motion*

After analyzing these various concepts that are involved in the understanding of change, Aristotle returns in Books V and VI of the *Physics* to the analysis of motion itself. He now defines motion more narrowly, excluding the most fundamental change, the generation or destruction of a substance or *ousia,* and confines himself to those motions in which there is a subject which persists and has at the end of the motion passed from one contrary to the other. This leaves him with three kinds of "motion" or *kinēsis* in the strict sense, change of quality, of quantity, and of position.

How can we determine when a motion is "one," and what are the limits of any particular motion? This has always been a problem for any attempt to analyze process. What constitutes a single process? This has perplexed Whitehead both in his early analysis into "events" and his later analysis into "actual occasions." And it is equally a problem for the analysis into "situations." How can we delimit an "event," an "actual occasion," or a "situation"?

A motion can be said to be "one," Aristotle points out, in many ways: it can be one generically, or specifically, or substantially, or numerically. But we say that a motion is one in the simple sense (*haplōs*) if it is one in substance (*ousia*) and in number (*tō arithmō*); that is, it must be the change of a single thing that remains identical in kind through a continuous interval of time. We know that we are dealing with a single motion or process when it has been completed (*teleios*); for anything that can be said to be a unity is always completed and whole. It is this feature of reaching a goal or end that makes a process self-delimiting. In contrast, the selection of any particular "event" is always made by an external observer, and involves an element of arbitrary choice. In one other case we say that a motion is one, adds Aristotle: when it is uniform (*homalēs*), that is, when it preserves the same velocity. How Aristotle would deal with the unity of a uniformly accelerated motion is not clear.

Since any single motion is continuous, Aristotle tries to analyze and define continuity (*to syneches*). He discusses it in terms far simpler than the logical confusion in which the calculus was at first involved. Those things are said to be "together" (*hama*) which are in a single place. They are said to be in "contact" (*haptesthai*) when their extremities are together. They are said to be "consecutive" (*ephexēs*) if in their serial order they are not separated by any intermediary of the same kind. Two things are "contiguous" (*echomena*) if they are both consecutive and in contact.

The continuous is one species of contiguity. I say there is continuity when the limits by which the two things are in contact are one and the same, and, as the name suggests, hold together (*synechetai*); that cannot happen when there are two different extremities. Such a definition shows that the continuous is found in things whose nature is such as to make them one when they are in contact.[16]

In other words, that is continuous which when cut has a common boundary. This seems indeed to be the essence of Dedekind.

It is interesting to find Aristotle restricting the distinction between motions in accordance with nature (*kata physin*) and contrary to nature (*para physin*) to local motion.

There is no alteration in accordance with nature, and another contrary to nature, since getting well is no more in conformity with or contrary to nature than becoming ill, nor growing white than growing black. The same holds for getting larger or smaller. . . . And this holds also for generation and destruction: for generation is not in accordance with nature, and destruction contrary (getting old is in accordance with nature).[17]

Aristotle is now prepared, in dealing with the divisibility of motions in Book VI, to give his answer to the puzzles of Zeno. He first makes it clear that lines are not composed of indivisibles, or points; nor is an interval of time composed of instants. Both points and instants are limits, and not magnitudes or parts of a line or of time. Magnitudes and time are always divisible, no matter how far we carry the division, into magnitudes, but not into such limits. Thus there can be no motion in an instant, but neither can there be any rest: Zeno's arrow is hence never at rest. And both magnitudes and time are infinitely divisible. Hence Zeno is right in holding that it is impossible to traverse an infinite distance in a finite time. But you can easily traverse an infinitely divisible distance in a finite time, for a finite time is itself infinitely divisible.

One puzzling conclusion in Aristotle's analysis brings out

[16] *Physics* V, ch. 3: 227a 10–15. [17] *Physics* V, ch. 6: 230a 21–28.

clearly his fundamental point of view. It occurs when he asks about the "first instant" of change. When has change "first" taken place? (*pote prōton metablēken?*) This is said in two ways, Aristotle points out: we can mean either, when is the change first completed, or we can mean, when has it first begun. The first instant of the completion of any change "can be said and is": for such an instant is a limit. But the first instant of starting to change "just is not at all." For as soon as a thing is changing, it has already been changing. In other words, it is easily possible for there to be a limit to change after it has been completed. But before the change is already taking place, there can clearly be no limit to it.

Aristotle leads up to his treatment, in Books VII and VIII of the *Physics,* of the First Mover of all the other motions in the cosmos. No change can be infinite, for it is always from one contrary to the other: it involves a limit and a completion. Only local motion is not always carried on between two such limits. But even local motion cannot traverse an infinite distance. It can be infinite in time, if it is a circular motion; and so the eternity of motion in the cosmos demands an eternal circular motion of the outermost heavens. But the First Mover has already been considered, as it appears in Book Lambda of the *Metaphysics.* It is significant that here in the *Physics* Aristotle confines himself to the physical function of the First Mover, and does not attempt to describe its activities in itself.

Chapter X

THE EMERGENCE OF NOVELTY:

THE ANALYSIS OF GENESIS

The *De Generatione et Corruptione (Peri Geneseōs ḳai Phthoras)*, *On Genesis and Destruction,* or, as the recent fashion has it, *On Coming into Being and Passing Away,* discusses at length the first and most fundamental kind of change, substantial change. Qualitative change, alteration (*alloiōsis*), merely changes the accidents or incidental properties of a thing, while it remains itself the same substance or *ousia,* the same kind of thing. But real "genesis" or "coming into being" creates a new substance, with new properties not to be found in the elements taken by themselves. Hence Aristotle's analysis of what is involved in genesis appears to us as strikingly modern. It is dealing with the issues which have been central in our own recent philosophies of "creative" or "emergent" evolution. It is examining the notions of "creativity," of the "emergence of novelty," and doing it with rather less of logical confusion than we have been guilty of.

Aristotle's analysis involves also a careful criticism of the atomism of Democritus. It examines the validity and the limits of the analysis of change into the motion of elements alone. It is dealing with what we call the method of reductive analysis, which takes all change to be the mere rearrangement of the constituent parts of a thing. Hence, as is the case whenever Aristotle is criticizing the concepts of Democritus' atomism, what he has to say is most pertinent to our own criticism of the method and the assumptions of a mechanistic Newtonian science.

Here are Aristotle's functional concepts really coming to grips with the concepts of reductive analysis.

1. Genesis and Destruction

Is there such a thing as real genesis, real coming into being, or is there only alteration?

On this question the early philosophers are divided. Some of them assert that so-called "simple genesis" (*haplē genesis*) is "alteration," while others maintain that alteration and genesis are distinct. For those who say that the whole is one something (that is, those who generate all things out of one thing) are bound to assert that genesis is alteration, and that whatever is generated in the proper sense of the term is really being altered. But those who make the material of things more than one, must distinguish genesis from alteration. To this latter class belong Empedocles, Anaxagoras, and Leukippos.[1]

For the monists all change will be alteration; for the pluralists, there will be a process different from alteration, as Empedocles recognizes in saying, "There is no 'nature' of anything, but only a mixing and unmixing of mixable things."[2] Empedocles did not recognize that alteration is different from this mixing and unmixing. But alteration is a fact of experience: "While the substance of the thing remains unchanged, we see it altering, just as we see in it the changes of magnitude called growth and diminution."[3]

Simple genesis therefore demands discussion. Is there such a process, and how does it take place? Now, only Democritus seems to have really tackled the problems. He seems not only to have thought carefully about all the problems, but also to have been distinguished from the beginning in the way he dealt with them (*en tō pōs*). "Democritus and Leukippos postulate the

---

[1] *De Generatione* I, ch. 1: 314a 7–13.
[2] Diels, fragment 8; quoted *De Generatione* I, ch. 1: 314b 7–8.
[3] *De Generatione* I, ch. 1: 314b 14–15.

'figures' (*schēmata,* atoms), and make both alteration and genesis result from them. They explain genesis and destruction by their coming together (*synkrisis*) and separating (*diakrisis*), but alteration by their order (*taxis*) and position (*thesis*)." [4]

The first thing in these difficulties is to decide whether all change is due to some new combination of "first things," taken as indivisible magnitudes or atoms; and then to determine whether these indivisible magnitudes are bodies, as Democritus and Leukippos maintain, or planes, as the *Timaeus* asserts. To resolve bodies into planes is irrational, and more is to be said for analyzing them into indivisible bodies, though this too involves a good deal of irrationality.

Lack of experience (*hē apeiria*) lessens our power of taking a wide view of the admitted facts. Hence those who have lived in intimate association with natural things (*en tois physikois*) are better able to lay down such *archai* as can be connected together and cover a wide field. Those on the other hand who from many words are unable to see the things that really are, are more easily detected as men of narrow vision. One can see, too, from this the great difference that exists between those who conduct their investigations as natural philosophers (*physikōs*) and as dialecticians (*logikōs*). For on the subject of atomic magnitudes, the one school [the Platonists] maintains their existence because otherwise the "ideal triangle" will be more than one, while Democritus would seem to have been convinced by appropriate and physical arguments.[5]

Here is a clear statement of the cardinal methodological distinction running throughout Aristotle, between treating a subject matter *logikōs,* in terms appropriate to discourse or *logos,* and treating it *physikōs,* in terms appropriate to natural processes, *ta physika.*

Despite this preference for Democritus, Aristotle cannot accept his atoms as literally "indivisible." He shows how such a notion arises from the paradoxes involved in dividing bodies through and through (*pantē diairesis*). But every perceptible body may

[4] *De Generatione* I, ch. 1: 315b 7–9.   [5] *De Generatione* I, ch. 2: 316a 5–14.

well be actually indivisible at any and every point, while it can continue to be potentially divisible. Hence Democritus is right in holding that there are both coming together (*synkrisis*) and separating (*diakrisis*), but not of indivisibles or atoms, and not involving a division through and through into points in contact. Rather, the coming together of "relatively small parts" is a necessary condition of all genesis: there can be no genesis without such a coming together, and in so far Democritus is right. But this coming together of small parts is not sufficient to define genesis.

But simple and complete genesis (*hē haplē kai teleia genesis*) is not defined by coming together and separating, as some say, while change in what is continuous is alteration. In fact, this is where the whole mistake lies. For simple genesis and destruction do not take place by coming together and separating, but when a thing changes from this to that as a whole (*hotan metaballē ek toude eis tode holon*). But some suppose that all such change is alteration; in fact there is a difference. For in the subject that underlies the change there is something that corresponds to the definition, and something that corresponds to the material. When, then, there is a change in these two, there will take place genesis or destruction. But when it occurs in the thing's qualities, and incidentally, there will be alteration.[6]

This position of Aristotle can be put in the language of more recent philosophizing. The coming together or "association" of relatively small parts described by Democritus is a necessary condition of all genesis: there can be no coming into being of a new substance without such coming together of elements. But it is at the same time creative of novelty, of a new "substance" or *ousia;* that is, in terms of the elements, of a new "kind" of thing. This creation of a new *ousia* involves a "change from this to that as a whole." That is, genesis is not to be understood as a mere combination of existing elements with their properties. In terms of our own, though not of Aristotle's chemistry, when

[6] *De Generatione* I, ch. 2: 317a 17–27.

hydrogen and oxygen unite to form H_2O, in the new combination the elements interact and are modified. The chemical combination H_2O manifests new properties not to be found in either of the elements taken by themselves, like "wetness," or "liquidity." Aristotle characteristically puts it, the elements continue to exist in the new whole "potentially"—that is, they can always be analyzed out again, with nothing left over. But when they are operating in combination in the whole, they display novel characteristics and powers. That is, a new "form," a new "nature," comes into being—a new kind of thing, with new "essential properties" and "powers," that is, with a new "nature."

The question remains, is there any genesis *haplōs,* simply or unqualifiedly, or is genesis always a coming to be "something" out of "something" (*ek tinos kai ti*)? For sheer genesis, sheer coming-into-being, would seem to mean a coming-into-being out of non-being (*ek mē ontos*), and that would seem to make "non-being" a something out of which things could come-to-be. Aristotle concludes:

In one sense things come to be out of what is sheer non-being (*ek mē ontos haplōs*). Yet in another sense they come to be always out of something that is (*ex ontos*). For coming into being necessarily implies the pre-existence of something which is potentially, but is not actually, and this is described in both ways.[7]

Aristotle is trying to generalize his analysis of alteration or qualitative change. It is clear that he is having some difficulty in making the distinctions that are found in motion (*kinēsis*) apply to the more fundamental kind of change, genesis.

Aristotle asks further, how can such new things come into being? What is the material employed in the eternal succession of processes of genesis? Assuming that the amount of material in the world is finite, why in the course of time has not this material been all used up? "Why, then, is this form of change

[7] *De Generatione* I, ch. 3: 317b 16–18.

necessarily ceaseless? Is it because the passing-away of *this* is a coming-to-be of something else, and the coming-to-be of *this* a passing-away of something else?" Aristotle answers his own question:

There is no need even to discuss the other question we raised—why coming-to-be continues, though things are constantly being destroyed. For just as people speak of a sheer "passing-away" when a thing has passed into something that cannot be sensed, and in that sense "is not," so also they speak of "a coming-to-be out of a not-being" when a thing emerges from something that cannot be sensed. Whether, therefore, the underlying substratum is or is not something, what comes-to-be emerges out of a "not-being": so that a thing "comes-to-be out of a not-being" just as much as it "passes-away into what is not." Hence it is reasonable enough that coming-to-be should never fail. For coming-to-be is a passing-away of "what is not," and passing-away is a coming-to-be of "what is not." [8]

2. What Underlies Genesis?
First Matter and the Elements

But what is it that can be said to "underlie" sheer genesis as a "substratum," in the way that some *ousia* is always the underlying and persisting "substratum" of the less radical forms of change? What is it that can be said to persist as the same "subject," the same *hypokeimenon,* in the case of such fundamental change as the coming-to-be of a new *ousia?* In this crucial case, are there not two contraries, but only one, the one that is achieved when the coming-to-be has been accomplished? Or is there an identical "material" that underlies all such fundamental changes?

The "material" out of which things are made is eternal, and persists throughout all change, even while it is assuming new forms: Aristotle clearly states the doctrine of the "conservation of matter." Yet when this material is organized in complex ways, novel properties are generated. The novelty lies not in the mate-

[8] *De Generatione* I, ch. 3: 318a 25–27; 319a 22–29.

rials but in the forms. It is new forms, not new materials, that
are generated by the coming together of elements. In this sense
we can distinguish "by reason" (*logō*) a material that persists
throughout all the comings-into-being and passings-away, a material that can be said to be a "first matter" (*prōtē hylē*), a material
that is wholly first (*hylē holōs prōtē*), a *materia prima,* a material
that can assume any form, and undergo any transformation.

Aristotle is very explicit that for him there is no "first matter"
that can exist as such by itself. Material can exist only with some
specific quality or form, like the material out of which the
statue is made, which before it becomes involved in the artist's
making of the statue has, by itself, its own specific form of bronze.
Ultimately, in terms of Aristotle's distinctive chemical analysis,
the material of the statue has the form of "water," since in the
last analysis all metals are for him transformations of "water."
And generally, when he uses the term "first matter," he means one
of these two things: either the "first" or immediate material of
the thing, like the bronze of the statue; or the material of the
thing that is "wholly first," its ultimate material, like the element "water."

Yet even these ultimate materials of production, earth, water,
air, and fire, seem to pass into each other. In these ultimate
transformations there seems to be a kind of quantitative equivalence which can be called "first matter," though Aristotle of
course has no means of measuring these equivalences. Aristotle's
view seems to be very close to that of the great nineteenth-
century exponents of the doctrine of the "conservation of energy."
This doctrine maintained that there is nothing that can be
called "energy as such," by itself: there are only specific kinds of
energy, mechanical, kinetic, potential, electrical, and the rest.
Yet in the transformations of one type of energy into another
we can discover formulae of equivalence, which in nineteenth-
century physics were susceptible of exact mathematical determination. Thus in Rumford's famous experiment, it was possible to

measure the kinetic energy consumed by the production of a measurable amount of heat generated by friction.

For the understanding of Aristotle's notion of "first matter" it is important to realize that this is the context in which he is led to such a concept. "First matter" is his way of referring to such equivalences in the most fundamental transformations of the elements into each other. It is also of importance to realize that for Aristotle the notion of "first matter" is of minor significance. The term is not even used in the discussion of the problem in the *De Generatione*. It occurs at most some dozen times in the whole corpus of Aristotle's writings, and only some three or four times in a sense clearly different from the other two senses mentioned above. "First matter" became, however, a major problem for the medieval "Aristotelians," who, being in their ultimate philosophical assumptions Platonists, were vitally concerned with the problem of creation. Like the author of the *Timaeus,* they wanted to know what God took to make the world out of. What material was there to use "in the beginning?"

But that is God's problem, which he must solve with the aid of the advice of the Platonists. It is distinctly not the problem of Aristotle. For him, there was never such a "creation," nor ever any "beginning." And for him material is always determined and relative. It is always the material involved in a specific process: its "Out of What," or *ex hou.*

He sums up:

When the change from contrary to contrary is in quantity, it is "growth and diminution"; when it is in place, it is "local motion"; when it is in property or quality, it is "alteration." But when nothing persists, of which the resultant is a property, or an "accident" in any sense of the term, it is "coming-to-be" or genesis, and the converse change is "passing-away."

"Matter," in the best and controlling sense of the term, is to be identified with the substratum which is receptive of coming-to-be and passing-away. But the substratum of the remaining kinds of

change is also, in a certain sense, "matter," because all these sub-
strata are receptive of contrarieties of some kind.[9]

There is no coming-to-be without a combination or *mixis* of
elements. Aristotle is hence led to a careful analysis of the process
of combination and of the elements that combine. By "combination" he means something like what we call "chemical combination," in contrast to a mere physical mixture. In such a thoroughgoing combination, in what sense can the elements be said to be
still present in the outcome?

Since some things are potentially, and other things are actually, it is
possible for things which combine in a mixture to be in one sense,
and not to be in another. The compound may actually be something
different from its constituent elements. Each element may still be
potentially what it was before they were combined, and the elements
may not be destroyed. This is the difficulty that arose in our earlier
argument. It is clear that the constituent elements that were for-
merly separate not only coalesce in the compound; they can also be
separated out again from it. The elements, therefore, do not actually
persist, as "body" and "white" persist; nor are they destroyed,
either one or both of them, for their power to be separated out again
is preserved.[10]

It remains to examine the elements of bodies (*ta stoicheia tōn
sōmatōn*). All natural processes take place "not without" (*ouch
aneu*) sensed bodies (*ta aisthēta*). But there is disagreement as
to the matter that underlies them. Is it one or many? Aristotle
agrees, the first things (*ta prōta*) whose change results in genesis
and destruction are *archai* and elements. But there is no single
"matter" besides the four bodies, which themselves are "bodily and
separable." Everything that is "separably existent" must be
determinate. There can thus be no "boundless," such as Anaximander assumed. There can be no "omnirecipient," as is set
forth in the *Timaeus*: for it is nothing definite (*oudena dioris-*

[9] *De Generatione* I, ch. 4: 319b 32–320a 6.
[10] *De Generatione* I, ch. 10: 327b 23–32.

mon). Such views would make all genesis a kind of alteration. There is, to be sure, a "kind of matter" (*tis hylē*). But it is never found separate (*ou chōristē*), but always together with contraries (*all' aei met' enantiōseōs*).

3. What Makes Genesis Happen?

What makes genesis happen? It takes place always in "the region around the center" of the world, never in the sphere beyond the moon, in which no subtantial change is ever observed to occur. Material and form are its necessary conditions. But they alone are not sufficient conditions of genesis: for neither matter nor form can generate anything. Neither cause as the material origin, nor cause as the For What, the form or *logos,* can be the sufficient condition of genesis. There must be a third *archē*. For neither form alone nor matter alone can account for coming-into-being, though matter is, as Aristotle puts it, "more natural" (*physikōteron*). For it belongs to matter to be acted upon and to be moved (*to paschein kai to kineisthai*). Matter is a "passive power," that is, a power of being acted upon; while moving and making (*to kinein kai to poiein*) belong to another power. And those who make matter the cause of genesis eliminate the more controlling cause, the form or essential nature (*to ti ēn einai*).

The third *archē* is motion in place (*phora*). Every other type of change or process always involves motion in place as a necessary agent or By What: motion in place, *phora,* is thus the primary kind of "motion." And it alone can be perpetual and continuous, without interruption or break. Now such a perpetual and continuous motion must exist, as the efficient cause of the whole world-process: Aristotle's whole conception of motion as "being moved" demands that every process must be moved by some cosmic motion, just as an intricate piece of clockwork must be moved by the motion of some spring, weights, or motor. The ultimate cause of all the processes of generation is thus the eternal circular motion of the sun, the "Generator" (*to gennētikon*). Thus motion in place, *phora,* and not genesis, is the first of all changes (*to prōton tōn metabolōn*).

We were right in the *Physica* in calling motion (*phora*) and not gene-sis the primary form of change. For it is far more reasonable that what is should cause the coming-to-be of what is not, than that what is not should cause the being of what is. Now that which is being moved is, but that which is coming-to-be is not: hence also motion is prior to coming-to-be.[11]

Now, the same, provided it remain in the same condition, always by nature produces the same. Hence, to account for both genesis and destruction, both birth and death, the motion of the sun must involve contraries, And thus the ultimate efficient cause of all processes of generation is the annual motion of the sun along the ecliptic, bringing it alternately nearer and farther from the earth, and thus causing the unceasing cycle of the seasons and the great pattern of birth and death, of all life, all generation and destruction.

Is any process of genesis necessary? It is clear that any particular generation may fail to occur: such natural processes exhibit only hypothetical necessity, not simple necessity. For the occur-rence of any one of them certain conditions are necessary, but it is not necessary that they should occur at all.

Then are all the things that come to be of this contingent character? Or, on the contrary, is it absolutely necessary (*anankaion haplōs*) for some of them to come to be? Is there, in fact, a distinction in the field of coming-to-be corresponding to the distinction within the field of being between things that cannot possibly not-be and things that can not-be? For instance, is it necessary that solstices shall come-to-be, and impossible that they should fail to be able to occur?

[11] *De Generatione* II, ch. 10: 336a 19–24.

Aristotle's answer is that only cyclical changes can be necessary with a simple necessity.

It follows that the coming-to-be of anything, if it is absolutely necessary, must be cyclical. . . . It is in circular movement, therefore, and in cyclical coming-to-be that the absolutely necessary is to be found. In other words, if the coming-to-be of any things is cyclical, it is necessary that each of them is coming-to-be and has come-to-be; and if the coming-to-be of any things is necessary, their coming-to-be is cyclical. . . . Thus precisely those movements which belong to and depend upon the eternal revolution of the heavens come-to-be of necessity and of necessity will be. For since the revolving body is always setting something else in motion, the movement of the things it moves must also be circular. Thus from the being of the upper revolution it follows that the sun revolves in this determinate manner; and since the sun revolves thus, the seasons in consequence come-to-be in a cycle. And since they come to be cyclically, so in their turn do the things whose coming-to-be they initiate.[12]

[12] *De Generatione* II, ch. 11: 337b 10–14; 338a 4–5, 15–17; 338b 1–6.

Chapter XI

ARISTOTLE'S FUNCTIONALISM ILLUSTRATED

IN BIOLOGICAL THEORY

From quotations which I had seen, I had a high notion of Aristotle's merits, but I had not the most remote notion what a wonderful man he was. Linnaeus and Cuvier have been my two gods, though in very different ways, but they were mere schoolboys to old Aristotle.—CHARLES DARWIN to William Ogle, on the publication of his translation of *The Parts of Animals,* 1882. *Life and Letters of Charles Darwin,* ed. Francis Darwin (New York, 1896), II, 427.

Aristotle may have been a pupil of Plato, and he may have modeled his conception of what a fully worked-out and completed science should be upon the geometry which the Greeks had by his day so successfully elaborated. And his intellectual interests may have been far-ranging, so that from his own vantage point very little of the Greek world of the life of man in nature failed to enter into his perspective. But as to what that vantage point is, and to where his heart lies, there can be little doubt. It is the great panorama of living things that enlists his central concern. Coming out of that Greek world of the Sophists and Socrates and Plato, that society of eager and indefatigable talkers, he may have devoted much energy to avoiding the pitfalls into which so many talkers had fallen, and to elaborating the best way of talking. But his central aim in doing so is to be able to talk about living things and their processes of generation and growth. That is why he is so anxious to defend and reconstruct the older notion of *physis* or nature against the atomists: the inescapable challenge to the man who desires above all else to know is to find a way of understanding and talking about *physis* in its root meaning of "growth." It is very evident that what Aristotle himself wants to be is a *physikos,* a natural philosopher. Of all living things man himself may well be the most interesting, in his own eyes at least. But Aristotle approaches man too with the attitude and the interests of the *physikos:* it is the behavior and activities, individual and corporate, of the human animal that call for inquiry and understanding, and Aristotle never forgets the place which that animate being that is man occupies in the great spectacle of living beings that the world displays. It is significant that even in his most Platonic moments, in describing the supreme "For What" that is divine, in Book Lambda of the *Metaphysics,* Aristotle cannot accept the impersonal Idea of the Good which the later Plato was trying to grasp in mathematical terms. For him even the divine, though deathless and eternal, as every Greek knew, has to be in some sense a kind of life.

1. The Biological Motivation of Aristotle's Thought

Aristotle's interest is rooted in living things. On the one hand, he extends his analysis to embrace all natural processes, the inanimate as well as the animate. On the other, he pushes it to deal with man and all the works of human art. But the central range from which his analysis springs lies in the fields and subject matters that we today should call "biological." Since the twelfth century at least, it has been traditional to approach Aristotle's thought through his logical and metaphysical writings. But in the corpus that has come down to us, neither logic nor metaphysics bulks very large in comparison with the pages devoted to biological inquiries. The biological treatises comprise some third of the entire corpus. Clearly Aristotle's interest in the direct study and analysis of living beings can hardly have been for him a matter of secondary importance. And it may well have been more than an accident that, of those great collections of factual reports that Aristotle is said to have compiled with the help of students and colleagues, the only one to come down to us is the *History of Animals*.

But we do not need to depend on inferences from the amount of writing Aristotle has left us about living things. His own words make clear his delight:

Of these beings that are works of nature there are two kinds; those that are ungenerated and indestructible throughout all ages, and those that partake of genesis and destruction. The former are of the highest worth and are divine, but they are less open to knowledge. The evidence that might throw light on them and on all the things we long to know about them is given but scantily through the senses. But as to perishable things, plants and animals, we have abundant information, living as we do in their midst. And a great deal about all their various kinds can be learned by anyone who will take enough trouble. Each of the two groups has its charm. For though we have little grasp of eternal things, it brings us because of their great worth more pleasure than all we know of what is about us, just as a chance and partial glimpse of those we love gives more pleasure than seeing accurately many other great things. But we can get more and better knowledge about the things near us. And their proximity and closeness to nature makes up somewhat for the philosophy that deals with the divine.

We have already treated such living things, as they appear to us. It remains to talk about the nature of animals. So far as possible we will not leave out any of them, mean or noble. For if some do not charm the senses, yet for scientific knowledge the nature which fashioned them provides a pleasure to all who can know their causes and are by nature philosophers. Indeed, it would be strange and absurd if we took pleasure in looking at likenesses of such animals, because we were seeing the art of the craftsman, the painter or the carver, and yet failed to delight much more in looking at the works of nature itself, provided we were able to discern the causes of their generation. We must therefore not draw back childishly from examining the meaner animals. In all natural beings there is something of the marvelous. It is said of Heraclitus that when strangers who came to visit him found him warming himself at the kitchen stove, and hesitated to go in, he bade them enter, saying, "There are gods even here." In like manner we should study every kind of animal without hesitation, knowing that in all of them there is something natural and beautiful.

For in the works of nature there is to be found the absence of chance (*to mē tychontōs*) and the presence of natural ends (*heneka tinos*) in the highest degree. The function and the ends for which those works have been constructed or formed have their place among what is beautiful. If, however, there is anyone who holds that the study of the other animals is an unworthy pursuit, he ought to think the same way about the study of himself. For it is not possible without considerable disgust to look upon the blood, flesh, bones, blood-vessels and suchlike parts out of which the human frame is constructed.[1]

The biological writings in the Aristotelian corpus have as their foundation one of those collections of recorded facts which Aristotle calls "histories," that is, "investigations" or "researches," *Forschungen,* into particular facts. The *History of Animals* comprises ten books, the last of which seems not to be by Aristotle; it is the longest of all the Aristotelian writings. Its aim is stated: "We shall speak in detail that we may first grasp the basic differences and common properties [of animals]. After this we must try to find the causes (*aitiai*) of these."[2] There is a fourfold division of likenesses and differences into modes of living (*bioi*), activities or functions (*praxeis*), characters or dispositions (*ethē*), and parts. In the theoretical works, modes of living, activities, and characters are largely fused together, so that the division becomes one between parts and functions. The first four books consider principally the parts and functions of animals, the next three their modes of generation, and the two last certain activities.

[1] *De Partibus Animalium* I, ch. 5: 644b 23–645a 31.
[2] *Historia Animalium* I, ch. 6: 491a 8–11.

On the basis of these observations, Aristotle proceeds to work out his biological theory. He states his aim: "I have already described with considerable detail in the *Histories* about animals from what parts and how many each of them is composed. Leaving aside what was said in the *Histories,* we must now investigate through what causes each animal is composed in this way." [3] Thus the title of his first major treatise on biological theory should be, *On the Causes of the Parts of Animals;* and Aristotle refers to it elsewhere by that title.[4] Since the major "cause" turns out to be the "For What" or final cause, the function the part performs, the title might more accurately run, *On the Functions of the Parts of Animals.* With this belongs the small separate treatise, *De Incessu Animalium,* on the functions of the various organs of locomotion. The *De Anima, On Life,* deals with the functions of the organism as a whole. The *Parva Naturalia* and the *De Motu Animalium* deal with various specific functions and problems. Finally, the extensive *De Generatione Animalium* treats in five books what Aristotle felt to be the most challenging problem of all, the reproductive functions.

Jaeger, Ross, and others, tracing in Aristotle an intellectual development from an early Platonism through his own naturalistic philosophical formulations to an increasing interest in empirical observation and scientific investigations, have assigned the *History of Animals,* together with the theoretical analyses based on its data, to the period of his other great "histories" or collections of facts, during his second stay in Athens as the head of the Lyceum as an institute of organized research. But D'Arcy W. Thompson, himself a distinguished biologist, suggested in 1910:

We know that Aristotle spent two years in Mitylene, when he was about forty years old: that is to say, some three years after the death

---

[3] *De Partibus Animalium* II, ch. 1: 646a 8–13.

[4] *De Generatione Animalium* V, ch. 3: 782a 21: *en tais aitiais tais peri ta merē tōn zōōn.*

of Plato, just after his sojourn with Hermias of Atarneus, just prior to his residence at the court of Philip, and some ten years before he returned to Athens to begin teaching in the Lyceum. Throughout the *Natural History* references to places in Greece are few, while they are comparatively frequent to places in Macedonia and to places on the coast of Asia Minor, all the way from the Bosphorus to the Carian coast. I think it can be shown that Aristotle's natural history studies were carried on, or mainly carried on, in his middle age, between his two periods of residence in Athens; that the calm, land-locked lagoon at Pyrrha was one of his favorite hunting-grounds.[5]

Thompson's view has been convincingly supported by a recent study by H. D. P. Lee of the place names in the *History of Animals*.[6] This would place Aristotle's factual researches on animals in the period during which he was living in the Troad, at Assos, in Lesbos, and in Macedonia, between 347 and 335.

If this be the case, it gives to Aristotle's biological studies a much more central place in the development of his thought than that to which they have been conventionally assigned. As Thompson puts it, "Then it would appear that Aristotle's work in natural history was antecedent to his more strictly philosophical work, and it would follow that we might proceed legitimately to interpret the latter in the light of the former."[7]

[5] *The Works of Aristotle Translated,* vol. IV (Oxford, 1910), p. vii.

[6] *Classical Quarterly,* 42 (1948), 61 ff.

[7] This view is accepted by A. L. Peck, translator of the *De Partibus Animalium* and the *De Generatione Animalium* in the Loeb Classics series. It is also the central theme of Harold D. Hantz, *The Biological Motivation in Aristotle* (New York, 1939), a dissertation written under F. J. E. Woodbridge. Hantz points out that the characteristic Aristotelian distinctions emerge naturally from the inquiry into biological problems of function and generation, and do not appeal to other inquiries or writings.

"The so-called four 'issues' are exhibited in the *De Partibus* as emerging from a consideration of natural productivity. There is no appeal to other works for their origin or justification. By this I do not imply that the study of living things first led Aristotle to the doctrine. But I do suggest that Aristotle endeavors to show that the naturalist is led to these basic factors if he is to have an adequate understanding of natural genetic processes. As Aristotle proceeds with his study of development, he finds increasingly useful two additional concepts, potentiality and actuality. These gain in prominence in the *De Generatione Animalium*

2. *Aristotle's Natural Teleology versus "Design"*

However it may stand with the biographical question of whether a consuming interest in the generation and growth of living things colored Aristotle's thinking from the very beginning, two facts are clear. Aristotle's functionalism is exhibited and illustrated most fully and completely, just as it is stated most explicitly, in his biological writings. Moreover, the concepts and distinctions he worked out to deal with the functioning of living things, and extended to include human and social living as well, are most suggestive and illuminating in grasping the traits and structures of biological and human processes. Here Aristotle's scheme for rendering the world intelligible can be seen at its best and most successful. The arguments for understanding in terms of functional and teleological relations, set forth in generalized form in the second book of the *Physics*,[8] are here revealed in their concrete meaning; such instruments are indispensable for the biologist in gaining an intellectual grasp upon his subject matter. Here is set forth and illustrated what Aristotle means specifically by "natural ends" as principles of intelligibility, and by the relations of "natural teleology" as essential conditions of any understanding of processes.

When Aristotle goes on from describing the various "parts" of which animals are made up, to investigate "through what causes (*aitiai*) each animal is made up in this way," that is, when he

and become dominant in the *De Anima* in the investigation of the factors productive of the functions of animals. . . . In short, in the biological works the reader witnesses the emergence of 'form,' 'matter,' 'end,' 'mover,' 'potentiality,' and 'actuality,' the terms which carry Aristotle's system of thought, biological and otherwise. . . .

"On the evidence of the corpus, irrespective of the tradition, Aristotle's philosophy appears to be a system of knowledge which grows from inquiries, conspicuously biological, into natural things, expanding into a problem like that of the *Metaphysica*, the problem of what it means to be. His philosophy seems to be this rather than a metaphysics imposed upon natural inquiries." (31–32, 42).

[8] *Physics* II, ch. 8; see pages 186–88 above.

attempts to state his biological theory, he is a thoroughgoing functionalist. He is interested throughout in the behavior of the organism and of its component organs. He is not primarily the anatomist or the histologist delineating in detail the structure of the various organs or of the "uniform parts" or tissues. In any event, without a microscope that task was impossible for him. Structures and tissues are to be understood in terms of what they do, the operations they perform. He several times repeats: "Our knowledge [of such structures] must come from a study of their functions" (*ek tōn ergōn*).[9]

For the natural philosopher who would understand living things and living processes, final causes are more important than either material or efficient causes. To be sure, Aristotle recognizes much spontaneous variation and much that has no function in biological processes, both alike due to the necessary consequences of mechanical or efficient causes. We must investigate and observe what the organism actually does, and then understand how its various structures and tissues enable it to do so. One is tempted to say, we must understand how these organs were "developed" to do so. We should not be falsifying Aristotle's own aim if we said this in reference to the development and growth of the individual organism from an embryo; the processes of generation, growth, and maturation fascinated him. And though Aristotle did not of course believe in the evolutionary development of the different types of animal life—for him species had no "origin"—his own experimental functionalism is so close to the teleological and functional concepts of evolutionary thought that at this point it seems to a modern to cry for such supplementation, and to be incomplete without it. For the ultimate function of every organ and arrangement for Aristotle is the "survival value" which for evolutionary thinking is the necessary condition of the process of natural selection.

Thus the last two chapters of the *De Anima* try to account for

[9] *De Partibus Animalium* II, ch. 9: 655b 21.

the various "parts" or functions of the *psychē* in terms of sheer
survival value:

Every living thing must have the nutritive *psychē* that it may live,
and have life from its birth until its death. For what has been born
must necessarily grow, reach maturity, and decline, and these processes are impossible without nutriment. . . . The animal must of
necessity possess sensation, if nature makes nothing in vain. For
everything in nature exists for an end (*heneka tou*) or else will be
accessory to things which exist for an end. An animal capable of
moving from place to place, if it had no sensation, would be destroyed, and would not reach the end which is its natural function.
For how could it be nourished? . . .

A being which has no sensation when it comes into contact with
other things will be unable to avoid some and seize others. And if
this is so, it will be impossible for the animal to survive (*sōzesthai*).
. . . Taste also must be a kind of touch, because it is a sensing of
what is tangible and nutritive. These two senses, then, are necessary
to the animal, and it is plain that without touch no animal can exist.
. . . If the animal capable of locomotion is to survive, it must be
able to sense things not only when in contact with them but also at
a distance. And this will occur only if it can sense through a medium,
the medium being capable of being acted upon and set in motion
by the sensed object, and the animal itself by the motion of the
medium. . . . Thus it is evident that touch is the only sense the loss
of which necessarily involves the death of the animal.[10]

This emphasis on survival value also makes clear that Aristotle's conception of "natural ends" and "natural teleology" is
very remote from the conception of "final causes" familiar in the
religious tradition, and employed in the conventional "argument
from design" for the existence of a creator. The eighteenth-century
instances of such "final causes" advanced by Bernardin de Saint-
Pierre may be rather extreme, but they serve to bring out the
differences between such a notion and Aristotle's natural teleology.
Bernardin suggested that melons are produced with ridges marked

[10] *De Anima* III, chs. 12, 13: 434a 22–25; 434a 30–434b 1; 16–18.

on their rind to facilitate division at a family meal, and that fleas are dark in color so that they may be more easily picked off the human skin. He failed to consider Africa. Such a notion of "final causes" was not unknown to Aristotle: for he could read in the *Timaeus* how the created gods, the stars, to whom the Supreme Craftsman assigned the generation of man's body, acted always from the best, and were guided by "final causes" or ends. Thus they made the liver in animals so that men might practice divination of the future and prophesy; they placed a thick thatch of hair on the head to provide shade from the burning sun; and they gave man eyes in the front of his head, so that he might see where he was going, and not in the back, where he could see only where he had come from. Plato—if he really wrote the *Timaeus*—was capable of being quite as uncritical as Bernardin de Saint-Pierre.

Since it was such notions of "final causes" and teleology that led the great scientific pioneers of the seventeenth century to reject final causes completely as principles of intelligibility, and since it has been the identification of all teleology with such views that has kept alive among scientists and indeed in popular thought the prejudice that any kind of appeal to ends is "unscientific," it is worth while to point out with some precision just where Aristotle's "natural teleology" differs from that kind of "design."

Since the various religious traditions not unnaturally identified "nature," the system of ends toward which natural processes are discovered to be directed, with the "will of God," as Plato's creation myth had already done, "final causes" were taken as the conscious *purposes* of the Deity, and as such were held to be *ipso facto* efficient causes, themselves acting to bring about their own realization. In sharp contrast, for Aristotle "final causes" and "natural ends" are in no sense whatever to be taken as "purposes": they involve no conscious intent, except in the one case where conscious intent is obviously involved, human action and art. And final causes or ends are for Aristotle *never* to be identified with efficient causes: *never* for him does what a process brings about itself bring about the process. For Aristotle a final cause is always a necessary condition of understanding, a principle of intelligibility; it is never a "whence of motion," an *archē* of action.

In the second place, "final causes," as they were developed during the predominance of the religious traditions, tended to become a way of showing how under the ministrations of God's providence everything in the universe conduces to the self-centered purposes of man. In sharp contrast, Aristotle's natural teleology is, in the technical sense, wholly "immanent." No kind of thing, no species, is subordinated to the purposes and interests of any other kind. In biological theory, the end served by the structure of any specific kind of living thing is the good —ultimately, the "survival"—of that kind of thing. Hence Aristotle's concern is always to examine how the structure, the way of acting, the "nature," of any species conduces toward the preservation of that species, and enables it to survive, to exist and to continue to function in its own distinctive way. This Aristotelian emphasis on the way in which kinds of living things are adapted to their environment brings Aristotle's thought very close to the functional explanations advanced by evolutionary thinkers: in both cases the emphasis is placed on the survival value of the arrangement in question.

It might be well to add, that such functional and teleological conceptions are just the notions that modern biologists, no matter how "mechanistic" their explanatory theory, actually have to employ in describing the subject matter they are attempting to explain. Teleological relations, the relations between means and ends, or "functional structures," are an encountered fact. Like all facts, they have to be explained in terms of certain mechanisms that are involved.

3. Aristotle's Functional Theory

We are now in a position to see what Aristotle himself has to say in stating and defending his functional emphasis in biology.

There is a further point which has not yet been decided: should the natural philosopher (*ho physikos*) follow the same sort of procedure as the mathematician follows in his astronomical expositions? Should he first of all consider the phenomena observed in animals, and the parts of each of them, and then state the reasons and the causes (*to dia ti kai tas aitias*), or should he follow some other procedure? Moreover, we see that there are several different causes involved in the genesis of natural things: there is that For Which (*hou heneka*) the thing comes to be, and there is that whence comes the beginning of the motion (*hothen hē archē tēs kinēseōs*). Therefore we must decide which of these comes first and which comes second. It is clear that the first is what we call the For Something (*heneka tinos*). For this is the *logos* of the thing, and the *logos* is the beginning, alike in things that are formed by nature as in those formed by art. The physician or the builder sets before himself something quite definite—the one views health with his mind, the other the house with his senses; and once he has got this, each of them can tell you the reasons (*logoi*) and causes for what he is doing, and why it has to be done in that way. But the For What and the good is more fully present in the works of nature than in those of art.[11]

We must also decide whether we are to discuss the processes by which each animal comes into being, which is what the earlier philosophers considered, or rather the animal as it actually exists. There seems to be a considerable difference between the two methods. I said earlier that we ought first to take the phenomena that are observed in each group, and then go on to state their causes. This applies equally to generation. Here too we ought surely to begin with things as they are actually observed to be when completed. Even in building, the stages of the process come about because the form of the house is

[11] *De Partibus Animalium* I, ch. 1: 639b 12–21.

such and such, rather than that the house is such and such because its building follows a particular course. The coming to be (*genesis*) is for the sake of what comes to be (*ousia*); what comes to be is not for the sake of the coming to be.

So Empedocles was wrong when he said that many of the characteristics animals have are due to some accident in their process of genesis, as when he accounts for the vertebrae of the backbone by saying "the fetus gets twisted and so the backbone is broken into pieces." He was unaware that the seed which forms the animal must to begin with have that specific power, and that the parent was there before the offspring; it was earlier in time as well as logically prior. For it is man that begets a man, and therefore the child's generation is what it is because its parent was a man.

The same may also be said of the products of the arts, and even of the sometimes identical results that are apparently produced quite spontaneously, like health. But normally, as in the sculptor's art, for example, there is no spontaneous production, and there must be to begin with an efficient cause which is similar in character to the product. The art is the *logos* of the work not yet embodied in matter. The products of chance are similar: they are formed as are the products of art.

So it would be best to say, that because this is what it is to be a man, therefore a man has such and such parts, since there cannot be a man without them. If we may not say this, then the nearest to it must do: that there cannot be a man at all otherwise than with them, or that it is well that a man should have them. And from this it follows: Because man is such and such, therefore the process of his generation must be such and such and must take place in such a manner: first this part comes to be, and then that. And the same way with all the things that come to be by nature.[12]

Whenever there is clearly some end (*telos ti*) towards which a motion goes forward unless something stands in its way, then we always say that the motion has the end as its For What (*toud' heneka*). From this it is clear that there really is something of this kind, that which in fact we call "nature" (*physis*). For actually we do not find any

[12] *De Partibus Animalium* I, ch. 1: 640a 10–640b 4.

chance being formed from a particular seed, but rather this here thing comes from this here seed (*tode ek toude*); nor does any chance seed come from any chance body. Therefore that from which the seed comes is the *archē* and agent of what comes out of it. These things are by nature: the offspring grows out of the seed. Nevertheless, prior to the seed stands that of which it is the seed, for the seed is a process of generation, while the end (*to telos*) is something that has come to be (*ousia*). But prior to both of them is that out of which the seed comes. For a seed is said to be the seed "of" something in two ways, which are not the same, but quite different. It is the seed "of" that out of which it came, as from a horse; and it is the seed "of" that which will come out of itself, as a mule. Again, the seed is only potentially what it will be; and how a power is related to its operation we know.[13]

In these passages Aristotle is spelling out just what he means by the natural teleology that so much impressed him in connection with his observation of living things and living processes. Such teleology is perfectly objective and empirically observable: it involves for Aristotle no dubious inference to unobservable "causes." As he puts it, such a natural end is an outcome toward which a process is *observed* to go forward unless something stands in its way. Acorns grow into oak trees, not into pine trees; human infants grow into men, not into donkeys. What acorns and human infants will grow into, under appropriate conditions, is an indispensable factor that must be known if we can be said to know what acorns and infants are. It is true that acorns grow into oak trees "because" they are the seed produced by oak trees, and that infants grow into men "because" they are begotten by men: "man begets man" is for Aristotle a basic axiom he never tires of repeating. We have to understand acorns and infants in terms of the completed and actualized *ousiai* they have the *power* to become, and under the appropriate conditions *will* become. But an acorn is not "made" to grow into an oak because of the oak tree it has the power to become. It grows into an oak tree

---

[13] *De Partibus Animalium* I, ch. 1: 641b 24–642a 2.

because it is the seed of a parent oak tree, and as such has been given the power—the particular structural determinations—to develop in that direction rather than in any other.

This is to say that for Aristotle all his "causes," his "whys" and "wherefores," including this basic "final reason why," are necessary conditions in nature for the human understanding of processes. They are principles of understanding, principles of intelligibility; they are not "efficient causes," that is, they are not factors the manipulation of which will produce significantly different outcomes. Taking the squirrel's point of view, we may indeed say that acorns are the most important ingredient in a breakfast. But this does not mean that acorns have been generated "so that" they may serve as a squirrel's breakfast. In ninety-nine out of a hundred cases, this may well be the outcome of an acorn's career. This fact tells us that squirrels are prone to eat acorns, and that, there being a good many squirrels, the vast majority of acorns may well end as raw materials in the teleological pattern of the diet habits of squirrels. We can even say that it is the "nature" of squirrels to eat acorns. But this tells us nothing about the "nature" of acorns, about "what acorns really are." To state the question in this wise means that we do not understand what acorns "really" are unless we understand what they have the power to grow into, oak trees, entirely apart from their very incidental traffic, however prominent statistically, as in the case of the squirrels, with processes that impinge upon their natural development "by violence" (*bia*)—like destructive squirrels.

But Aristotle goes beyond the natural teleology exhibited in biological processes to give a more generalized statement of his functionalism.

If, then, each animal and each of its parts is what it is in virtue of its figure and its color, what Democritus says will be correct. For that seems to be his view, if we understand him aright when he says that it is plain to everyone what "man" is like as touching his shape, for a man is known to be a man by his figure and his color. Now a corpse has the same fashion of figure as a living man, but it is still not a man. Again, a hand formed in any and every manner, out of bronze or wood, is not a hand except in name, and the same applies to a painted physician. It cannot perform the function appropriate to the thing that bears the same name, any more than a flute carved in stone can perform the function of a flute, or the painted physician perform the physician's art. Likewise the eye or the hand or any other part of a corpse is not really an eye or a hand. The statement of Democritus, therefore, needs to be qualified, or a carpenter might as well claim that a hand made of wood really is a hand.

The early writers on nature (*hoi physiologoi*), however, when they describe the generation and the causes of the figure of animal bodies, talk the same way. Suppose we ask the woodcarver, "By what agency (*hypo tinōn dynameōn*) was this hand fashioned?" Perhaps his answer will be, "By my axe," or "By my auger," just as if we ask the natural philosopher, "By what agent was this body generated?" he will answer, "By air," or "By earth." But of the two the craftsman will give the better answer, because he will not judge that it is enough to say merely that a cavity was made here, or a level surface there, by a blow from his tool. He will state the reason why (*dioti*) and that for which (*tinos heneka*) he made the strokes he did; and the answer will be, so that the wood might finally be formed into this or that shape.[14]

Aristotle sums up his functional theory:

Now, as each of the parts of the body is for something (*heneka tou*), just as every instrument or tool is for something, that is, for some action, it is evident that the body as a whole must be constituted for some complex action. Just as the sawing is not there for the sake of the saw, but the saw is for the sake of the sawing, because sawing is the using of the instrument, so in some way the body is for the sake of life (*hē psychē*), and the parts of the body for the sake of those functions for which they are naturally suited.[15]

[14] *De Partibus Animalium* I, ch. 1: 640b 30–641a 14.
[15] *De Partibus Animalium* I, ch. 5: 645b 15–20.

We must understand living organisms and their parts, therefore, in terms of how they act and operate as a whole, and how their component organs and tissues function and behave. It is just here that Aristotle introduces the other major "cause" that needs to be taken into account in the analysis of living processes, Necessity. Natural necessity relates the materials and parts of animals to their functioning: it designates the means that are necessary for the ends of natural processes. It is in this central relation of means to ends that Aristotle finds the necessity exhibited by natural things.

There are two kinds of cause; and in our treatise both must be set forth, or at least an attempt made to do so. It is clear that those who do not treat both tell us practically nothing about nature. For the nature of a thing is much more the *arché* for understanding it than its matter. . . .

We have then these two causes before us, the For What (*to hou heneka*) and the Necessary (*to ex anankēs*), for many things come into being because they are necessary. Perhaps one might ask which kind of necessity is meant by those who say that some things are necessary, since here it can be neither of the two kinds defined in the books *Kata Philosophian*. There is in things that are generated a third kind; as when we say that nourishment is necessary, we mean neither of these two kinds, but that without nourishment no animal can be. This is a kind of hypothetical necessity. For example, an axe in order to split wood must of necessity be hard; if it is to be hard, it must of necessity be made of bronze or of iron. Now the body like the axe is an instrument: each of its parts, and the body as a whole, is For Something. The body must therefore of necessity be such and such, and made of such and such components, if that function is to take place.[16]

Necessity is not present in all natural things to an equal extent. Almost all thinkers try to carry back their reasons to necessity; but they do not distinguish how many ways there are of saying "neces-

[16] *De Partibus Animalium* I, ch. 1: 642a 2–14.

sary." Simple necessity (*to haplōs*) belongs to eternal things; hypothetical necessity (*to ex hypotheseōs*) belongs to everything that comes to be by natural generation as well as to the products of art, such as houses and the like. If a house or any other end is to come to be, it is necessary that there be such and such material. One thing must be formed first, and set in motion, and then another, and in this order and this way up to the end which is that For Which each of these things comes to be and is. It is just the same with the things that come to be by nature.

However, the way of demonstration and of necessity is different in natural science (*hē physikē*) and in the theoretical sciences. In the theoretical sciences the beginning is with what already is (*to on*), in natural science it is with what is going to be. Thus because something like health, or a man, is of such and such a character, it is necessary for some particular thing to be or to come to be. It is not the case that because that particular thing is or has come to be, it is necessary for that other thing, health or a man, to be or to come to be.[17]

Note how Aristotle here sharply contrasts "physics" or natural science with the theoretical sciences. Normally, as in the beginning of the *Physics,* he classifies physics as itself one of the three theoretical sciences. But here in considering living organisms his sense of the process of generation and coming to be is so strong that he treats physics as a "productive science." He regards it as an *art,* the art of natural production, and concentrates on the relation between means and ends, the fundamental functional relation that is central also in human production, and its discoverable necessities. In "physical" science *physis* retains its root meaning of "growth": we might call it here "biology." Thus in biology Aristotle definitely subordinates the formal distinctions and relations of discourse to his functional distinctions and relations of living processes.

The central place of function and activity in Aristotle's scheme

---

[17] *De Partibus Animalium* I, ch. 1: 639b 21–640a 7.

of understanding can be perhaps most strikingly exhibited in a criticism he makes of Anaxagoras.

Since man stands upright, he has no need of legs in front; instead of them nature has given him arms and hands. Anaxagoras indeed asserts that it is his possession of hands that makes man the most intelligent of the animals. But surely it is reasonable that it is because he is the most intelligent animal that he has got hands. Hands are an instrument; and nature, like an intelligent man, always assigns an instrument to the animal that can use it; as it is more in keeping to give flutes to a man who is already a flute-player than to provide a man who possesses flutes with the skill to play them. Thus nature has provided that which is less as an addition to that which is greater and superior, and not the other way round. If, therefore, this way is better, and if nature always does the best among possible courses, it is not through possessing hands that man is the most intelligent animal, but it is because he is the most intelligent animal that he has hands. We should expect the most intelligent to be able to use the greatest number of instruments well. Now the hand would seem to be not one single instrument, but many, as it were an instrument that represents many. Thus it is to that animal which has the capacity for acquiring the greatest number of crafts that nature has given that instrument whose range of uses is the most extensive.[18]

It is very difficult for us not to approach a passage like this with our ingrained evolutionary attitude, and not to sympathize with Anaxagoras. But Aristotle is telling no story of any kind of creation, supernatural or evolutionary; he is supremely uninterested in how man got that way. Rather, we empirically encounter man as the most intelligent animal. In the light of that indisputable fact, we can understand the conditions that are necessary for that to be the case. The character of the existence of the parts of an organism is to be understood in the light of what they do, of what they make possible, living, and in the case of man, living well and intelligently.

[18] *De Partibus Animalium* IV, ch. 10: 687a 5–23.

Not all the parts of living things serve a function. "There are those parts which result necessarily because others are present." [19] There is a kind of brute necessity of matter, illustrated by the bile. In general, bile is a waste product, a residue, which is produced necessarily but itself performs no function. "Now and then nature does use residues advantageously; yet on account of this fact one ought not to seek a For What for all of them. But while some things serve a function, many others are present of necessity because of these things." [20] Aristotle's illustrations make clear the difference between this kind of necessity and hypothetical necessity. The latter always characterizes a relation of means to ends, of conditions "necessary for" some outcome: it signifies a teleological or functional relation. This other kind of necessity indicates the absence of function, and looks to the origin rather than the function of parts. Hence it may be called "material necessity."

4. The Generation of Animals

The third of the three major Aristotelian biological writings (unless we include the *De Anima* as a fourth), the *De Generatione Animalium,* treats of the parts concerned in generation and their functions, and of the general problems involved in reproduction. For Aristotle this is the most challenging problem of all; we have already seen how in his books on *Genesis and Destruction* it strained his analysis almost to the breaking point. Reproduction is the most fundamental of all biological phenomena. Aristotle's analysis is of slighter methodological and philosophical interest than his clear statement of his controlling functionalism in the *De Partibus Animalium.* But his positions on definite biological problems that have become central in modern times interest the biologist, and give a concrete content to his approach. In dis-

---

[19] *De Partibus Animalium* I, ch. 5: 645b 32.
[20] *De Partibus Animalium* IV, ch. 2: 677a 16–19.

cussing these problems Aristotle now works out a precise meaning for his cardinal distinction between powers and their operation, between potentiality and actuality.

Aristotle divides the general problem of development into the two problems of the genesis or beginning of development, and the subsequent growth or course of development. As to the first, Aristotle holds that the semen or *sperma* comes from both the male and the female, and hence the contributions of both are *archai* of generation. Democritus, Empedocles, and Anaxagoras had all held that the semen comes from the whole body. Aristotle finds insoluble objections to this view. He maintains that instead of coming from the whole body, the semen *goes to* the whole body of the offspring. Each parent supplies a different factor. The material of the embryo and of its growth comes from the female; the activation of this material and the form it will acquire are derived from the male. For the female does not produce unless impregnated by the male. Just as the carpenter and his tools do not become a part of the material fashioned, so the semen does not become a part of the female secretion. Again, as the form of the product comes to be in the wood by means of the carpenter's art and his tools, so the form of the offspring comes to be in the female secretion by means of the semen, which nature uses as a tool, much like a sculptor's chisel. Thus the process of generation begins when the female secretion is activated by the male, and in this genesis of a new animate being the materials are supplied by the female, while the power and character of development are derived from the male.

On the problem of the course of development, Aristotle holds to the view of epigenesis rather than preformation. Sex is determined at the time of conception, but the various parts of the embryo develop in succession: originally undifferentiated, the embryo becomes differentiated in the course of its development. Thus the lungs develop after the heart. Growth or development exhibits a serial order. Materials are transformed in accordance with a definite temporal order of succession, until in the end the new organism becomes like the parent. This order is unintelligible without the notion of powers coming into operation, of the emergence of actuality out of potentiality. This distinction points to the conditions of development; materials must have the power of being transformed into something other than what they in fact are at any time, and these possibilities of the materials must be activated and set in operation by something actual. "Matter" is necessary for generation, but the notion in itself has no reference to the possibilities inherent in it: in Empedocles and Democritus there is nothing to account for the successive and transformative character of natural growth, and all such observed development is attributed to "chance." "Matter" must be regarded as potentially what it can grow into, if we are to understand the serial regularity of the pattern of embryonic development. "We must take first of all as our starting point this *arché;* whatever comes into being either by nature or by art, comes into being by means of something which *is* actually, out of something which *is* potentially of that character." [21] What exists actually at first is the adult male, which produces the semen. The generator sets the semen in motion, and imparts to it an *arché* and *logos,* which are in turn transmitted to the female secretion, and become its *arché* and form. The reason for the characteristic order of development is this form or *logos* which comes from the parent: each part derives its traits from this *logos* transmitted in the semen. Thus the organization of the parts of the hand, or of the whole body, comes from the preexisting organization in the parents; that organization is potentially in the *logos* transmitted by the semen. Aristotle rejects the view that particles from all the organs somehow collect in the male and female secretions, and grow into the adult by simple accretion of material. This would deny or leave unintelligible both the fact of successive development, and the fact of the transformation of materials.

[21] *De Generatione Animalium* II, ch. 1: 734b 20–22.

Aristotle holds a recapitulation theory of embryonic development. The most general character is formed before the more specific ones. Thus, in viviparous animals, the heart appears first. The heart is the origin and *arche* of growth, which is the first activity and the very being of the embryo. The heart is also the source of the regulation and orderly differentiation of the simple and complex parts, hence it must develop first. For Aristotle the heart is also the seat of sensing, and since it is sensing that distinguishes the animal from the plant, this organ must take form first. Hence Democritus was in error in saying that the external parts take form first, and the internal ones later.

The efficient cause of this process is heat, but heat or cold alone will no more suffice to make a hand than to make an axe.

Heat does not make flesh or bone from anything whatever nor in any chance way; but from what is naturally fitted, when and where it is naturally fitted. For that which is potential will not come into existence by means of that which can move but is not active, nor will that which is active produce from any chance thing, just as a carpenter would not make a box except out of wood, nor without the carpenter will the box come from the wood.[22]

The fifth and last book of the *De Generatione Animalium* deals with those secondary characteristics of animals that are due not to any final cause, but to necessity alone, that is, to material and efficient causes. These are the traits that have no discoverable function. Now, some traits are characteristic of an entire species of animal, others occur at random. Those products of growth which are characteristic of all animals, or of all of a species, have come to be "for something," they serve a function. Thus the existence and the formation of an eye is For Something, but its being blue is not, unless this is proper to that particular species. The color of eyes has no function, and comes into being as a result of their material composition, and of the presence of other

[22] *De Generatione Animalium* II, ch. 6: 743a 21–26.

parts; it contributes nothing to the maintenance of the life of the organism.

There is no need to go here into the details of Aristotle's account, nor to single out those aspects of his theory which have more or less close counterparts in our own biological theory, like his view of homologous organs, for example, or his general classifications. The aim here has been to exhibit how completely Aristotle's functional concepts and scheme of understanding are exhibited in his biological investigations, and how he finds all his most characteristic distinctions and emphases growing naturally out of the intellectual demands of the subject matter of living processes. Whatever may be the case in other fields, in biology the Aristotelian functionalism is not artificially imposed from without, in the interests of some systematic unity.

As a scientist, Aristotle is clearly at his best where organization and function count most, in biology and psychology, just as he is notoriously at his worst where they count least, in astronomy and cosmology. Yet it is well to remember that he is a rather better philosopher of mathematics than Plato. And today, of course, our own electrical world is forcing physicists to turn to organic and functional concepts like those of Aristotle in physics also. But since his scheme of understanding applies to life, and may well have been elaborated during his investigation of living processes, it will be illuminating to see how he fits human living into his general pattern. For in human conduct and in human art means and ends and their relation are of transcendent importance.

Chapter XII

THE PRACTICAL SCIENCES:

KNOWING HOW TO CHOOSE

RELATIVE GOODS

1. The Aristotelian Method and Concepts in Practical Affairs

Aristotle's thought is primarily functional and biological: it aims above all to understand life. His whole philosophy is built around the categories of life. And his thought is teleological: life is to be understood, not in terms of its elements and origins alone, but in terms of its ends. Hence we should expect Aristotle's treatment of human life to be the most illuminating part of his philosophy. And this is indeed true. His ethics and politics are actually his supreme achievement. But they can be so regarded only if they are rightly understood. For of all the Aristotelian writings, the architectonic science of conduct, in men and in cities, is the most difficult part of Aristotle's thought to understand. That is because in this analysis Aristotle is most limited by the materials he is working with, the materials furnished by Greek culture, Greek mores, and Greek institutions. In this analysis, it is most difficult to disentangle the essential Aristotelian method and concepts from the specific subject matter of Greek culture and values. We are hence tempted to judge the *Ethics* and the *Politics* in the light of Aristotle's conclusions, instead of viewing them in the light of his starting point, his *archai*. We are not so tempted in the *Physics,* for example, where we normally expect the conclusions to be primarily of historical significance.

In consequence, the *Ethics* and the *Politics* have never been Aristotle's most popular books, save during those few periods to which he seemed to be describing a cultural situation like that with which the readers were themselves familiar, and hence to be suggesting an appropriate program: during the Renaissance in Italy, and during the late nineteenth century, that period of "liberalism" from which we are ourselves just emerging.

Even today, when the *Ethics* still appeals to us as refreshing and liberating after our own long struggle to emancipate ourselves from the limitations of our own recent moral tradition, it is apt to seem disappointing on first reading. Is that all? we ask. Where is the fire, the enthusiasm, the compelling force, the *erōs* of Plato? We find ourselves in a position to appreciate today the Greek view of life as an art, an achievement to be attained by intelligence and skill. But we are drawn to that approach to the moral life, away from our centuries of legalistic and Puritan morality, even from our own recent debauch of Romantic self-expression, by Plato's enthusiasm for the art of life. Aristotle has no enthusiasm, no *erōs;* he exhibits only sober sanity and wisdom. And sanity and wisdom seem the last things in the world to which our Age of Anxiety can be driven.

There is a certain attitude in practical affairs, a certain "Aristotelian" approach and temper in dealing with conduct, which forms a great contrast to the "Platonic" attitude toward practice, the "Platonism" in conduct and social life we find critically but very sympathetically portrayed in the dialogues. This Aristotelian attitude and approach are not indeed opposed to that Platonic temper: they rather supplement it. Now, this Aristotelian attitude is the most characteristic, and probably the most valuable element in Aristotle's practical philosophy. But without considerable experience it is very difficult to feel and appreciate it. Readers are usually first fascinated with the

Scholastic Aristotle: they get hold of the logical side of his thought, rather than of his functional foundation for all the statements of logic. They miss entirely the fact that Aristotle is not a system, but a spirit, a method, an intellectual technique. They find in Aristotle another possible world. But they miss the primary and controlling Aristotelian conviction, that we must understand the actual world, the world we discover and must work with. They find the dialectic, but they miss the wisdom of experience, the sheer empiricism of Aristotle, the sheer acceptance of brute facts as given, as the only possible starting point for our thought and action. They fail to discover Aristotle's basic conviction that wisdom is learning how to deal, not with what might be, but with what is.

And so the Schoolmen, and the modern bright young undergraduates, find in Aristotle intellectual imagination, intelligibility, the answer to all the questions, a gorgeous rationalization of the world. But they find it much harder to feel the obstinacy of matter, the importance of fact, the sheer thereness of what is, the weight of existence, of life itself, of the rich world in which we find ourselves placed, the weight of existing institutions and opinions, making sport of all our neat little systems and theories, all our abstract scientific schemes, and our confident programs of reform and revolution. In Aristotle's own terms, they have plenty of "intellect," of *nous,* but they do not have enough "sense."

Now, as contrasted with earlier modern scientists, with the age of Newtonian thought, Aristotle has a wealth of intellectual imagination, of *nous.* He himself got it from Plato, and we do indeed need it ourselves. It is our science today that seems to display far more of such intellectual imagination than our philosophizing. But Aristotle's whole life, as the scholars have now reconstructed it for us, was the realization that intellectual imagination, having plenty of brilliant ideas, is not enough. We need sense also, the humility in the face of encountered facts.

That is indeed the trouble with what Aristotle calls, somewhat condescendingly, the *dialektikos* and the *logikos*—the "intellectual," in our language. He has ideas galore, but very little sense.

And so, as an attitude in practical affairs, "Aristotelianism" does not mean dialectic, discussion, vision alone—though that is what the medieval religious traditions found in Aristotle, and that is what nearly all those willing to call themselves Aristotelians today have learned from him. "Aristotelianism" in practice means the wisdom of experience, the acceptance of encountered facts, the investigation of what is given to us.

Like all the great Knowers, Aristotle is interested, not in the radical remolding of life, in what might be, but in understanding life as it is and will be. He is concerned to see man's life in the world, and to explain it, not to change it into something else. So we find him saying, in the *Ethics,* "It is proper to state the accepted views on the subject, and after thoroughly discussing them, to establish the truth of all, or at least the most important of the popular opinions." [1] This surprises us, for we are not accustomed to thinking of ethics as concerned with understanding what is, what men do and say, and why they are right in doing and saying it. When we do look for facts in moral experience, it is to show how they conflict with the "accepted views," and not, like Aristotle, to show how they confirm and justify them. When we find him accepting as facts the moral judgments he finds prevailing, and giving them a rational interpretation and defense, this strikes us as a mere "rationalization," as we put it—as though Aristotle ought to be proving that established standards are really all wrong, and need "reconstruction," or "transvaluation"; as though he ought to have been a John Dewey, or a Nietzsche, or a Felix Adler, a critic of traditional morality.

The Aristotelian attitude toward the problems of human con-

[1] *Nicomach. Ethics* VII, ch. 1: 1145b 3–6.

duct may be stated quite simply. The life of man is the life of an animal both "political" and "rational"—an animal who lives in a city, a *polis,* and who is endowed with *nous* and *logos* —in our modern terms, an animal both "gregarious" and "intelligent." The practical sciences of politics and ethics aim to discover the end or function of such a social and rational animal, and to calculate the means to achieve that end. The best life is the life of the most complete operation of all the powers of such an animal: it is the life of a social animal lived on a rational level. Intelligence is capable of perfecting animal life into the "life of reason" or *nous.* The natural materials of living —impulses, desires, the accepted customs and ideals—and the inherited social institutions of living—the family, slavery, the city-state and its political organization—can all be made excellent by intelligence.

It is to be noted carefully, that the materials Aristotle starts with are the materials he finds at hand, the materials of Greek culture and civilization. This is obvious in the *Politics,* where he starts from a slave economy, from the Greek form of the family, from the Greek status of women, from the Greek city-state political organization. But it is equally true in the *Ethics,* where he begins with the norms, standards, and ideals of Greek culture and Greek tradition—moderation, self-control, intelligence, justice and right.

The very core of the Aristotelian attitude toward the conduct of man's life is this insistence that we must start with what we find at hand, and perfect the tendencies that are actually there. We must set out with our own particular cultural heritage. In comparison with Plato—with the Plato of the dramatic dialogues, the Plato of the *Republic*—this gives the impression of a much more limited horizon. There is in Aristotle none of the free play of the imagination to be found in the *Republic,* there is no talk of "remolding human nature" in the light of a more perfect model than that used by God in creating man. There is a sense of the limits imposed by the encountered facts of experience, and of a bondage to them.

Now, such a statement of course suggests what is the most important point of all in the understanding of Aristotle's practical philosophy. "Aristotelianism" is a method that can be applied to *any* social and cultural materials, to *any* set of institutions and standards, to *any* cultural heritage. It can be applied to Soviet Russia, to medieval Christendom, to India, to New York City. In each case the results will be quite different from Aristotle's own application of his method to the materials presented by Greek culture. The fundamental fact about this "Aristotelianism" is that it is a method that can be generalized.

Thus it is certain that were Aristotle to write today an *Ethics* and a *Politics* for contemporary Americans, he would not elevate knowing above practical action, he would not find the "life of *theōria*" superior to the "life of *praxis*," and take it as most divine. He would do this no more than he would try to perfect the city-state as a form of government, or try to prescribe for an economy in which there is no "market," or develop a distinctive and subordinate type of excellence for American women.

The particular Aristotelian excellences or "virtues" are of course the values, the norms or ideals of Greek culture, just as are the particular social institutions Aristotle discusses in the *Politics*. And neither these particular values which Aristotle defends, nor the particular conclusions about social institutions with which he comes out in his analysis, are the central or the really important thing in Aristotle's practical philosophy. It is undoubtedly true that the Aristotelian ethics is the ethic of an upper class in a slave society—in its conclusions. When we have made this rather facile observation, however, we must also remember that it is the ethic of a functioning upper class, and not of a "leisure class," in the Veblenian sense. In the fourth century the Greek upper class had not yet degenerated and lost its social function, as happened in later Hellenistic and Roman times. And we must remember also that in Attica slaves were always in a minority: their total number was about 106,000 out of a population estimated roughly at some 260,000 in 323 B.C.[2]

But in a deeper sense, the Aristotelian ethics is in its conclusions the ethics of the detached intellectual—it expresses the values of Aristotle himself. And the conflict that is never clearly resolved by Aristotle between the life of practice and the life of *theōria,* is ultimately the conflict between what Aristotle observed about him in Greek life, and what he himself was—between the values of the Athenian citizen, and the values of Aristotle the Knower. The excellences he describes on the basis of his observation are the rather individualistic ideals and values Athenian citizens actually cherished, not the more socialized and functional ideals and values they sometimes, with an eye on Sparta, thought they ought to cherish. It has even been suggested, with some plausibility, that Aristotle's "high-minded man" is actually the intellectual's satire of the practical man of affairs and politician.

In any event, these excellences described by Aristotle are obviously not the socialized ideals and values possible and necessary in our own world today. It is hardly enough to say, let us abolish our form of slavery—perhaps, as Aristotle suggests, through automation—and then let all men live like Athenian citizens, then let us set up a whole society of "high-minded men." This is to confuse Aristotle's conclusions, inescapably rooted in the facts of his own Greek culture, and necessarily alien to our quite different way of life, with his starting point, his *archai,* with his method and his concepts.

When Aristotle is himself speaking of the excellences that *ought* to be cherished, he is speaking for the detached and irresponsible intellectual, not for the socialized expert. That is why his ethics has always been so beloved of intellectuals,

[2] See the estimate of A. W. Gomme in the *Oxford Classical Dictionary* (chart, p. 718).

so appealing to the medieval teachers, and to the whole tradition
of liberal, humane education growing out of the Renaissance,
a tradition for which, for better or for worse, there seems to be
little place in our own socialized world.

To understand Aristotle's practical philosophy, it is extremely
important to recognize the inevitable limitations of Aristotle's
own *conclusions.* For only by so doing can we disentangle his
method, and apply it to our own cultural heritage. The failure
to effect this disentanglement marks many attracted by the
Aristotelian humanism. They assume that "man," and "human
nature," remain always and everywhere the same—that Aristotle's
definition of "human nature" is really definitive. Hence the same
Aristotelian method, when applied to the natural and social
materials of this unchanging "human nature," will always lead
to the same Aristotelian conclusions about ethics. These conclusions are eternally valid, and can hence be identified, as St.
Thomas identified them, with the Stoic "natural law."

Such supporters of the universal validity of Aristotle's conclusions in ethics and politics have not yet learned the facts of
life—of man's social and cultural life—as the historian and the
anthropologist know them today. There is indeed a "unity of
all mankind." But it is scarcely so easily won.

2. *Aristotle's Application of His Method*
to Greek Culture

In the practical science of conduct, or *praxis,* the *archē* is the
good at which conduct aims. This good is something done, not
for the sake of something else, but for its own sake. This best
of goods will be the object of the ruling science, the supreme art,
political science. For though the good is the same for the individual citizen and for his city or *polis,* the good of the *polis*
is obviously greater and more perfect and complete, and to
secure it is nobler and more divine.

Now, the highest of all goods at which conduct can aim, all men agree, is the Good Life, or Acting Well, *eu praxein:* it is *eudaimonia,* that is, "well-being" or "welfare." The end of conduct is human welfare. So that human welfare is the one and only *arché* of ethics and politics, the one "principle" in terms of which all conduct is to be understood and judged. Any other ideal—any "transcendent" ideal, like the "idea of the Good" of the Platonists, any ideal that is "apart," *chōristos,* and unrelated, *haplōs,* not relative to the conditions of human living, is quite irrelevant to ethics and politics. For such a good would not be practicable or attainable by men, and ethics and politics deal with an attainable good, not with empty abstractions such as the Platonists love. An unattainable or "absolute" ideal, Aristotle points out, is not even of any value as a criterion or standard for judging the goods that men can obtain. For no science and no art ever uses such "transcendent" standards. The physician does not study "health" in the abstract, unrelated to his particular patient; his concern is always how to make this man here healthy. Just so, ethics does not seek "the Good in itself," *auto to agathon,* but how this man here can act well in this situation.

Now each kind of living thing has its own good, relative to its own specific nature. There is thus one good for fish, and another good for birds, and still another for men. And the specific good of men, say, is likewise always "relative"—relative to the particular man facing his particular problems, choices, and situations. There is no good common to all living beings: the good of fish is not the good of birds, and neither is or could be the good of men. Likewise, there is no human good that is or could be common to all men on all occasions—save that of always acting intelligently. What is good is always something plural, specific, and relative to a particular situation or context.

The goods of different kinds of being differ, just as do the goods of different men and of different human situations. Each of these goods is determined by, or "relative to," the specific context or situation, so that no uniform generalization about human goods is possible. There is to be found in the practical science of ethics no invariable structure that is true "always or for the most part," as is the case in the theoretical sciences, and is indeed the defining mark of those inquiries.

But this does not mean for Aristotle that the good of any particular situation is "subjective," or "personal," or dependent on the mere "feelings" of the participants in the situation. It does not at all mean that statements about the several goods of different situations are not objectively determinable and discoverable, that such statements are not "scientific," but are merely "emotive," expressing the subjective "feelings" of men, or expressing their "existential commitments." Each situation has a good which intelligent inquiry can hope to discover. Aristotle is in ethics a complete and thoroughgoing relativist—an objective relativist, in our present-day classifications.

This objective relativism of Aristotle's is clearly a reaction on his part against the claim of the Platonists—and if our recent scholarship is sound, of the later Plato himself—that we can acquire a theoretical science of the Good that will hold for all cases, and will be like mathematics, so much so, indeed, that it can be expressed in mathematical terms, as is supposed to have been set forth in Plato's famous "Lecture on the Good." This is the view that has been at times defended in modern philosophy, that the methods of physics can determine questions of value. This claim of the Platonists, which seems to have been maintained by Speusippos and Xenocrates in the Academy, seemed as absurd to Aristotle as does its counterpart to anybody today —to both positivists and idealists, who for quite different reasons summarily reject it. In opposition to this view that the science of conduct is like mathematics, Aristotle holds that deliberation about the good—in our language, inquiry into "questions of value"—is not a theoretical science like mathematics or physics, but is what we should call an "applied science," and what he himself distinguishes as an "art," like medicine or architecture or engineering. Ethics is an art which applies scientific knowledge to the needs of particular cases. As a physician, Aristotle treats ethics, not, like the Platonists, as a science like geometry, but as an art like medicine, which is concerned with the health of the soul—a rather modern conception. In this position, he is of course returning from the later Plato to Socrates, who recognized real knowledge only in the craftsman, the cobbler, the navigator, and the rest, and in his long search was seeking a craft of living well.

Now, to find what characteristics any human good must possess—that is, to find what "human welfare" must mean, concretely—we must ask, What is man's distinctive function? What is the distinctive activity of man's specific "nature"? What is distinctive about man is the possession of *logos,* discourse and reason: it is man's talking and thinking that set him apart from the other animals. And hence man's specific function is the operation of all his powers and capacities in accordance with *logos;* that is, it is to act intelligently. The good man is the man who performs this distinctive human function *eu kai kalōs,* "well and beautifully"; he is the man who acts most intelligently. Any function is well performed when it is performed in accordance with its own proper excellence or "virtue." Hence the good of man—human welfare—is the functioning of man's various powers under the guidance of intelligence, and in accordance with their own proper and respective excellence or "virtue."

These individual excellences or *aretai* demand conditions: length of life, riches, a proper society to function in. Social organization, the *polis,* provides the means of training in these individual excellences, and it also furnishes the field in which they can operate: it provides the materials and conditions for training in, and for the exercise of, the good life. Ethics and politics are hence two aspects of the same "architectonic" science. The excellences or *aretai* of the individual are formed in the *polis*, in society, and they can function only in the *polis*. In the individual citizen, they can be considered as *hexeis* or "habits," as powers possessed by the individual. A "habit" or *hexis* for Aristotle is a kind of "second nature," an acquired power: like human "nature" itself, a habit is a determinate power to act in a specific way.

Hence "society," the *polis*, exists "by nature," *physei;* and man is "by nature" a social animal, *a zōon politikon,* an animal who lives in a *polis*. That man who is "by nature" solitary and un-social, who is *apolis*, is either a beast or a god. The "reason why" man lives in a *polis, to dioti*, is that alone of all animals man possesses *logos,* the power of speech. It is significant that the same *logos* that makes man a "rational animal" in its sense of "reason," also, in its sense of discourse and language, makes him a "political" or social animal. For speech serves to indicate the advantageous and the harmful, and hence also the right and the wrong. Through speech it is man alone who has a sense of good and bad, of right and wrong. And it is partnership in these things that makes every human association, from the family to the *polis*.

Hence the *polis,* or "society," is "prior in nature" to each of us. For all things are to be defined by their powers and functions. And the individual man displays and exercises his powers and functions only in the *polis*. That is, society is "prior" in under-standing any particular man.

Now the *polis* comes into being for the sake of living, *tou zēn heneken:* the end or final cause of its "genesis" is to provide the conditions necessary for any existence that will be human. But the *polis* continues to exist for the sake of living well, *tou eu zēn heneken*. Its continuing function is to serve human welfare or *eudaimonia*. As the supreme partnership or *koinōnia,* which includes all the other lesser partnerships, it serves the most supreme of all human goods, human welfare. It provides not only the essential conditions necessary for men's existence as men: defense, trade and exchanging goods. These functions, necessary as they are, are not enough to constitute a genuine *polis,* a *polis* that has become all that a *polis* has the power to become, and like the perfected oak tree has come to realize its true form, has come to put into operation the very "nature" of a *polis.* To do that, a *polis* must provide all the conditions that are necessary for human welfare, for acting well—that is, for the proper functioning of the various human excellences or *aretai.*

Such a *polis* must exist for the sake, not merely of common living, but for the sake as well of "worthy and beautiful actions," *tōn kalōn praxeōn heneken.* A true *polis* is one that has achieved its entelechy, that is, that has actually become a partnership in a perfected and complete life, and hence in living well and beautifully, *to zēn eudaimonōs kai kalōs.* The best *polis* is the one that best fosters all human excellences, all conduct in accord with moral excellence and intelligence.

This is the way Aristotle carries his functionalism into human affairs, and applies his categories of process to ethics and politics. Aristotle thus stands for the omnicompetence of the state. There is nothing that political government must refrain from doing, if it makes for human welfare. Aristotle thus quite literally is stating the theory of the "welfare state." In his view he stands at the opposite pole from Hobbes, for whom the sole and unique common good to which the commonwealth must devote itself is the preservation of social peace, among men who are by nature asocial.

It is significant and ironical that both these poles as to the function of government have possible totalitarian implications. For neither Aristotle nor Hobbes recognizes anything in the nature of an independent "spiritual" power standing outside the control of the state, like the Church, or like the University, which might well join the churches today as an independent spiritual power, to safeguard us from the perils of creeping totalitarianism. Aristotle thus states the theory of the rights and duties of the citizen of some particular state. No proclamation of the rights and duties of man, quite in independence of his *polis,* was made in Greece till the appearance of the Stoics, though the Cynics had come close to it. The two theories have often collided, though the French Revolution tried to combine them both in its Declaration of the Rights of Man and of the Citizen. In American history the classic collision was occasioned by the Dred Scott decision.

3. The Science of Politics: Aristotle's Empirical and Functional Naturalism

Aristotle's *Ethics* is a practical science that approaches very closely to an art, and is clearly modeled on the physician's art of diagnosis and healing. The practical science of politics, in building up the conception of a perfected welfare state, continues this concern with an ethical art for fostering an "arrangement of citizens" or a mode of life which shall direct the external organization of the *polis* toward establishing such conditions as will best promote the moral excellence and training of the citizens.

But a large part of the *Politics* (Books IV, V, and VI in the traditional numbering) sets forth a conception of political science which is much less in the spirit of the moral physician of the soul, and much more in the spirit of the *physikos,* the natural philosopher observing and analyzing nature's way with human governments, the natural processes of the generation and the destruction of organized human societies. And it is in this spirit that the historical account of Athenian constitutional history in *The Constitution of Athens* is set down.

The *Ethics* is written not only in the temper of the moral

artist; it is close to the spirit of the *logikos* in its long and detailed analysis of ethical language and terms. This brings it near to the treatment of the language of ethics as practiced in present-day Oxford Wittgensteinian elucidation of language; and in fact the careful study of the *Ethics* by Oxford classicists seems to have exerted great influence on their present moral philosophy. The contrast is great between this temper displayed in the *Ethics* and in parts of the *Politics,* and the empirical and functional naturalism of other portions of the *Politics,* in which Aristotle accepts with extraordinary detachment and resignation the political process as Greek history had exhibited it. In modern scholarship it has led to repeated efforts to rearrange the traditional order of the several books of the *Politics.* And since Jaeger it has seemed to point to a cardinal case where tracing a chronological development in Aristotle's thought, away from Plato to a biological empiricism, would illuminate the encountered discrepancies.

It has long been recognized that our text of the *Politics* seems to have been put together from several different bodies of manuscript, either by Aristotle himself, by his school, or by later editors.[3] On the hypothesis advanced by Jaeger, and endorsed by Sabine,[4] the text belongs to two different stages of Aristotle's intellectual development. There is first an earlier treatment of the ideal state and theories about it, in Books II, III, VII, and VIII. This Jaeger assigns to a time not long after Aristotle's first departure from Athens. There is secondly a treatment of actual Greek cities, the causes of their decay, and the best means of giving them stability, in Books IV, V, and VI. This realistic study was clearly carried out on the basis of the

[3] Sir Ernest Barker, in his *Political Thought of Plato and Aristotle* (London, 1906), p. 259, held: "There are three sets of lectures, on distinct subjects, in distinct styles." Sir David Ross, in his *Aristotle* (Oxford, 1924), p. 236, said: "The work is a conflation of five separate treatises."

[4] Werner Jaeger, *Aristoteles* (Berlin, 1923), pp. 237–70; tr. Richard Robinson (1934), ch. 10. George H. Sabine, *A History of Political Theory* (New York, 1937), pp. 90–92.

collection Aristotle made of the constitutional history of one
hundred fifty-eight Greek cities, of which one, *The Constitution
of Athens,* presumed to be by Aristotle himself, was discovered
in 1890. These studies were primarily historical and empirical
in character; with them as a basis, after his opening of the
Lyceum, Aristotle undertook a theoretical analysis of political
structures and functions, and inserted it in the middle of the
original draft. Then, Jaeger suggests, he wrote the present Book
I as a general introduction to the whole work, but never completed the required harmonizing of the different parts.[5]

Sabine sums up as follows this view of Jaeger's. Aristotle began
by seeking to construct an ideal state on the lines laid down in
the *Statesman* and the *Laws;* he conceived political science in
ethical terms, and the end of the *polis* was to produce the morally
highest type of man.

At some date not far removed from the opening of the Lyceum, however, he conceived a science or art of politics on a much larger scale.
The new science was to be general; that is, it should deal with actual
as well as ideal forms of government and it should teach the art of
governing and organizing states of any sort in any desired manner.
The new general science of politics, therefore, was not only empirical
and descriptive, but even in some respects independent of any ethical

[5] But Sir Ernest Barker, in his translation of *The Politics of Aristotle* (Oxford,
1946), pp. xlii-xlvi, writes: "The present writer was at one time attracted to the
view that the *Politics* contained different chronological strata. . . . But five years
spent in the constant company of the *Politics* during the preparation of this
translation have irresistibly compelled him to change his views." Barker has become convinced, "It is certain that the results obtained by one disciple of the
[genetic] method contradict, and contradict flatly, the results attained by another.
The fact is that the use of the genetic method is vitiated by subjectivity." Thus
von Arnim concluded that Books VII and VIII on the ideal state are the latest
part of the *Politics,* and exhibit Aristotle's furthest departure from the tradition
of Plato. Barker concludes: "We can abandon the attempt to apply a genetic
method to the composition and structure of the *Politics,* and we can renounce
the search for chronological strata. . . . We can adopt the view that the six
'methods' of the *Politics* all belong to the period of the Lyceum, and are all—so
far as chronology goes—on exactly the same footing. There is really no valid
reason why we should adopt any other view."

purpose, since a statesman might need to be expert in governing even a bad state. . . .

The complete art of the statesman must take governments as they are and do the best it can with the means it has. It might even divorce itself from moral considerations altogether and tell the tyrant how to succeed in tyranny, as Aristotle actually does later.[6]

The more completely Aristotle approached the attitude of the *physikos,* the natural philosopher of politics, the nearer he came to the similar attitude of Machiavelli.

However it may stand with the chronological order of our text —and like Barker, the present author is skeptical of the too neat hypothesis of Jaeger—it is true that in Books I, IV, V, and VI Aristotle does state an aim for political science significantly different from the ethical attitude of Socrates and Plato. He there is clearly applying his general biological and functional naturalism to the life of Greek cities.

It is clear that in the case of the constitution . . . it is the business of the same science to study which is the best constitution and what character it must have to be the most ideal if no external circumstance stands in the way; and what constitution is adapted to what people, since for many it is doubtless impossible to attain the best one. So that the good lawgiver and the true statesman must be acquainted with both the form of constitution that is best of all, and also with what is best under actual conditions. Thirdly, he must also consider the sort of constitution that depends upon an assumption: he must be able to study a given constitution, with a view to explaining how it may have arisen, and, taking it as it stands, in what way it may be preserved for the longest time. I mean for example where a city has neither the ideally best constitution, or even the elementary conditions needed for it, nor the best constitution possible under the actual conditions, but has only a constitution of an inferior type. And beside all these matters, he must ascertain the form of constitution best suited to states in general; most of those who write about the constitution,

[6] George H. Sabine, *History of Political Theory,* pp. 91, 106.

even if the rest of what they say is good, fail when they come to deal with matters of practical utility.

For it is proper to consider not only the ideally best constitution, but also what is the one possible of achievement; and likewise, what is the one easiest to work, and most suitable to cities generally. . . .

The proper course is to bring forward an organization which men can be easily persuaded, and will be readily able, to graft onto the one they already have. For it is no less a task to reform an old constitution than to frame a new one from the beginning, as hard to unlearn a lesson as it was to learn it originally. In addition, therefore, the student of politics must also be able to improve any existing constitution.

Hence he must take in view the different varieties of the several kinds of constitutions, and know how many there are and how many are their combinations. And after this it needs this same discrimination also to distinguish the laws that are best of all from those that are appropriate to each of the forms of constitution. For laws ought to be made to suit the particular constitution, as indeed in practice they always are, and not constitutions made to suit laws. . . . If we assume that there is not one single form of democracy, or one single form of oligarchy, but a number of varieties of both, the same laws cannot possibly be beneficial equally for all oligarchies or all democracies.[7]

In addition to distinguishing the laws from the political structure of a city, Aristotle also adds a class analysis, as throwing light on the different possible combinations reflected in actual constitutions.

Cities too, as we have repeatedly noticed, are composed not of one but of many parts. One of these parts is the group of persons concerned with the production of food, or, as it is called, the farming class. A second, which is called the mechanical class, is the group of persons occupied in the various arts and crafts without which a city cannot be inhabited—some of them being necessities, and others contributing to luxury or to the living of a good life. A third part is what

---

[7] *Politics* IV, ch. 1: 1288b 22–1289a 25.

may be termed the marketing class; it includes all those who are occupied in buying and selling, either as merchants or as retailers. A fourth part is the serf class composed of agricultural labourers; and a fifth element is the defence force, which is no less necessary than the other four, if a city is not to become the slave of invaders. . . . The four original parts . . . will require some authority to dispense justice, and to determine what is just. If the mind is to be reckoned as more essentially a part of a living being than the body, parts of a similar order to mind must equally be reckoned as more essentially parts of the city than those which serve its bodily needs. And by parts of a similar order to mind we mean the military part, the part concerned in the legal organization of justice, and, we may also add, the part engaged in deliberation, which is a function that needs the gift of political understanding. . . . The seventh part is the group composed of the rich, who serve the city with their property. The eighth part is the magistrates, who serve the city in its offices. No city can exist without a government; and there must therefore be persons capable of discharging the duties of office and rendering the city that service, permanently or in rotation. There only remain the two parts which have just been mentioned in passing—the deliberative part, and the part which decides on the rights of litigants. These are parts which ought to exist in all cities, and to exist on a good and just basis; and this demands persons of a good quality in matters political.

The different capacities belonging to the other parts may, it is generally held, be shown by one and the same group of persons. The same persons, for example, may serve as soldiers, farmers, and craftsmen; the same persons, again, may act both as a deliberative council and as a judicial court. Political ability, too, is a quality to which all men pretend; and everybody thinks himself capable of filling most offices. There is one thing which is impossible: the same persons cannot be both rich and poor. This will explain why these two classes —the rich and the poor—are regarded as parts of the city in a special and peculiar sense. Nor is this all. One of these classes being small, and the other large, they also appear to be opposite parts. This is why they both form constitutions to suit their own interests. It is also the reason why men think that there are only two constitutions —democracy and oligarchy.[8]

It is against such a pluralistic and empirical background that Aristotle undertakes to explain the natural processes by which cities come into being, and the equally natural processes by which their forms of government are overthrown by revolution and *stasis,* or "sedition."

In this subject as in others the best method of investigation is to study things in the process of their growth from the beginning. The first coupling together of persons then to which necessity gives rise is that between those who are unable to exist without one another. Such is the union of female and male for the sake of begetting off-spring, and this not out of forethought (*proairesis*) but with man as with the other animals and with plants there is a natural instinct to desire to leave behind one another being of the same sort as oneself. And such is also the union of natural ruler and natural subject for the sake of security; for he that can foresee with his mind is naturally ruler and naturally master, and he that can carry out these things with his body is a subject and naturally a slave. So that master and slave have the same interest. . . . The partnership (*koinōnia*) that comes about in accordance with nature (*kata physin*) for the satisfaction of daily needs is the household (*oikos*). . . .

The partnership made up of several households for the satisfaction of something more than daily needs is the village (*kōmē*). . . . The partnership finally composed of several villages is the *polis;* it has at last attained the limit of virtually complete self-sufficiency (*autarkeia*), and thus, while it comes into existence for the sake of life, continues to exist for living well. Hence every *polis* exists by nature, since the first partnerships so exist; for the *polis* is the end of the other partner-ships, and nature is an end, since that which each thing is when its growth is completed we speak of as being the nature of each thing, for instance of a man, a horse, a household. Again, the object for which a thing exists, its end, is its chief good; and self-sufficiency (*autarkeia*) is an end and a chief good. From these things therefore

[8] *Politics* IV, ch. 3: 1290b 38–1291b 14.

it is clear that the *polis* belongs to the things that are by nature (*tōn physei hē polis esti*), and that man is by nature a political animal (*politikon zōon*).[9]

Aristotle distinguishes five main varieties of democracy, and four of oligarchy, the two chief principles of political organization, depending on the varying combination of the "parts" of the *polis,* or social classes. Both democracy and oligarchy are in a condition of unstable equilibrium; each has a natural tendency to be pushed to its extreme, oligarchy to government by an oppressive faction, democracy to rule by the mob. Both thus tend to degenerate into the worst of all forms of government, tyranny, which is also the least likely to be successful or to endure. Hence the statesman governing either a democracy or an oligarchy finds his chief task to keep it from following out the logic and the natural process of degeneration of its particular form.

In consequence of this analysis, Aristotle judges that the best practicable form of government for most states, assuming no more than the common run of moral excellence and political skill, will be a judicious mixture of the democratic with the oligarchic principle. It will be what he calls *politeia,* "polity" or constitutional government, and may lean either toward a moderate democracy or a moderate aristocracy.

If we adopt as true the statements made in the *Ethics*—(1) that a truly happy life is a life of goodness lived in freedom from impediments, and (2) that goodness consists in a mean—it follows that the best way of life is one which consists in a mean, and a mean of the kind attainable by every individual. . . .

In all cities there may be distinguished three parts, or classes, of the citizen-body—the very rich; the very poor; and the middle class which forms the mean. Now it is admitted, as a general principle, that moderation and the mean are always best. We may therefore conclude that in the ownership of all gifts of fortune, a middle con-

[9] *Politics* I, ch. 1: 1252a 24–1253a 3.

dition will be the best. Men who are in this condition are the most ready to listen to reason. Those who belong to either extreme—the over-handsome, the over-strong, the over-noble, the over-wealthy; or at the opposite end the over-poor, the over-weak, the utterly ignoble —find it hard to follow the lead of reason. Men in the first class tend more to violence and serious crime: men in the second tend too much to roguery and petty offenses; and most wrongdoing arises either from violence or roguery. It is a further merit of the middle class that its members suffer least from ambition, which both in the military and the civil sphere is dangerous to cities. It must also be added that those who enjoy too many advantages—strength, wealth, connections and so forth—are both unwilling to obey and ignorant how to obey. . . . But there are also defects in those who suffer from the opposite extreme of a lack of advantages: they are far too mean and poor-spirited. . . .

A city aims at being, as far as it can be, a society composed of equals and peers; and the middle class, more than any other, has this sort of composition. It follows that a city which is based on the middle class is bound to be the best constituted in respect of its elements of which, on our view, a city is naturally composed. The middle classes enjoy a greater security themselves than any other class. They do not, like the poor, covet the goods of others; nor do others covet their possessions, as the poor covet those of the rich. Neither plotting against others, nor plotted against themselves, they live in freedom from danger. . . .

It is clear from our argument, first, that the best form of political society is one where power is vested in the middle class, and, secondly, that good government is attainable in those cities where there is a large middle class—large enough, if possible, to be stronger than both of the other classes, but at any rate large enough to be stronger than either of them singly; for in that case its addition to either will suffice to turn the scale, and will prevent either of the opposing extremes from becoming dominant. It is therefore the greatest of blessings for a city that its members should possess a moderate and adequate property.[10]

[10] *Politics* IV, ch. 9: 1295a 36–1296a 1.

In Book V Aristotle's natural history of the Greek political progress reaches its culmination: his mastery of Greek political experience is most impressively revealed in this pathology of the different types of city, the natural tendency of each type to degenerate and be corrupted.

We have to consider the particular way in which each kind of constitution is liable to degenerate—i.e., to explain *from* what a constitution is most likely to change *to* what. In addition we have to suggest the policies likely to ensure the stability of constitutions, collectively and individually, and to indicate the means which may best be employed to secure each particular form of constitution.[11]

Hence Book V is the analogue in the *Politics* to Book VII of the *Ethics,* in which the various forms of "sin" are analyzed. The difference in temper between the two inquiries is profound, and Aristotle is revealed as the perfect *physikos* in political science. The climax of this attitude is his willingness to offer advice on how to preserve and maintain a tyranny. "Tyrannies can be preserved in two ways, which are utterly opposed to one another. One of them is the traditional way; and it is also the method of government still followed by the majority of tyrants."[12] Aristotle lists the devices: liquidating leaders, forbidding common meals or clubs, or any social meetings, requiring all residents to appear at the palace, where they can be observed, setting up a secret police to secure dossiers, sowing mutual distrust and discord, and impoverishing their subjects.

Such are the arts of the tyrant, and such are the means he uses in order to maintain his authority; but they plumb the depth of wrongdoing. . . . We have here three principles to which the ordinary policies of tyrants may be reduced—three ideas to which their measures may all be referred: (1) to breed mutual distrust among their subjects, (2) to make them incapable of action, and (3) to break their spirit. Here too we have one of the two main methods for the preserva-

[11] *Politics* V, ch. 1: 1301a 22–25.   [12] *Politics* V, ch. 9: 1313a 34–37.

tion of tyrannies. But there is also a second method, where the line of action followed is almost the very reverse.[13]

The second way consists in acting as much like a legitimate and respectable king as possible; and this is the way Aristotle himself counsels. The tyrant must retain the power to govern, or else the tyranny is at an end. But in everything else he should act, or at least appear to act, the part of king. He should be a wise administrator, use taxes for the public benefit, exercise restraint in his personal behavior, avoid giving personal offense, adorn his city, show zeal in the public cult of the gods.

A tyrant should appear to his subjects not as a despot, but as a steward and king of his people. He should show himself a trustee for the public interest, not a man intent on his own; he should make moderation, and not excess, the aim and end of his life; he should seek the society of the notables, and yet court the favor of the masses. The benefit which he is bound to gain by such methods will be twofold. In the first place, his rule will be a nobler and a more enviable rule: his subjects will be men of a better stamp, free from humiliation, and he himself will cease to be an object of hatred and fear. In the second place, his rule will also be more lasting; and he will himself attain a habit of character, if not wholly disposed to goodness, at any rate half-good—half-good and yet half-bad, but at any rate not wholly bad.[14]

Aristotle's whole treatment of tyranny seems typical of his willingness to accept the institutions he finds, and to try to make the best of them. W. L. Newman suggested that he may have wished to amend the worst of Greek institutions, and that he may also have desired to keep Macedonian kingship on the right track. Barker adds: "The doctor in him (we have always to remember his medical ancestry and interest) was attracted to the diagnosis of symptoms and the suggestions of cures; and the problems of one-man government, especially in its tyrannical

[13] *Politics* V, ch. 9: 1314a 13–14, 30–32.
[14] *Politics* V, ch. 9: 1315a 42–1315b 11.

form, afforded him curious and abnormal material."[15] In fairness it should be added, that while Aristotle devotes a single chapter in Book V to the method of ensuring the stability of a tyranny by making it as little tyrannical and "despotical" as possible, he gives the whole of Book VI to the methods of constructing democracies and oligarchies with a special view to their greater stability and their immunity to the natural tendency of all polities toward *stasis* and corruption.

4. Practical Intelligence and Greek Norms

Returning then to the *Ethics,* we can say that in Aristotle's analysis excellences (*aretai*) or "virtues" are twofold. For there are two levels of human behavior, two "parts of the *psychē,* or "soul": there is the part that "has *logos,*" intelligence itself, the part that knows and chooses; and there is the part that, though it does not "have *logos*" and is therefore "non-rational," is not "irrational," but can still "participate in *logos*" and obey it, the human impulses and desires which can either resist and fight *logos* or intelligence, in those who lack *sōphrosynē,* or self-control, or else be guided by it, in those who exhibit such *sōphrosynē,* the "continent." There are thus two kinds or sets of human excellences or virtues. There are the excellences of desires, of natural impulses and habits, which when brought under the intelligent control of practical *nous* or "reason"—that is, when directed by foresight of consequences, by *proairesis* or "forechoice"—become "excellences of character" or "moral virtues." Secondly, there are the excellences of intelligence itself, the "intellectual excellences" or "virtues."

The first set, the excellences of character, are acquired and fixed moral states, settled habits or *hexeis,* acquired powers or "second natures." They are habits of using foresight (*hexeis proairetikai*). They are habits of seeking and following the mean

[15] *The Politics of Aristotle,* translated by Ernest Barker, p. 242.

(*to meson*)—the mean not of the thing itself, but the mean relative to ourselves, as determined by reason (*logos*), or as an intelligent man, a man of foresight, *ho phronimos,* would determine it. These habits of following the mean are habits of making choices that are relative to, and proportional to, adjusted to, the time, the place, the individual, the resources in the situation, etc. They are habits of adapting natural impulses to appropriate ends. Such habits must be ingrained in character by a proper training, so that they may truly become *hexeis,* habits or fixed moral states. But they must function flexibly: it is impossible to lay down general rules, "moral laws," that will cover all situations. Conduct is determined in any particular situation not by *nous,* intellectual insight, but by *phronēsis,* practical intelligence or "prudence," the perfected excellence of practical *nous.* Moral deliberation, like art, deals with particulars, with what choice to make in this situation. It is significant that what is the right action in specific situations is not arrived at for Aristotle by *nous,* by moral intuition, by insight or hunch, by "conscience," but by *logos,* reasoning, and *phronēsis,* foresight or "prudence." It is arrived at by practical intelligence or "moral deliberation," *boulēsis.* And this right choice is something objectively determinable, something that can be discovered; it is not the result of "subjective" preference.

Aristotle is clearly thinking here in terms of medical diagnosis, a process which, though it may be ultimately what we mean by having "hunches" and "insight," and though such hunches may well enter into it, is at least open to public and objective checking. There are for Aristotle no general rules, no universal moral laws, no "principles" in ethics, save the one and single *archē,* always to act intelligently in any individual situation, and thus to realize human welfare, *eudaimonia.* The function of the intelligent or "prudent" man, *ho phronimos,* and hence of the good or the "moral" man, is never to create the havoc that comes from acting on universal moral or political "principles," never to be so stupid as to "follow the right, *ruat caelum*," but rather, to make the very best he can out of every situation.

These moral excellences are founded on intellectual excellence. One needs brains to lead the good life, as one does not need brains to do one's duty, or to act "on principle." "Theirs not to reason why, Theirs but to do and die." If Tennyson is here accurately portraying the soldier, then, Aristotle would say, no soldier could be a moral man. That is "brutality," not being intelligent, not being a man at all. If you do not have any brains yourself, says Aristotle, go find someone who has. Consult the "prudent man," the *phronimos,* the man of intelligence and foresight, the man who has acquired *phronēsis.* He is clearly anticipating the wisdom of the Catholic confessional and moral director: the wise priest plays in it the role of the Aristotelian *phronimos,* being by training and profession in possession of "prudence" or *phronēsis.*

But intelligence alone is not enough: Aristotle knew his Greeks. Socrates, he is convinced, was wrong: to know what is the good thing to do is not to do it. Men are "incontinent," *akrateis;* they lack self-control. They know what is the intelligent thing to do, but often they do not do it. Aristotle, indeed, knew almost as much about "sin" as our theologians. But he attempted to analyze it and its causes, and did not leave it as a brute encountered unanalyzed fact, to be employed for religious purposes.

In Book VII of the *Ethics* Aristotle analyzes three kinds of "sin": "vice," *kakia;* "brutality," *thēriotēs;* and "incontinence," *akrasia.* Vice is the failure to hit the mark in seeking for the mean; brutality is the lack of the intelligence to know how to choose the good. These two are failures of intelligence. The third form of "sin," *akrasia,* is something more:

For as man is the best of animals when perfected, so he is the worst of all when sundered from law and right. For unrighteousness is most pernicious when possessed of weapons, and man is born possessing weapons for the use of wisdom and excellence, which it is possible to employ entirely for the opposite ends. Hence when devoid of excellence man is the most unholy and savage of animals, and the worst in sexual indulgence and in gluttony.[16]

Excellence of character is necessary for moral deliberation, *boulēsis,* to be effective. And such excellence is produced by the proper training, by moral education: hence moral education will be the chief end of all wise legislation. If we bring up the young to direct their impulses by intelligence, we can then trust them to have acquired the habit or *hexis* of acting intelligently as a "second nature." But such a *hexis* is not the kind of thing that can be taught through words spoken by a teacher: it does not belong to *ta mathematika,* the things that can be taught by oral instruction, like geometry. It is only through the practice of performing good acts that we can become good ourselves, only through practical moral experience. But by right training and experience men can hope to acquire *phronēsis,* the habit of acting with foresight and intelligence. Such moral insight is a natural perfecting of human nature.

This takes us to the "life of reason" or *nous,* which has two aspects. In the first, reason is a means, an instrument: it is the organ of discerning what is best, of perfecting the possibilities resident in natural impulses, and adjusting them to each other, and to the conditions under which they must function. The second aspect is that of reason as an end in itself, the supreme "for what" or *hou heneka.* The best life is the life of sheer knowing, of *theōria;* and from the standpoint of this best of lives, the life of practice, acting intelligently, is ultimately "for the sake of" knowing.

Thus for Aristotle the fullest and most intense activity of man's characteristic function, the completest fulfillment of man's distinctive "nature," is the operaion of *nous,* of reason, in knowing. This is the satisfaction of the supreme desire with which man is endowed by nature, the desire to know. The philosopher who enjoys "wisdom," *sophia,* which is the union of "science,"

---

[16] *Politics* I, ch. 1: 1253a 32–36.

epistēmē, the demonstration of the reasons why things are as they are, with *nous,* the intellectual vision of the beginnings, the *archai,* of demonstration, of the sources of intelligibility—the philosopher who has come to "know truth" possesses the fullest *eudaimonia,* the fullest exercise of human powers, and is hence most completely "human" and at the same time "most godlike and divine." Aristotle ends the *Ethics,* as he ends most of his treatises, on the Platonic note. The fullest development of human nature, of human *nous,* leads men beyond human nature itself to the "life of the gods," to participation in what is "deathless and eternal"—to the supreme, continuous, and never-ending blessedness of sheer *nousing,* sheer knowing.

Felix qui potuit rerum cognoscere causas.[17]

[17] Vergil *Georgicon* II. l. 490.

Chapter XIII

THE PRODUCTIVE SCIENCES:

KNOWING HOW TO MAKE THINGS

1. Aristotle's Theory of Art

In addition to the sciences of *theōria*, which deal with how to understand what is always or for the most part, and include first philosophy, mathematics, and physics; and in addition to the sciences of conduct or *praxis*, which deal with how to choose relative goods in order to become a good man or a good *polis*, and include ethics and politics; there are for Aristotle the sciences of production or *poiēsis*, which deal with how to make things. There are three such productive sciences[1] in the Aristotelian corpus: the *Topics*, which treats how to make a good argument, the *Rhetoric*, which treats how to make a good speech, and the *Poetics*, which treats how to make a good poem, especially a dramatic poem—only the part dealing with tragic poems is preserved. These inquiries are Aristotle's excursions into poultry raising, short story writing, or advertising and public relations—arguments, speeches, and poems were just as practical to Greeks, and our modern inclusion of such courses in the *universitas scientiarum* is hence in an ancient tradition.

Now the *Poetics*, while thus intended primarily as a kind of manual for the Hollywood producer, has had an enormous critical influence since its virtual rediscovery in the sixteenth

[1] Occasionally Aristotle even includes physics among the productive sciences, so impressed is he by the fact that Nature is the supreme maker or "poet"; though of course normally physics is for him a theoretical science.

century. For it is based on a theory of dramatics and poetry which is part of a larger and more comprehensive theory of art that is implicit in Aristotle. We should not, perhaps, expect Aristotle the scientific philosopher to be at his best in talking about the specific practice of any art, except the art of inquiry, and of course his own beloved art of medicine; though we should expect a student of Plato and an observer of the ways of the Greeks to try to understand the process of art. As a matter of fact, what Aristotle has to say about art is far more penetrating than anything Plato lets his characters say, especially in the *Republic,* where the discussion, to be sure, is not about art itself but rather about the moral and political effects of art, and is deeply involved in the various layers of irony that masterpiece exhibits. Plato talks about poetry rather than about "art," and his own attitude is colored, in the *Republic* as well as in the satirical *Ion,* by the fact that the poets were the Greek sacred writers, authors of their Scriptures. To take the poets literally as moral and religious teachers was for Plato rather like taking the Bible literally today: rhapsodes like Ion were the counterpart of our Fundamentalists. And Plato was very critical of the Olympians, opposing to them his own religion of reason or *nous.* Perhaps Plato, with a premonition of aesthetic discussion and its terrors, judged it wiser not to talk about art, but to illustrate it. He does say, in the *Ion* and elsewhere, that poetry is a kind of divine inspiration, or madness, hardly to be given a rational explanation, thus anticipating the Romantic philosophy of the artist as inspired prophet and divine creator.[2]

Where Plato develops the implications of the fact of art, and of the artist's experience and outlook, for knowledge, the good life, and the nature of the cosmos in general, Aristotle makes "art" or *technē* a fundamental category of his thinking, a basic concept for understanding any existential subject matter. In his analysis, art or *technē,* human production or *poiēsis,* is the

[2] See Milton C. Nahm's suggestive *The Artist as Creator* (Baltimore, 1956).

clearest illustration of what a natural process is, of what nature can do. Nature in general is an order of productive enterprises, and human production, human art, is not a completely novel and unique addition to nature, but rather an instance of nature at work, the most complex, and in a certain sense the most successful instance, carrying nature's enterprises to a happy fruition. Hence most of the many penetrating comments Aristotle has to make about art he makes in talking about nature—in the *Physics*, which is as much an analysis of the "processes by art" as of any other natural processes; and when he is analyzing what is involved in any process or *kinēsis*, in the *Metaphysics*, Book Theta.

"Art" or *technē* meant to Aristotle, as to any Greek, "making" something, realizing some form in some matter. The artist is a *poiētēs*, a "maker," and nature is clearly the great Maker, the great "poet" or artist. The only difference between nature and the human artist is that nature herself makes something out of her own materials, while the human artist makes something out of something else, some materials outside himself, to which he is an external *archē*. But "processes by nature" and "processes by art"—*kinēseis kata physin* and *kinēseis apo technēs*—are not two quite different kinds of process. "By nature," *physei*, a tree is made out of a seed; "by art," *apo technēs*, a man makes a house out of wood and bricks. "But," says Aristotle, "if a house had been a thing made by nature"—if the wood and bricks had grown into a house—"it would have been made by nature in the same way as it is now made by art; and if the things made by nature were made also by art"—if men could make a tree—"they would come to be in the same way as they now do by nature." There is in each case a necessary order of means and ends that would have to be followed.[3] Both are processes whereby natural materials are made by a natural agent to realize the forms potential in those materials, made to

[3] *Physics* II, ch. 8: 199a 11–15.

realize their implicit ends. And while nature cannot make a house in any other way than houses are made, and hence must work through man as her agent in housebuilding—which is next to the art of medicine Aristotle's favorite illustration of a process "by art"—and while man cannot make a tree, and hence must leave the making of trees to nature, we do · not have here two radically incompatible kinds of process, but rather a natural cooperation.

Hence, when the Christian says,

> Poems are made by fools like me,
> But only God can make a tree

Aristotle would say, "There is a sense in which that is obviously true. But there is a deeper sense in which God or nature and I are just alike: we are both artists. And when I make a poem, God or nature is making it, just as much as when he—or she— is making a tree, only through different agents: through me, and not through the wind, the sun and the rain." "In general, then, art in a sense completes what nature is unable to finish, and in a sense imitates nature." [4]

Art, that is, overcomes the difficulties of matter. Aristotle does not mean that art "mimics" nature: art does not imitate nature's products—that would be quite impossible. Art does better, more successfully, just what nature does or tries to do: it brings that which is possible in materials to a realization, and thus "completes nature." The distinction between "imitating" and "mimicking" is important, since Aristotle's formal definition of art or *technē* is that art is an imitation of nature, a *mimēsis*. It is necessary in order to understand what Aristotle means by this definition, to realize that art does not imitate nature's products: it could not possibly make an oak tree or beget a man. Rather, art does imitate nature's productive activities. It must be remembered that "nature" for Aristotle is a way of acting,[5] and what art

---

[4] *Physics* II, ch. 8: 199a 16–18.   [5] See pages 173 ff.

imitates is that way: art does the kind of thing that nature does. "So the best example of how nature acts, is the man who cures himself," [6] doing without deliberation or conscious purpose what the physician would consciously direct him to do.

This is what Aristotle makes out of the Greek discussion of art as *mimēsis* or "imitation," a discussion which took its start from the fact that in Greek a dramatic spectacle was called a *mimos,* an "imitation." This is as though we should develop the theory—as in point of fact we have—that art is essentially "play," from the fact that we call a dramatic presentation a "play." [7]

Aristotle says little about the actual process of imitating. But certain distinctions are clear. In "imitation" the artist separates some form from the material with which it is joined in nature, some sensible form, and realizes it in the materials of his art, in his medium; just as the shipbuilder or the housebuilder realizes the form or function and end of his art in another material or under other conditions than those that are "naturally" encountered. But the new material or medium imposes its own conditions on that form: a house of wood, to function as a shelter made by art, must have a different structure from a natural shelter, like a cave, a structure dictated by the wood.

Likewise, a poem or a picture will have a different structure from the actions of men that it imitates, a structure imposed by its materials, words or colors respectively. The action "imitated" may be "natural" to the actor. But the artist must convey, not its natural appropriateness and rightness, but rather a "necessity or probability" inherent in the materials of his art. The man sitting for a portrait assumes a posture determined by the laws of gravitation, anatomy, etc. But the painter must justify his picture, not in terms of physics or anatomy, but in terms of the composition of colors and lines. A man acts, as a consequence

[6] *Physics* II, ch. 9: 199b 3–32.
[7] See Richard McKeon, "Literary Criticism and the Concept of Imitation in Antiquity," *Modern Philology,* 34 (1936), 1–35.

of his character, his heritage, his habits, etc. But the poet has
to make his action appear necessary by means of his medium,
words, through developing the man's character, expressing his
thoughts, narrating or depiciting incidents. "Imitation" is therefore the presentation of an aspect of things in a matter other
than its natural matter, rendered inevitable by reasons other
than its natural reasons. The form "imitated" in art is a natural
form, a natural way of acting. But the materials and their
structure belong not to nature but to the art.

Art is also considered by Aristotle not in relation to other
natural processes, in the similarities and contrasts between
"processes by nature," *kinēseis kata physin,* and "processes by
art," *kinēseis apo technēs,* but as a human capacity, as a power
or *dynamis* in man. Art in this sense is a "productive state" or
"habit," a productive *hexis,* under the guidance of right reason
or intelligence. Art is thus the power to make something intelligently. We can make things by mere "experience": we can
make Socrates healthy again, because we know what cured
Callias of the same symptoms. But we do not possess "art"
unless we know why it cured him, and why it will cure every
man with that same disease—unless from many instances gained
by "experience" we have formed a universal judgment about a
certain kind of ailment.

"Experience" is a knowledge of individuals, and in making
things it is not at all inferior to "art." Indeed, since what you
make is always an individual thing, if you have only a knowledge of universal rules, without any experience of particular
cases, you will often bungle, like the young interne, for you will
not know the individual materials. But actually there is no
conflict, since we always acquire an art *through* experience:
we cannot acquire it, as we acquire "science"—"theoretical"
science—through *logos,* through words or oral instruction. Art,
like good conduct or *praxis,* living well, does not belong with
the things that are teachable through *logos* by a teacher to his

pupils: it does not belong with *ta mathēmatika*. This is the difference between art and practical intelligence, or *phronēsis,* on the one hand, and science, or demonstrated knowledge, on the other. Just as we can become morally excellent or "virtuous" only through performing virtuous acts, so we can acquire an art only through making particular things—through the practice of that particular art.

But we have not really acquired the "art" until we have learned, not only that things are so, but also why they are so. In this sense, though "art" makes individual things, and is concerned with what is variable, contingent, and relative, and not always or for the most part—since their cause lies in their maker, the artist, and not in themselves, in the process of production—art involves a knowledge of universals. In other words, says Aristotle, like "science," and unlike "experience," "art is of universals."

It is to be noted as fundamental for the understanding of Aristotle's theory of art that not only is art not an anomaly in nature, an arbitrary addition to nature made by man, so that its very existence inevitably constitutes a problem to be solved, as in most modern theories of art, but is rather an illustration of the productive processes of nature, a natural fact to be analyzed and understood. In addition, for Aristotle there is no distinction at all between what have come to be called in modern times the so-called "fine arts" and the "practical arts." Such a distinction would have been quite unintelligible to a Greek thinker. For Aristotle and the Greeks, the "artist" is a maker, a craftsman, like the shipbuilder or the physician. The different and separate arts are distinguished only by the fact that they make different kinds of thing: the shipbuilder makes ships, the physician makes health, the poet makes plays. Good ships, good health, and good plays are all a delight to behold, because each does something well: the ship sails and parts the waves, the tragic poem arouses pity and fear, and thus purifies the soul. The effect in each case is "an innocent joy and pleasure."

2. How to Write a Speech

The longest of the productive sciences in the Aristotelian corpus is the *Art* or *Technē of Rhetoric*. Manuals on speech writing were an old story in Greece long before Aristotle; in this field he was keenly aware of standing in a long succession of writers, and he uses the development of the art of rhetoric to illustrate the continuous growth of knowledge (see passage 20 cited on p. 53). Hence while he could sum up and round out an extensive effort to formulate the rules for a favorite Greek practice, he could here scarcely display the originality he does elsewhere. Of the two Platonic dialogues dealing primarily with the ideas and the practices of the rhetoricians, the *Gorgias* and the *Phaedrus,* the latter in particular, the central theme of which is the criticism of a speech by the rhetorician Lysias, makes clear the existence of a well-developed theory of public speaking with clearly formulated rules. According to Cicero,[8] Aristotle, in his lost history of rhetoric, the *Synagōgē Technōn,* claims that the "art" of rhetoric originated in Sicily after the expulsion of the tyrants in 467 B.C., when citizens had to present claims for property illegally confiscated by the tyrants, and appealed to two rhetoricians of Syracuse, Corax and Tisias, to draw up rules for their appeals. Corax was the author of the first of the numerous *technai* or Arts of Rhetoric, and to him is attributed the definition of it as "the artificer of persuasion" (*peithous dēmiourgos*). His pupil Tisias was in turn the teacher of Gorgias, Lysias, and Isocrates; by the third generation they were joined by many others.

Against his predecessors, Aristotle complains that they all

[8] Cicero *Brutus* xii. 46.

emphasized forensic speaking, defense in the law courts, although deliberative rhetoric, dealing with questions of policy in the legislative assembly, is nobler and more worthy of a statesman. And they all concentrated on the ways of arousing prejudice, compassion, anger, and similar emotions in the judges, instead of on the instrument of rational proof of a case, the enthymeme.

Aristotle starts by defining rhetoric as the counterpart (*antistrophos*) of dialectic, since both have to do with matters that are in a manner within the cognizance of all men, and not confined to any special science. Hence all men in a manner have a share of both; for all, up to a certain point, endeavor to criticize or uphold an argument, to defend themselves or to accuse others.

It is clear that rhetoric is useful: if the true and the just do not win the decision, their supporters lack the requisite skill to support them rightly. If it be argued that rhetorical skill can also support the false and the unjust, this is true of all good things except excellence (*aretē*).

Rhetoric may be defined as the power of discovering the possible means of persuasion in reference to any subject whatever. It furnishes three types of proof. The first type tries to establish the moral character of the persuader, so as to create confidence in his integrity. The second type tries to put the hearer into a receptive state of mind. The third type tries to persuade by means of the speech itself, through its rational or seemingly rational proof of its contentions. Hence the effective speechmaker must be a master of logical reasoning, of the characters and virtues of men, and of the emotions they will feel. All three concern the effect or function his speech will have: here too Aristotle's analysis is thoroughly functional.

Thus it appears that rhetoric is as it were an offshoot of dialectic and of the science of ethics, which may be reasonably called politics. . . . Rhetoric is a sort of division or likeness of dialectic, since neither of them is a science that deals with the nature of any definite subject matter.[9]

The function of rhetoric is to deal with things about which we deliberate, but for which we have no systematic rules. That is, we deliberate about human actions, none of which are necessary.

There are three kinds of rhetoric, depending on the nature of those to whom it is directed. The hearer of speeches will be either a mere auditor or a judge, and if a judge, a judge of things that have happened, or of things to come. There are hence three kinds of rhetorical speeches, deliberative, forensic, and epideictic (in the political assembly, in the law courts, and as show pieces). The deliberative speaker can freely admit that what he advocates is unjust; he cannot admit that it is inexpedient. The forensic speaker can freely admit that his action was harmful, but not that it was legally unjust.

The deliberative speaker must know the nature and extent of the City's resources; he should know the City's military power; he should have a special understanding of proposed legislation. Aristotle carries through a brief examination of the good and the expedient in general, since men deliberate not about the end, but about the means to the end, which are the things that are expedient in our actions.

Let us assume good to be whatever is desirable for its own sake, or for the sake of which we choose something else; that which is the aim of all things, or of all things that possess sensation or reason; or would be, if they could acquire the latter. Whatever reason (*nous*) might assign to each, and whatever reason does assign to each in individual cases, that is good for each; and that whose presence makes a man fit and also independent; and independence (*to autarkes*) in general; and that which produces or preserves such things, or on which such things follow, or all that is likely to prevent or destroy their opposites.[10]

Aristotle proceeds to enumerate such goods: health, the virtues, pleasure, happiness, wealth, friendship, honor and good repute,

[9] *Rhetoric* I, ch. 2: 1356a 25-34.   [10] *Rhetoric* I, ch. 6: 1362a 23-29.

justice, "since it is expedient in general for the common weal."
In the case of more doubtful goods, that is good the opposite
of which is evil, or is advantageous to our enemies. That which
is not in excess is good; and also that which many aim at and
compete for, and that which is praised. Generally speaking, all
that is deliberately chosen is good. All these are the material
from which we must draw our arguments in reference to good
and the expedient. Aristotle is here listing the unquestioned ends
of the audience to whom an effective deliberative or political
speech must be directed.

Since deliberation often has to consider which of two useful
courses is the more useful and expedient, Aristotle offers much
shrewd advice on comparative values.

That which men of practical intelligence (*hoi phronimoi*), either
all, or more, or the best of them, would judge, or have judged, to
be a greater good, must necessarily be such, either absolutely or in
so far as they have judged as men of practical intelligence (*phronēsis*).
The same may be said in regard to everything else; for the nature,
quantity, and quality of things are such as would be defined by science
(*epistēmē*) and practical intelligence (*phronēsis*).[11]

The most important and effective of all the means of
persuasion and good counsel is to know all the forms of government and to distinguish the manners and customs, institutions,
and interests of each; for all men are guided by considerations
of expediency, and what preserves the City is expedient.

There are four kinds of government, democracy, oligarchy, aristocracy, and monarchy. . . . Democracy is a form of government in
which the offices are distributed by the people among themselves by
lot; in an oligarchy, by those who possess a certain property-qualifica-
tion; in an aristocracy, by those who possess an educational (*kata
paideian*) qualification, meaning an education that is laid down by
law. In a monarchy, one man alone is supreme over all; if it is subject
to certain regulations, it is called a kingdom; if it is unlimited, a

[11] *Rhetoric* I, ch. 7: 1364b 12–16.

tyranny. . . . Now the end of democracy is liberty, of oligarchy wealth, of aristocracy things relating to education and what the law prescribes, of tyranny self-protection.[12]

In forensic speeches, which have to do with accusation and defense in a law court, we must consider the motives that lead men to act unjustly, their state of mind, and the character of those exposed to injustice.

Let injustice be defined as voluntarily causing injury contrary to the law. Now, the law is particular or general. By particular, I mean the written law in accordance with which a city is administered; by general, the unwritten regulations which seem to be universally recognized. . . . By general laws I mean those based upon nature (*kata physin*). In fact, there is a general justice (*dikaion*) and injustice (*adikon*), as all men in a manner divine, even if there is no community or agreement between them. This is what the Antigone of Sophocles seems to mean, when she says:

> For neither today nor yesterday, but from all eternity,
> these statutes live and no man knoweth whence they came.[13]

. . . .

And as Empedocles says about not killing that which has life (*to empsychon*), for this is not right for some and wrong for others,

> But a universal precept, which extends without a break
> throughout the wide-ruling sky and the boundless earth.[14]

Alcidamas also speaks of this precept in his *Messeniacus*.[15]

It is significant that this clear reference to natural law and natural justice does not mention Plato.

The motives that lead men to do injury and commit wrong actions against the law are vice (*kakia*) and incontinence or lack of self-control (*akrasia*). There are four causes of voluntary action: habit, reason, anger, and desire; and three of involuntary action: chance, nature, and compulsion.

---

[12] *Rhetoric* I, ch. 8: 1365b 29–1366a 6.

[13] Sophocles *Antigone* l. 456.   [14] Empedocles fr. 135 (Diels).

[15] *Rhetoric* I, chs. 10, 13: 1368b 7–10; 1373b 6–18. The commentator supplies the line from Alcidamas, a pupil of Gorgias: "God has left all men free; nature had made none a slave."

As for those acts which men do of themselves and of which they are
the cause, some are the result of habit, others of desire; and of the
latter some are due to rational desire (*logistikē orexis*), others to
irrational desire. Now wish (*boulēsis*) is a desire for the good, for
no one wishes for anything unless he thinks it good; irrational
desires are anger and appetite (*epithymia*).[16]

All things that men do voluntarily either are or seem to be
good or pleasant; appetite is the desire for what seems to be
pleasant. This leads Aristotle to a discussion of pleasure and a
list of pleasant things, from revenge, to friends and learning
things.

And since things which are akin and like are always pleasant to one
another, and every man in the highest degree feels this in regard to
himself, it must needs be that all men are more or less selfish
(*philautoi*); for it is in himself above all that such conditions are
to be found. Since, then, all men are selfish, it follows that all find
pleasure in what is their own, such as their works and words. That
as a rule is why men are fond of those who flatter and love them,
of honor, and of children; for the last are their own work.[17]

A successful speaker must know how to show himself to his
audience to be of a certain character, and how to put the
audience or judge into a certain frame of mind. In deliberative
speaking the former is the more important, in forensic, the
latter. In order to produce conviction in the assembly, the
speaker must seem to be possessed of practical intelligence
(*phronēsis*), moral excellence (*aretē*), and good will (*eunoia*).

For either through want of intelligence they form incorrect opinions,
or, if their opinions are correct, through viciousness they do not say
what they think, or if they are intelligent and good, they lack good
will; wherefore it may happen that they do not give the best advice,
although they know what it is. These qualities are all that are necessary, so that the speaker who appears to possess all three will necessarily convince his hearers.[18]

[16] *Rhetoric* I, ch. 10: 1369a 1–4.   [17] *Rhetoric* I, ch. 11: 1371b 16–24.
[18] *Rhetoric* II, ch. 1: 1378a 11–16.

The emotions are all those passions that cause men to change their opinion in regard to their judgments, and are accompanied by pleasure and pain, like anger, pity, fear, envy, emulation, shame, love, and the like. Aristotle undertakes a detailed analysis of these emotions, much in the spirit of the seventeenth-century thinkers like Descartes, Hobbes, or Spinoza, though with the practical motive of showing how to arouse them in an audience or a judge.

Aristotle proceeds to the "commonplaces" of all argument, the possible and the impossible, and the future, especially appropriate to speeches in the assembly; the past, useful in the courts; and amplification, valuable in display speeches. This leads him to the instruments of rhetorical proof: these are examples, which are either past incidents, or incidents invented by the speaker, taking the form of comparisons, or of fables like Aesop's; and enthymemes. Enthymemes include maxims (*gnomai*) or general statements: the enthymeme is the syllogism dealing with the subject, while the maxim is the premise or the conclusion without the reasoning.

It is the third book of the *Rhetoric*, which as Diels suggested may well have been originally an independent writing, that displays most clearly the character of being a practical manual or handbook for the speaker. Aristotle has much sound practical advice. He here considers briefly delivery, which is of the greatest importance, but has so far been hardly treated by any rhetorician; style (*lexis*), and arrangement. The two chief excellences of style or diction are clarity and appropriateness. Propriety of style will be obtained by the expression of emotion and character, and by proportion (*analogon*) to the subject matter. "Style is proportionate to the subject matter when neither weighty matters are treated offhand, nor trifling matters with dignity, and no embellishment is attached to an ordinary word; otherwise there is an appearance of comedy." [19]

The form of diction should be neither metrical nor without all

[19] *Rhetoric* III, ch. 7: 1408a 12–14.

rhythm. If it is metrical, it seems artificial and fails to persuade, distracting the hearer's attention. If it has no rhythm at all, it is without any limits (*aperanton*); and the unlimited (*to apeiron*) is unpleasant and unknowable. Now all things are limited by number, and the number belonging to prose is rhythm.

The other theme treated is the arrangement (*taxis*). A speech must have two parts: it is necessary to state the case, and then to prove it. Aristotle ridicules the elaborate divisions into parts the rhetoricians had worked out. At most he will admit Isocrates' addition of exordium (*prooimion*) and peroration (*epilogos*): and the peroration is often unnecessary.

The epilogue is composed of four parts: to dispose the hearer favorably towards oneself and unfavorably towards the adversary; to amplify and depreciate; to excite the emotions of the hearer; to recapitulate. For after you have proved that you are truthful and that the adversary is false, the natural order of things is to praise ourselves, blame him, and put on the finishing touches.[20]

The *Rhetoric* of Aristotle, as some of the difficulties of its composition make clear, is undoubtedly a compilation of several different sets of notes. Its intention is extremely functional and practical: it is designed to tell a speaker how to deliver a successful and effective speech, that will influence an assembly or win the decision in a court of law. Much of it belongs to the Aristotle who wrote the *Realpolitik* of Books IV to VI of the *Politics:* that is, to the observer of men who had no illusions about how to appeal to them. But the later historical influence of Aristotle's *Rhetoric* was enormous, not only on all subsequent Greek Arts of Rhetoric, but on the controlling ideas of Cicero and Quintilian as well. Above all, it established the central line of the Western tradition, that rhetoric cannot be a merely formal discipline, as Gorgias had contended. With Plato's *Gorgias* it transmitted to Cicero the all-important notion

[20] *Rhetoric* III, ch. 19: 1419b 10–16.

that the effective speechmaker must possess ethical and political intelligence or *phronēsis* in addition to technical skill, and that any training in speaking well must include training in the art of living well and of advising the city how best to act. This made Roman education, which was largely rhetorical, and carried on by the rhetoricians, like the later Varro and St. Augustine, a training in moral and political wisdom, and not merely in history and polite letters. And it is hardly too much to trace back through Cicero to Aristotle the central conviction running through the whole tradition of literary humanism in medieval and modern times, which derives from Roman educational practice, that the study of good writing and good speaking must be indissolubly wedded to the study of good living, and that the pursuits of the arts of letters are *ipso facto* pursuits of humane wisdom.

3. How to Write a Tragic Poem

Against the general background of what art is, Aristotle undertakes to tell how to make a good play. To know when something has been well made, we must know what that kind of thing does, what its function is. Specifically, to know what is a good poem, we must know what poems do; and to know what is a good tragic poem, we must know what tragedies do. When we understand what their effects are, we can then contrive to make them most effective.

Now, poems, says Aristotle, are made by men for two reasons, each of which is a "part" of human nature. In the first place, men love to "imitate" human actions: they love from childhood to make believe, they love to imagine they are somebody else, and to behave accordingly. Secondly, they take delight in recognizing "imitations": they like to see pictures of what they are familiar with, just as they like to exercise their senses, to see and to hear, in harmony and rhythm. The seeing and the hearing are joys in themselves; and when they are seeing and hearing what they can recognize, there is a double delight. For then there is an intellectual delight added to the purely sensory delight. If you have not seen the thing before, your pleasure will be entirely in the execution or the coloring, in the tune and rhythm. But if you "recognize" it as something you are already familiar with, you gain an added intellectual pleasure. For, says Aristotle the Knower, who is clearly speaking at this point, you are also "learning" something: you are learning the "meaning" of something, you are seeing what you already knew in a novel light. Thus we love to see a picture of a dead dog, even though to behold the actual dead animal would be repugnant to us.

Above all, men delight in "imitations" of human actions, in the portrayal of the characters of men in action—that is, of human powers in operation. They love to observe what men do and what they suffer in interaction with the operation of the powers or characters of other men. Men love to "imitate" human actions in playing the flute, or the lyre, or in the rhythm of the dance. Music, in fact, can "imitate" character and its operating or functioning better than any other art: music is the most "imitative" of all the arts, while painting is the least "imitative." In painting there are no actions at all, no operation of characters: painting is completely static, it portrays only a single moment halted (see *Politics* 1340a 18–b 19).

It is clear that Aristotle means by "imitation" something quite different from mere representation, the mere reproduction of the surface of the finished products of nature. He is not even thinking of program music. He is indeed opposing his functional concepts and attitude to the Greek love for representation in painting: he had a very low opinion of Apelles, whose paintings of fruit were said to have deceived the birds and the insects. Rather, in calling music the most "imitative" of the arts, Aristotle means that music produces by its sounds *the same effects* that nature produces by human character in action. A good poem or a good song arouses in us the same feelings and emotions as do the actions of a man. We might put it today in our language: music is the most "expressive" of all the arts; were it not that this term has a flavor of the subjectivism of modern theories of art that is utterly lacking in Aristotle's perfectly objective functionalism.

Every art—the art of shipbuilding, the art of healing, the art of poetry, and all the rest—is thus an imitation of the work and action of nature. Poetry does not use form and color, as painting does, but the voice, like music: it employs rhythm, harmony, and language to imitate the actions of men, what men do and suffer, their happiness and misery. It does not use rhythm alone, like dancing, nor rhythm and harmony alone, like fluteplaying. Epic poetry and dramatic poetry are the highest forms of poetry, because they are clearly the most "imitative" of men's actions, the most living and functional. Empedocles, for instance, is according to Aristotle, no poet, even though he employs the means of poetry, but a *physikos,* a natural philosopher; for there is in his verse no imitation of human actions. Thus for Aristotle, Lucretius would be no poet, though Milton would be—Aristotle might relent, however: for Lucretius could be said to "imitate" the actions of nature!

Tragic poetry, in particular, imitates men's actions in such a way as to arouse pity, or *eleos,* and fear, or *phobos,* as comic poetry arouses ridicule and laughter. Tragedy aims to arouse pity and fear for the hero, the protagonist, and thus to purge, heal, and lighten the soul of the auditor, and thus delight it. Tragedy aims to produce pleasure by giving relief from the pity and fear it arouses. Hence the best tragedy will be the one that best produces that effect. Aristotle's is certainly a medical, almost a Freudian theory of the function of tragedy. But it has many of the overtones of the ritual *catharsis,* the purification and "purging" of the soul, of the cult of Dionysos out of which

Greek tragedy developed. Tragedy remained a religious cult for the Greeks, and Aristotle's analysis is reminiscent of that underlying background.

Now art imitates nature by doing consciously and with full knowledge of why it is done, what nature does without awareness, without conscious intent or "purpose," without any "end-in-view." Art imitates nature by doing better what nature is prevented from doing fully and completely. Hence art, in imitating what men's actions do to produce pity and fear, can do it much better and more effectively than can the actual and contingent actions of the men produced by nature and not by the poet. Hence the function of the poet is to describe, not what has actually happened, but rather the kind of thing that might happen, what is probable or necessary. Herodotus in verse would still be merely "history," not poetry; it would remain an account of particular facts, while poetry is of the nature rather of universals,[21] of what such a man would probably or necessarily say or do. Poetry is just the kind of thing Thucydides puts into the speeches of his characters: Thucydides is clearly from Aristotle's point of view a true poet.

In real life, in history, we can hardly discern *why* things have to be as they are: there are far too many complicated and chance or accidental factors. The universal that is implicit there does not stand out clearly. But in tragedy the poet can improve on nature, and show the inevitable dependence of destiny on character. He can make plain not the mere bare event, the "fact that," *to hoti,* but also the "reason why," *to dioti:* he can disclose how it had to be the way it was. "In the characters and the incidents, what is said must be the probable or necessary outcome of character, and what happens must be the probable or necessary outcome of what has gone before." [22] Tragedy, that

[21] "Poetry is something more philosophic and of graver import than history, for poetry speaks rather of the universal, while history speaks of the particular." *Poetics* ch. 9: 1451b 5–7.

[22] *Poetics* ch. 15: 1454a 35–37.

is, must be "universal," not in dealing with universal types, as the neo-Classicists of the seventeenth and eighteenth centuries misinterpreted Aristotle, but in being "intelligible," in making us understand, in exhibiting men, as it were, *sub specie aeternitatis*. On all these counts, Thucydides is a true "poet," while Herodotus is clearly not.

The poet thus makes the universal pattern of nature clearer than nature unaided by art is able to do, "just as a good portrait-painter reproduces the distinctive features of a man, and at the same time, without losing the likeness, makes him handsomer than he is." [23] The poet clarifies nature's pattern. The poet depicts things as they are, or as they are said to be, or as they ought to be—as they ought to be if nature's aim is to be fully realized. Sophocles, who was Aristotle's favorite tragic poet, just as he was to be Hegel's,[24] said, he drew men as they ought to be, while Euripides drew them as they actually are—as they "ought" to be if they were to be fully men. Since the aim of poetry is to "convince," a convincing impossibility is preferable, and certainly far more effective, than an unconvincing possibility. In other words, it is no answer to the critic to say, "It actually happened! I knew a man who did just that!" If his model is in fact improbable, the poet ought to improve upon nature.

Now, if this is what a tragic poem does, the best tragedy will be the one that does it most effectively and convincingly. How

[23] *Poetics* ch. 15: 1454b 11–14.

[24] Aristotle's favorite Sophoclean tragedy was clearly *Oedipus Tyrannus*, just as Hegel's was *Antigone*. Hegel's judgment was based on his own essentially historical theory of tragedy, in which the tragic hero—in this case Antigone—is defeated because he is defending an ideal for which men are not yet ready, and which will triumph only in the future. Thus for Hegel, whether Woodrow Wilson is a tragic or only a pitiable figure depends on whether the United Nations manages to establish itself. It is interesting that Aristotle has a rather low opinion of the *Antigone*. Both Haemon and Creon, according to Aristotle, are with full knowledge on the point of doing a harmful deed, and then leave it undone. "This is odious and also, through absence of suffering, untragic." *Poetics* ch. 14: 1453b 35–39. But compare passage 14 in section 2 in this chapter.

should he set about his task? Aristotle has a great deal of practical advice to give, based on a careful analysis of existing Greek drama.

"The tragedy should be based on a single action, one that is a complete whole in itself, with a beginning, a middle, and an end, so as to enable the work to produce its own proper pleasure, with all the organic unity of a living being." [25] It must be a perfected and completed process, a life made whole, with a finished and close-knit design or pattern, transparently intelligible. There must be no brute chance or contingency, no coincidence or accident about it. If any chance be involved, it must appear, not in the play itself, but in the postulates of the action, so that if they be once granted, everything else in the play follows of necessity. The more concentrated the action is, the more effective the play will be, and the more pleasure it will give. That is why tragedy is a "higher" art than that of epic poetry: it is more concentrated, and thus more effective.

The plot or fable, the *mythos,* must be the outcome of character. It is plot, the combination of incidents, that is the most important element in a play. For it is in action, in the operation of their powers, that men actualize the qualities of their characters: activity, *energeia,* and not power, character, *hexis,* is that at which life aims, its "for what" or *hou heneka.* Characters exist "for the sake of action," not vice versa. "Character" is potentiality, character in operation, or action, is actuality. "Character" is here defined as character revealed in speeches, in talk, where it has not become obvious in the action. It is clear that Aristotle would not have considered Eugene O'Neill's *Strange Interlude* a very good play, in which the characters have to stop acting and talk.

To arouse pity and fear most effectively, the protagonist must pass from happiness to misery, not out of vice and depravity, and not wholly undeservedly, but because of some great error

[25] *Poetics* ch. 23: 1459a 19–21.

of judgment on his own part. If the protagonist were wholly evil, he would excite no pity; Hitler could hardly serve as the protagonist of a tragedy. And if he were wholly good, his fate would not seem pitiable, but hateful and monstrous: Calvary would not be a tragedy for Aristotle. This error of judgment, or "tragic guilt," is thus suggested by Aristotle as a necessary condition of making the play effective.

Aristotle's whole treatment is a characteristic combination of his fundamental functional concepts, and of a realistic analysis of the subject matter—of his permeating notion of the nature of art, *technē,* and of what Greek plays actually were and did, and by what means they did it. Aristotle is at his best in his freedom from the muddled notions of modern "aesthetic" theory, which divorce "art" from "nature," and the "fine arts" from the "practical arts"—which admit, "As a play it is effective, but is it really 'art'?" That is the one question it would never occur to Aristotle to ask.

At times, to be sure, the *Poetics* sounds a little like a correspondence course in scenario writing. But Aristotle's method here, as in all the productive sciences, is a very suggestive method. Here is something men make, Aristotle points out. Why do they make it? What does it do to the audience? In terms of that function it serves, how can it do what it does, and is intended to do, most effectively? This is a very fruitful method for dealing with our own arts, even with those we do not ordinarily think of as "fine"—like the movies, for example, or football, or religion.

Chapter XIV

THE HERITAGE OF ARISTOTLE

We have been emphasizing Aristotle the natural investigator, the *physikos,* who was concerned to work out a thoroughgoing philosophy of process. The distinctions and concepts bound up with Aristotle's functionalism have been at the center of attention. This strain in his thinking might also be called the "Aristotelianism" of Aristotle, in which he pushes his analyses *physikōs:* quite literally, therefore, it might well be called the "naturalism" of Aristotle. He developed this strain in his thinking in criticizing Democritus and the structural mechanism of atomistic thinking. For us, the parallelism is pretty complete with our own criticisms of the structural mechanism of the Newtonian "philosophy of nature." It is this criticism, this analysis, these concepts, that seem suggestive to a present-day student of philosophy. They are suggestive for our own "naturalism," and for our own philosophy of nature. It is this strain that might be called the most living part of the heritage of Aristotle's thinking.

The other strand in Aristotle's thinking is the product of the *logikos,* the *dialektikos,* the "syllogistic gentleman with a category for every emergency." This is Aristotle's Platonic side, his concern with an intelligible structure "separated in thought, *logos,*" as he usually puts it. This is the formalism of Aristotle. It represents his own heritage from the Platonists, which remained a living part of his thought even when he was engaged in his other great critical enterprise, directed not against the atomists but against the Platonists.

Aristotle's formalism is historically of the greatest importance. It played a central role in later Greek Aristotelianism, and dominated medieval concern with Aristotle's writing and thinking. This later predominance of the formalistic or Platonistic side of Aristotle is due in part to the historical accident that the "Old Logic"—the *Categories* and the *De Interpretatione*—came down to the West in direct tradition, and that the rest of the *Organon* was assimilated as early as 1150, some two generations before the more "physical" and functional writings. It is due in part also to the difficulty of expressing functional concepts in scholastic Latin: it is very hard to be a functionalist in that language of abstract nouns. And finally, formalism is the easiest beginning for any intellectual movement, as it is also the natural ending, when thinking has become institutionalized, and as we say "academic"—that is, specialized, divorced from any concrete subject matter or any living issue. This occurs when the problems themselves are inherited, as well as the intellectual tools and methods: in the West, the classic example is fourteenth- and fifteenth-century terminism, as well as our own twentieth-century formalisms.

But this same Platonic formalism is of course tremendously important in the historical Aristotle himself, and in the writings of the corpus. It is the source and indeed the locus of the rigidity of Aristotle's own formulations of structure, a rigidity greatly assailed by post-evolutionary temporalists like Dewey and Whitehead, Peirce, Heidegger and Boas. Such a formalistic rigidity is there, and richly deserves the criticism it has received of late. That criticism began with Aristotle himself, but he did not carry it far enough.

The actual documents of the corpus are a combination of "Platonism" and "Aristotelianism." Or rather, they contain a core of Platonism set in the context of the more distinctively Aristotelian ideas. The outcome is a "formalistic naturalism," or a "structuralistic functionalism." What is needed today is an

Aristotelianism more Aristotelian that Aristotle's own *concordantia* between Platonism and Aristotelianism: a more thoroughgoing critique of Platonic formalism in the context of Aristotelian thinking. In genetic terms, there is needed a further advance away from Platonism in the direction Aristotle himself took but did not pursue far enough. There is a sense in which this enterprise was first seriously undertaken by Hegel in modern times. It has been carried on by various pluralistic left-wing thinkers in the Hegelian tradition, like John Dewey and Whitehead; and, in a somewhat different tradition, by Heidegger, before he bogs down in his "crisis atheology."

Aristotle himself criticized the "Platonists"—just whom he has in mind is a vexed problem for the scholars—for their "separating" of the structure they had discovered from experienced things, from what "we see." They separated not merely the quantitative, in mathematics, but also the forms and ends of things from the things themselves, "which are much less separable." Aristotle tried to bring this structure back to the context of the experienced world from which the separation had been made. However, he did not then analyze in detail the relations to its context of the structure the Platonists had discovered. He merely left the two side by side. He provided a functional frame of reference, but failed to make the most of it—he did not really use it.

Our own formalism has achieved greater flexibility, and criticizes the too great rigidity of Aristotle's—quite rightly. But this flexibility is often achieved at the price of losing relevance. The positivists at least began by finding so much structure irrelevant and "meaningless," instead of, like Hegel or Dewey, looking carefully for what it is relevant to. It is doubtless true that we can consider formal logic without bringing in questions of ontology. But a logic that had literally no relevance to ontology, to what there is, would be about as "meaningless" an enterprise as the wit of man could devise.

We are far from here proposing to throw out the formalism

that is Aristotle's heritage from the Platonists. Structure has an essential place within process. But with all our concern today with words and language we have scarcely yet carried through the much needed functional analysis of *logos* that is missing from our Aristotle. Its absence is ultimately the reason why the formal or "logical" strand is too rigid and inflexible. *Logos* must be analyzed as itself a process, a verb: *to dialegesthai,* communication.

We may then freely admit that of the long line of philosophers in the Western tradition to undertake the enterprise of in some way harmonizing Platonism and Aristotelianism, the first is clearly Aristotle—unless we reserve that priority for the author of the dialogues himself. And with the same reservation, Aristotle is clearly the most successful. But just what do we mean by the "Aristotelianism" in the combination? Here is surely a living part of the Aristotelian heritage. Can we attempt a brief summary?

1. "Aristotelianism" certainly means an emphasis on the primacy of the subject matter, the experienced world encountered. This subject matter is what is experienced "directly," as we say. The ultimate test for Aristotle is in the end always what "we see." But the world encountered is also the world experienced reflectively, as Hegelians like Dewey put it: the world formulated in language, and understood in terms of our concepts and hypotheses—our *archai,* or beginnings of understanding. These too we encounter, though not at the outset. For Aristotle's Aristotelianism, there is never any question of creating the subject matter: it is always encountered as there. "How to create a world" is a Platonic, not an Aristotelian question. It is explored in the great creation myth of the *Timaeus,* and became central in the Platonic religious "metaphysics" of the Middle Ages. That question is the ultimate reason why so little of medieval "Aristotelianism" is Aristotelian.

2. Aristotelianism uses a factorial analysis, and does not fall

into the seductive snares of reductive analysis. The latter finds certain elements in a subject matter, and proceeds to try to reconstruct that subject matter out of these elements, invoking them as demiurges with which to create a world. Factorial analysis, in contrast, seeks for factors and structures it can distinguish within a subject matter, but understands them always in terms of the way they are found to be functioning within the context of the subject matter. It starts with what we find and encounter. For it, reality, or "being," or "nature"—whatever be chosen as the inclusive term—is what inquiry starts with, not something discovered at the end of a long search. By inquiry we can always find more of it, but we never lose what we had in our possession at the beginning. Aristotle's criticism of the "Platonists" is always not of what they have found and discerned, but of what they have lost and forgotten.

3. Aristotelianism has a definite position on the status of man in the world—the core of any philosophic "naturalism." Man is a distinctive illustration of what any natural process is like. Man's relation to the world is that of human "art" to "nature." "Art," *technē,* is the Aristotelian term for what present-day philosophies call "experience" or "culture." That is, art is an interaction or transaction between an intelligent animal and an intelligible world. Man is a "rational animal"—that is, he is an intelligent living being who uses *logos,* language. Man can grasp the structure and relations of things, and express them in *logos;* he can say what things are, and things are what they can be said to be.

4. Knowledge is a matter of language and saying, of words and sentences, of verbalized distinctions and of precise statements. It is not a mere opening of the eyes, a looking and seeing—though it must start from and be about what we can see. This is why it is so difficult to translate what Aristotle is saying into any other tongue, and also why what his Greek says seems usually so clear. This emphasis on language makes

Aristotle seem exceedingly relevant today, when we likewise start out from a critique of other men's language. But Aristotle's view of language is naturalistic, like that of Dewey and Mead, and not the supernaturalistic view that language is something imposed on nature from above—from the Oxford dictionary, perhaps. We talk. The problem is, have we said anything? Who can tell? What on earth have we said? This is the problem of the "application" of a language. For Aristotle, in contrast, the problem is, How can we best state what we have found out? It is the problem of expression.

5. Aristotelianism means also a logical realism, a structuralism. Knowledge is a discovery, a finding of something. It is not a human invention. This is important today, as a necessary corrective to our common view that since knowledge involves an element of construction, it is wholly a fiction made. But the construction of knowledge is out of materials discovered, and the way to construct knowledge best is also a discovery and not an invention. This Aristotelian view is opposed to the view that knowledge is purely a human creation, the view of Idealism; and also to the view of Romantic Irrationalism, that knowledge is a free choice of the will. Aristotle in a sense can be said to be a "voluntarist": he holds that *hormē, orexis,* desire, is the only mover, *to kinoun.* But in man the moving desire is the "desire to know." And Aristotle is opposed to traditional "Empiricism," with its assumption of a world completely without structure. This logical realism of Aristotle places him at the center of the "classic tradition." That tradition needs criticism and extension, but it is important to know what is being criticized.

6. Aristotelianism means a functional realism, a philosophy of process: Aristotle is the major functionalist in the Western tradition. The structures found are always those of determinate processes, functioning in determinate contexts: Aristotle is clearly a contextualist. The medieval Aristotle was hardly taken

as a functionalist and contextualist, until the fifteenth- and sixteenth-century Italians got busy upon him.

Clearly Aristotle did not say everything; though without what he first said, all words would be meaningless, and when it is forgotten they usually are. His view of the relation of *logos* to things is far too simple. Actually *logos* is highly selective, being relative to its context. And *logos* is an art, a *technē:* it rearranges and manipulates, in constructing its products, sentences and questions and the rest; though what it makes it makes out of discovered materials. Again, there is the fact that languages natural and philosophical change historically, a fact that in his historical innocence Aristotle did not have to consider. But since Hegel and history we have to consider it. And above all, there is the changing subject matter of philosophical criticism itself, cultures and their progressive and cumulative growth in knowledge. But on all these fundamental matters it is the Aristotelianism of Aristotle that will tell us where to set out. And with Aristotle as a guide —perhaps the Aristotle who did not forget Plato but also remembered the world—did Plato ever forget it?—we may hope to arrive at last where he so often arrives himself in the end, at the Platonic *nous* which he shared to the full—the imaginative vision of truth.

INDEX

Academy, 13-14, 153, 252
Accidental, the, 35, 46
Action, single, in tragedy, 292
Activity (*energeia*), 129-30
  two kinds of, 130-32
Adler, Felix, 246
Aesop, 285
Africa, 228
Age of Anxiety, 244
Agnosticism
  of empiricists, 96
  of Thomas Aquinas, 96
Albertus Magnus, 30
Alcidamas, 283
Alexander, Samuel, viii
Alexander of Aphrodisias, 24, 100, 108
Alexander the Great, 17, 19
Alexandria, 25-26, 108
Alien world, 5
Allan, D. J., 25, 167
Amyntas, King, 12-13
Analysis, factorial, 297-98
Analytics, 6, 30, 61
Anaxagoras, 92, 99, 103-4, 208, 237, 239
Anaximander, ix
Andronikos of Rhodes, xi, 14, 23-26, 108-9
Animals, parts of, 222-23
Animate, the (*ta empsycha*), 61
Antigone, 283, 291
Antipater, 19
Antiphon, 177
Apelles, 288
Apellikon, 23
Apollo, 12, 178
A priori, 35, 41

Archai
  common, 36
  how judged true, 44
  how learned, 42, 43
  of demonstration, 35-36, 42
  proper, 36-37
Architectonic science, 254
"Aristotelianism," 297-300
Aristotelian school, 25*n*, 26*n*
Aristotle
  attitude in practical affairs, 244, 246-47; generalized, 248-50
  development of his thought, 10-11, 20-21, 24-29; in *Politics,* 257-59
  dialogues, 13-14
  early writings, 11, 24
  genealogy of, 12
  life of, 9
  marriage, 17
  method in practical sciences, 243-50
  naturalism of, 27, 103
  religious interests, 13, 16, 18, 27, 108, 136-37, 148
  Wanderjahre, 16-18
  writings, character of, 22; history of, 23
Aristoxenos, 26
Arnim, J. von, 258
Art (*technē*), 77, 187-88, 273-74
  as a habit, 277
  definition of, 274-75
  is "of universals," 278
Asia Minor, 23, 224
Asklepios, 12
Assos, 17, 224
Athenaeus, 23
Athens, 108, 191, 224

The philosophy of Aristotle lies at the very base of our modern civilization. It was with the rediscovery of Aristotle's writings in the twelfth century that the culture of Western Europe began. Thereafter the human mind could systematically explore the world of nature.

How was this due to Aristotle? He provided a way of understanding both nature and human life in the same terms. For him, man is a natural being, one kind of living thing amongst many others, set off from the rest by his possession of the distinctive power of reason. This Aristotelian combination of naturalism and humanism, when harmonized with Christian faith by Thomas Aquinas and the other great Schoolmen, made the thirteenth century one of the two great Ages of Reason in Western cultural history.

This lucid book is a brief, general introduction to the philosophical achievement of Aristotle. Mr. Randall, one of the most distinguished philosophers of our time, has tried to presuppose no previous knowledge of the thinker who has been called "the second of the two major philosophers" produced by Western civilization. He sets forth what seems to him the significance for the present day of the thought of Aristotle.

Many another distinguished modern scholar has attempted to elucidate the text of Aristotle. But most recent interpreters have approached it either as confirmed Platonists, or else from a philologist's point of view, and hence have been more interested in a literal accuracy or in questions of Aristotle's intellectual development, than in the pretty con-

(Continued on back flap)